Risk, Failure, Play

Risk, Failure, Play

What Dance Reveals About Martial Arts Training

JANET O'SHEA

Oxford University Press is a department of the University of Oxford. It furthers the University's objective of excellence in research, scholarship, and education by publishing worldwide. Oxford is a registered trade mark of Oxford University Press in the UK and certain other countries.

Published in the United States of America by Oxford University Press
198 Madison Avenue, New York, NY 10016, United States of America.

Library of Congress Cataloging-in-Publication Data
Names: O'Shea, Janet, 1968– author.
Title: Risk, failure, play : what dance reveals about martial arts training / Janet O'Shea.
Description: New York, NY, United States of America : Oxford University Press, [2019] |
Includes bibliographical references and index.
Identifiers: LCCN 2018007212 (print) | LCCN 2018022324 (ebook) |
ISBN 9780190871550 (updf) | ISBN 9780190871567 (epub) |
ISBN 9780190871543 (pbk. : acid-free paper) | ISBN 9780190871536 (cloth : acid-free paper) |
ISBN 9780190871574 (Oxford Scholarship Online).
Subjects: LCSH: Martial arts—Psychological aspects. | Martial arts—Social aspects.
Classification: LCC GV1102.7.P75 (ebook) |
LCC GV1102.7.P75 O74 2019 (print) | DDC 796.801/9—dc23
LC record available at https://lccn.loc.gov/2018007212

For my instructors and my training partners.

Contents

Prologue–Taking Play Seriously: A History of this Project

THIS BOOK REPRESENTS my attempt to account for the personal transformation and community-building generated by martial arts practice. It constitutes an effort to delve into the paradoxes of play—its simultaneously competitive and cooperative elements, its ability to foster mastery and to negotiate danger—as they inform experiences of individual and interpersonal development. In doing so, I rely on theories of play, games, and sport. And yet I also have based this inquiry on my experience in dance and dance studies, making a case for the particularity of kinetic play in contrast to other forms of play. This project is thus an attempt to bring dance studies, martial arts studies, and sports studies into conversation. *Risk, Failure, Play* is intentionally and ambitiously interdisciplinary. This brings with it its own perils; I intentionally tread outside, sometimes far outside, my home ground. I sweep broadly through some of the disciplines I invoke rather than delving deeply into them. I enter into exchanges with scholars in a friendly sparring match but one in which our skills differ radically.

Four years ago, I returned to martial arts practice after a long hiatus and began training seriously for the first time in my life. As a dancer, yoga practitioner, and rock-climber, I adjusted swiftly to the physical rigors of martial arts. The greatest challenge I faced was in adapting to the simultaneously competitive and cooperative practice of sparring. I'm not alone in this: it's not uncommon for newcomers to join a martial arts class only to abandon it when exposed to the unpredictability of fighting. Unlike some other beginners, however, I took immense pleasure in sparring, despite its many frustrations.

Initially, I thought this project might take form as a martial arts life narrative. However, I found that my interests in martial arts training opened out to larger social, political, and philosophical questions. The idea of martial arts as play captured my imagination, and in it I found an arena in which philosophy, psychology, ethnography, and biological science came together.

As I considered the relationship of this project to the martial arts life narrative, I came upon a conundrum particular to that genre. Martial arts memoirs often follow the trajectory of a neophyte practitioner who puts him or herself through the paces of rigorous training; recounts struggles, injuries, and bouts of self-doubt; grapples with failure; and ultimately emerges transformed. Almost invariably, however, the collision of mastery and doubt, accomplishment and failure play themselves out in the fight to which the narrative leads.

I faced a quandary: Did I want to structure this book as leading up to a single fight? I admit to a certain practical reluctance: the idea of getting into the ring well into my fifth decade was daunting. But it was far from impossible. Sport fights, like other athletic events, vary in their intensity and difficulty. Plenty of other authors have taken up the challenge of that one fight, and some enjoyed it so much that they continued to compete. I have not rejected the idea of eventual competition.

However, I began to suspect that while ring fighting might spark insights specific to competition, I was most interested in discovering what training had to teach me. After all, far more martial artists, like other amateur athletes, train than compete. I was interested in the experiences of those of us who dedicate hours every week to training whether we step between the ropes or not. This devotion to training suggests that it carries its own merits and yields its own benefits. The pleasure and immersive experience of training operates, in some ways, in tension with the emphasis in competition on a goal.

My emphasis on training fits well with my experience in dance studies and its ability to take seriously what movement has to tell us. However, critical dance studies has, until recently, largely focused on representation and on choreography as a means through which representation occurs. As expansive as the concept of choreography can be, including decisions made in teaching, rehearsal, and in improvised performance, it relies on the idea of an individual person making decisions, perhaps in response to others, but planning their actions, enacting them, and building on them. The concept of choreography becomes less effective when one participant foils the actions of another. Indeed, this is the crux of martial arts, and especially its live training practices: plans crumble and tactics fail when they come into contact with the will of another.

While some practices within martial arts—namely forms and self-designated dances—are choreographed in the sense of being planned, the arts I practice do not rely heavily on forms. Drills are set but, in their typically close contact and the many variables they introduce in terms of speed and dynamics require a continual adaptation to one's partner. Sparring and grappling require a greater sense of continual adjustment. The mastery acquired in martial arts, and particularly in modern sport fight genres, is a relational one; it is a sense of accomplishment that rests upon an ability to respond to ever-changing variables.

The primary research on which this project is based is on an experiential reality that is so close to me that I am reluctant to label it as ethnographic. As in my previous research,[1] I delved deeply into a practice only to see it as a site for research when the practice raised questions I found hard to answer without recourse to cultural and social theory. Because it comes out of my own experience it is local in its focus, as the martial arts training I experienced comes largely through the legacy of Bruce Lee and the training networks affiliated with the Inosanto Academy of Martial Arts in Marina del Rey, California. (My involvement with the empowerment self-defense community has introduced me to martial arts and self-defense training beyond the local but still within the United States, as I participated in trainings in Lansing, Michigan, Huguenot, New York, and Vashon Island, Washington.)

I draw from English-language accounts of sport fight training in sites including the United States, Australia, the United Kingdom, China, and Thailand, while relying on a body of martial arts scholarship emerging out of Great Britain. My arguments regarding the complex relationship between play, games, and sport as well as between opportunities for mastery and intersubjective engagement in contrast to sedentary experiences that isolate us from one another draw largely but not exclusively from American data. The claims I put forward here apply primarily to politically democratic but stratified societies with "developed" capitalist economies, those most influenced by neoliberalism.[2] However, this inquiry is not exclusive to the Western capitalist countries: the refiguration of violence through play, games, and sports, and its potential to produce pleasure through mastery, insight through failure, and enhanced interpersonal awareness through vulnerability appears across a range of societal contexts, albeit in strikingly different ways.

As with most projects of this scope, thanks are due to far too many people than I can mention individually. I am grateful to my instructors, training partners, and fellow students, especially those at the Inosanto Academy of Martial Arts without whose warmth and kindness this project would not have been possible. I also extend my thanks to UCLA's Jeet Kune Do club for rigorous training and a sense of community. My thanks are due specifically to Vicent Pham and Hao Zhiwang for being among my first training partners. I am grateful to my martial arts instructors: Guro Alain Rono, whose figure-of-four takedown introduced me to the interconnections between multiple martial arts and whose skill in sparring both delights and terrifies me, Guro Tim Becherer and Guro Anna Bolgonese who in different ways taught me to see clarity in complexity, Guro Conrad Cayman, whose meticulous eye deepens my understanding of this practice, Coach Kathy Long whose rigorous sparring trainings continually test the parameters of interaction, Kru Attiucus Todd who always reminds me of the depth that can be found in doing the reps, and Professor Gary Padilla for an introduction to the complexities of ground fighting. My deepest gratitude extends to Guro Dan Inosanto whose spirit of inquiry runs through this book.

Thanks are also due to the international empowerment self defense community, whose insightful and analytical approach to addressing violence is matched only by their dedication and inclusivity. I am grateful in particular to Yehudit Zicklin-Sidikman, whose interjection of humor into self-defense training provides a model not just for ESD teaching but for navigating a troubled and contentious world. Thanks are also due to Susan (George) Schorn, fellow fighter-writer and dedicated self-defense advocate, for the profound insights that run through her witty prose; her support of my self-defense advocacy and martial arts teaching; and for commenting on the early drafts of this project. Thanks also to Stephanie Phillips, another fighter-writer, for providing the cover photo on short notice. I am deeply grateful to my second local fight community, IMPACT Personal Safety Los Angeles. Those who have taught me, offered me challenging fights, and learned alongside me in IMPACT trainings have informed and supported this project in myriad ways. Among those whose support calls out for acknowledgment are Johnny Albano, Jen Bunting, Don Hart, Michael Peñafiel, and Ellen Snortland. My profound gratitude goes to Lisa Gaeta, who has supported my self-defense advocacy, my self-defense learning and teaching, and my writing in far too many ways to mention.

Thanks are also due to my dance studies colleagues who welcomed this new area of research and to authors outside my field who encouraged the development of this project. Specifically, I am grateful to dance colleagues Royona Mitra, Anurima Banerji, Aparna Sharma, Lionel Popkin, and Susan Foster, discussions with whom encouraged the emergence of this project. Thanks to Robert Bilder who collaborated on the neuroscience project that formed my first academic study of martial arts. Thanks are also due to the Martial Arts Studies Network, specifically Paul Bowman and Alex Channon, as well as to the members of the Theater and Performance Research Association Performance and the Body Working Group, for welcoming me and for reflections on the smaller projects that informed this larger one. Thanks also to author Niva Dorrell for comments on the early articulations of this project.

I am also indebted to Ann Lane, first and closest reader of the full manuscript. Likewise, my deepest thanks are due to my research assistant Mana

Hayakawa. My gratitude also goes out to my editor Norm Hirschy for his support and his numerous insights. Special thanks are also due to Tim Shireman and Ellington O'Shea for putting up with my relentless training schedule and for turning patient ears and curious thoughts to yet another discussion of the merits of play.

Introduction

WHY DO YOU DO THIS? EXPERIENCING HUMANITY IN COMBAT PLAY

"WHY DO YOU do this?"

I struggled to answer my training partner's question. We stood on the springy elevated mat of UCLA's Yates Gym, a cavernous space cluttered with gymnastics equipment. My training partner was a UCLA undergraduate and newcomer to martial arts. It was my second time enrolling in a weekly jeet kune do class through Recreational Athletics. By this point, I was familiar enough with JKD's elemental boxing strikes—jab, cross, hook—that I could coach my partner through the sequence of punches. I held the focus mitts for him as he worked the series of three-punch combinations. As we switched off and he prepared to hold for me, he asked this question, one that bore no relationship to the drill: Why do you do this?

Why *do* I do this, I thought? Even after a mere three months of training, the question seemed more why *wouldn't* I do it? With a short stint of training behind me, it seemed that practicing JKD, the modern, hybrid martial art invented by Bruce Lee, was the most obvious thing in the world.

In retrospect, I shouldn't have been puzzled by his inquiry. As a woman who launched myself into martial arts training at midlife, kickboxing, grappling, and stick fighting with highly skilled people, some of whom are half my age, I encounter this question with regularity.[1] That I train in martial arts like it's a second job when I'm not a competition fighter but a writer, a dancer, and a parent yields this question or its variant, "What got you into *that*?" When I'm recovering from one spectacular contact injury or another I confront these questions daily, alongside their companion, "Are you going to stop?"

As a dancer and dance writer, however, I was surprised to have a conversation about utility. When it comes to dance, particularly in the United States, the assumption is that movement has no function, no tangible purpose, and indeed, that the very point of dancing is that it has no utility. Especially in conversations with nondancers, the difficulty lies not in explaining why I dance, for no one has ever asked me this question, but in getting across the idea that in some contexts, dance has a very clear function.

Moreover, as a dancer, and possibly as a woman, when I speak of martial arts, a listener tends to assume that I refer to the esoteric and refined practices of East Asia, practices such as tai chi chu'an or aikido, where violence is abstracted or redirected. To clarify, then, when I speak of the martial arts I've devoted myself to, I refer to modern sport practices such as muay Thai, Western boxing, and Brazilian jiu jitsu as well as to Bruce Lee's "scientific street fighting" practice jeet kune do and the guerilla-warfare derived Filipino martial arts.[2]

Combat sport genres tend to sit outside a conventional understanding of martial arts *as* arts. This is partially a matter of insufficient terminology: "martial arts" refers to a range of practices, from the stylized and individuated internal systems to combative games to training based on organized revolution and designated self-defense practices. I suspect, however, there is also an assumption that combat sport is for men and for young people and that adult women, especially those with intellectual and artistic inclinations, would be drawn to the more performative and choreographic elements of martial arts.

FIGURE I.1 Monique and I practicing muay Thai's basic drills.
Photograph courtesy of Tim Becherer.

What I have found so compelling about martial arts is not their similarity to concert dance training but their differences. While thinking with the body undergirds both martial arts and concert dance, the exchange between human beings that is so central to combat sport has largely been absent in my dance training. My devotion to martial arts came about because it provides what concert dance does not: oppositional, intensely physical interactions with other human beings.

Despite my initial defensiveness—why wouldn't I sport fight?—I have to admit that there is something extraordinary about the human ability to hit, kick, and grapple with each other in the absence of malice. Although recreational sport fighting has come to feel like the most natural thing in the world for me, "natural" is never as self-evident as it seems. The joy that comes from hitting another human being not out of anger but out of respect, and the satisfaction that comes not just from landing a strike but being able to take one with aplomb, signals something distinctive about how people interact.

In the gym, on that Monday evening, I offered a convoluted reply as to my training background: that I had done a little traditional kung fu decades ago but found it uninspiring and had practiced wing chun kung fu with sincere but inconsistent dedication. I had always wanted to learn the art of Bruce Lee. I said what it wasn't: I didn't practice martial arts for self-defense and I didn't do it just for fitness.[3] But what I meant to say eluded me.

Even the well thought-out explanation I came to later—that I practice fight sports because they are so enjoyable that they are worth risking injury and investing seemingly endless amounts of time—sparks curiosity but rarely understanding. Untangling that lack of understanding and trying to address it led me to research in phenomenology, neuroscience, sports ethnography, and social psychology. Ultimately, it led to the writing of this book.

What I meant to say on the mat that evening is that I train in martial arts because it provides a pleasurable depth of focus that I find hard to access in other arenas of my life. Enjoyment as an explanation ends a line of questioning because pleasure is subjective: no one can reasonably insist that I am not having fun in any particular situation. At the same time, however, an appeal to play seems insufficient in light of the time, effort, and danger of martial arts training. It appears to reduce this practice that inspires my devotion, to trivialize something to which I, and many others, dedicate hours of every day. Is play so important that an otherwise reasonable person would devote the equivalent of a part-time job to it? Is something that frequently scares me and leaves me wracked with self-doubt really a high point of enjoyment? Aren't the experiences of pain, fear, and self-doubt the antithesis of play?

If I were the only one to hug an opponent and mean it even as my face still stings from the impact of his gloves, if I were the only one to thank a training partner sincerely after she threatened my ligaments and my airways, that might suggest something peculiar about me but reveal little about fight sports. But I'm not alone in confronting this paradox: every martial artist I talk to offers similar reflections, a tale of how martial arts changed him; how the practice made her calmer, more focused, less prone to flare-ups of temper; how fight training enabled her to make a difficult change in her life; how martial arts encouraged him to stand up for himself while also allowing space for others to do the same. Nearly every account I read emphasizes a journey, a transformation in the trainee's sense of self that emerges from the rigors of the practice.[4]

Most martial art life narratives track this transformation. Initially, I thought that would be my aim as well. As I developed this project, however, I became more interested in the components of this oft-referenced transformation and its meanings. How, specifically, does martial arts training induce a transformation in a sense of self? How does participation in simulated, one-on-one combat build a sense of community? I became interested in what this transformation might mean on a larger societal level, especially since this happens through a practice that uses elements of violence and logically should be the opposite of self-building and community developing.

Indeed, a typical assumption, one that comes up in common conversation, is that people indulge in violence through fight sports. Senator John McCain's description of mixed martial arts (MMA) as "human cockfighting" represented a particularly prominent disparagement of full-contact combat sport but hardly an isolated one.[5] Those who take such a position reference sport fighters who act in violence outside the ring or the cage.[6] Other commentators treat the relationship of sport fighting to violence as self-evident but insist that combat sport is a steam valve, an arena in which human beings, usually men, can indulge their propensity toward violence so that it doesn't spew over into other areas of life.[7] On the flip side is the assumption that martial arts create a peaceful yet powerful self and a respectful community *in spite of* their engagement with the components of violence.[8] The association of martial arts with spirituality is a way of side-stepping this question, allowing practitioners and viewers to distinguish between traditional martial arts, which are respectful and disciplined, and modern combat sports, which are, basically, fighting.

There are a few problems with each of these lines of reasoning. Although like most martial artists, I feel a release from training and leave the mat feeling calmer and more focused than when I stepped on it, the after-effects don't seem to be a sufficient motivation for all I, and everyone else there, pours into training. The risk of practicing combat sport is such that it can't fully be justified simply by its afterglow. Although I'd like to say that the pleasure of martial arts comes through in spite of its use of the components of violence, I question whether this is really the case. The value of martial arts—for me and, I'm near certain, for others—is intrinsic and not extrinsic.

Sociologists and ethnographers have signaled the many ways in which sport fighting differs from violence.[9] Scholars with a more quantitative bent have examined the statistics surrounding sport fight participation: Does martial arts training mitigate or promote violence? The data varies. Research suggests that the aesthetics of the martial art practiced do not define its effects; rather its conventions for interaction determine its outcomes: a respectful boxing gym can produce calmer, more peaceful students than an aggressive karate dojo.[10] Publically engaged researchers, such as those associated with the Love Fighting Hate Violence initiative, aim to develop the inclusive elements of sport fighting and enhance its abilities to foster consent and cooperation.

My goal is not to add to the debate as to whether martial arts traffic in violence or oppose violence. Instead, my interest lies in how and why sport fighting *feels* so profoundly different from real-world violence. I consider what questions an investigation of combat sport raises about the cultural and historical context in which we find ourselves. I'm interested in whether kinetic play offers us models for interacting outside the parameters of the game and whether asking questions about physical play might help us envision alternate ways of engaging with others. Reflecting on the importance of play allows us an opportunity to rehearse how we want to live and interact. Such considerations have implications for kinetic play of all sorts: team sports, individually oriented lifestyle sports, partner dancing, and other physical practices.

Because it is so tangible, it seems that regardless of the codes and conventions of respect that surround it, sport fighting ought to feel like violence: after all, a punch thrown in play stuns in earnest.[11] The aggressive elements of fight sports, as opposed to the codification of violence in traditional martial arts, demand a consideration of the relationship of martial arts to violence as well as a reflection on so-called dark or edge play, topics I take up later in this book. Moreover, the element of danger that is central to combat sport, in contrast to esoteric martial arts, also begs questions around the pleasure of risk, the interpersonal consequences of vulnerability, and the relationship between mastery and failure. The contrast between the perception of the spectacle and the lived experience of fight sports led to the investigation of competitive pleasure, risk, vulnerability, mastery, and failure that I lay out here.

Play provides this context for exploring vulnerability, risk, danger, failure, competitive pleasure, and interpersonal interaction. Despite its association with frivolity and ease, play is not the opposite of danger, rigor, or failure. Dogs at the dog park and children on a play structure display a gravitas at odds with the absence of an end goal for their actions. Sports from the ordinary team variety to the so-called extreme hinge not on the avoidance of risk, nor the mindless courting of it, but on the management of danger through expertise.[12] Games, from chess to video games, demand a degree of skill that, paradoxically, depends upon a continual confrontation with one's own limitations.

Martial artists are not unique in their embrace of practices that evoke conflict. Pick-up games of basketball and soccer enact a playful, artificial disagreement between friends and associates. Martial arts are not the only recreational activities fraught with risk, replete with danger, and rigorous in their demands. Lifestyle sports, such as hang-gliding, spelunking, and deep-sea diving, explore the dangers of the natural environment and human vulnerability in relation to it. Combat sports are not the only practices that require seemingly excessive trust of other players and the context of play; rock-climbers and mountaineers rely on the skills of their partners and team as well as on their own abilities to manage risky situations.

Adherents of combat sport are not the only ones who exhibit a remarkable dedication to something that is, for many of them, only ever an avocation. Play inspires a dedication that can be remarkably serious as we aim to get good at what we play. And yet play exists as play and not as something else because it does not serve a purpose in the outside world.[13] This tension between seriousness and the absence of a goal as well as between pleasure and risk compels a loyal, sometimes obsessive attention. Kinetic play, in particular, inspires devotion because of its immersive and intensely intersubjective nature. Like improvised music, physical play requires a mobilization of a player's skills in order to access the immediacy of the event.

In the pages that follow, then, I suggest that play, especially intense, physical play, allows us to contend with difficult aspects of life experience. Play consists of techniques and practices that enable us to manage fraught realities with intelligence.[14] Play does this not because it operates as a steam valve, releasing tensions that would otherwise build up unchecked, nor because it functions as a rehearsal for real life. Play is not the opposite of danger or of failure;[15] rather, play provides opportunities to explore vulnerability alongside the experience of mastery. Play allows us to contend with troubling aspects of experience because of its intrinsic properties: its pleasurable nature, its structured interactions, and its absence of a utilitarian purpose give us the opportunity to experience mastery, to contend with other people's subjectivities, to manage risk, and to reflect on the meaning of success and failure. In the process, it teaches us how to cooperate and how to disagree with respect.

Play, Movement, and Volition

I'm partnered with a teenage boy for muay Thai class. When time comes for sparring, we circle and I throw a few jabs, to gauge his response. I evade his first kick. But he comes in a second time, fast and hard, landing on my flexed guarding arm. I fake a return kick on my right and switch to my left. I land it.

He's fourteen and I'm an adult, so I'm going at 40 percent to his 80 percent. I attack with a modicum of precision but little force; meanwhile, he wails on me with something resembling full power. Finally, I've had enough; I get him in a clinch. I'm shorter than him and heavier; I figure I can use my closer relationship to gravity to wrest a break from his hard Thai kicks.

I forgot he's trained in judo. He turns before I complete the clinch and flips me onto the mat as he lands on my ribs. I muscle up to a seated position and work my way around him. I take his back, hooking my flexed feet around his thighs and moving in for a rear naked choke. My boxing gloves fail me and he escapes. By the time we're back on our feet, the round is over. We touch gloves and hug, all smiles. Those arriving for the next class had gathered around, watching us. We had turned what was supposed to be light sparring in a kickboxing class into an MMA-style fight. And we were delighted.

When we walked off the mat, a senior student clapped both our shoulders. "Next time," he said. "I want to play with you guys."

The word "play," in English, has multiple connotations. Play, in its most common definition, means "to engage in an activity for enjoyment and recreation rather than for a serious or practical purpose."[16] Play is voluntary.[17] Play typically separates itself in some salient way from the activities of daily life.[18] Play serves no outside purpose and, although some games have a goal that concludes the state of play and results in a win, that goal typically serves no function in the world beyond the game.[19] Play stands in contrast to work in that work hinges upon accomplishing an end goal while play is not efficacious, at least not in an identifiable way. It is not utilitarian.

Play, as we'll see, is not necessarily the opposite of work, however. The intensity of focus, the merging of action and attention that are central to play, is not exclusive to it. Although a wholesale incursion of goal-oriented action into games deprives them of some of their most beneficial qualities, contemporary researchers on play and the flow state insist that the autotelic state—that of complete immersion in the activity at hand—is not antithetical to work, but can undergird it. Indeed, psychologist Stuart Brown maintains that the opposite of play is not work but depression;[20] philosopher Elaine Scarry contrasts not work and play but work and pain.[21] While the immersive state that psychologist Mihaly Csikszentmihalyi calls flow can focus our attention toward the action at hand without an eye toward a goal, it can also include an acute awareness of criteria by which a goal is accomplished, a sense of time or distance, for example.[22]

Playful activities, such as board games, card games, and sports, are not necessarily low stakes.[23] In more structured games and, even more so, in sports, the outcome is not overtly practical but there is a goal: to win. Sometimes this goal, even bearing no relevance outside the game, takes on an almost desperate importance. We need only think of a fight breaking out over the accusation of cheating at cards or fans rioting in the stands at a sports match to realize that an activity without practical purpose is not necessarily one of low investment.[24]

Play's other definitions reinforce this sense of seriousness that the connotations of recreation and enjoyment would belie. Arts and African American studies scholar Sarah Lewis,[25] in her investigation of creativity, failure, and mastery, points to the use of the word "play" to describe the ability to perform with a musical instrument, in which physical skill merges with the deft use of an implement. Lewis points out that the term "to play" is used not just to characterize an action, but also to appraise ability.[26] Play in the sense of participating in a sport combines the connotations of joining an activity without an obvious, practical outcome and demonstrating skill and dexterity. In English, playing a sport typically refers to acting as part of a team: we play soccer and basketball, but we don't play gymnastics or swimming. However, we speak of judo players and, more rarely, of jiu jitsu players.[27]

Play also refers to modulation and adaptation. We talk of play in the system when we mean that there is room to maneuver.[28] Play, in this sense, suggests moving between two or more things, extending the implication of skill to an ability to negotiate or contend with elements beyond oneself.

Play carries connotations of improvisation. This is not inherent within the term, but it accompanies many of its meanings. For instance, the pretend play of children hinges on extemporizing. Playing a game means improvising within a structure; the whole point of a game is to follow the rules while adjusting one's actions to a changing scenario. To play music doesn't always require improvisation, but many forms of music include opportunities for impromptu exploration. Likewise, an actor playing a role, like a classical musician, may have a script (score) to work with but the nuances that make the rendition a performance and not a read-through are subtly changing and adaptive. Playing with someone in the sense of tricking them is always improvisational: it is live and responsive.

When "to play" means to fool someone, it hinges on the sense of play as pretending to be someone that one is not. In this regard, it can mean to manipulate someone, as in "don't play me." In a more extreme sense, "to play on" means to exploit or capitalize on, as in to play on someone's fears. In line with such associations of play with trickery, theater director and performance studies progenitor Richard Schechner proposes the (problematically named) category of dark play to encompass both trickery and an implication of unwitting participants in a joke or prank.[29] Psychologist Stuart Brown sees this use of the term play to refer to exploitation and manipulation as unfortunate, a misconstruction of play's benevolent qualities.[30] I agree with the play theorists who argue that play hinges on consent; it you don't agree to it, you're not playing, even if you're entangled in something that another person sees as a game.[31] Consent is particularly important when play becomes dangerous, and even more so in fight sports where the ground of exploration is violence.[32]

While consent is central to my understanding of play, I nonetheless think authors such as Brown are too hasty in their dismissal of play's complexities. Play's potential to mess with perception, to alter perspectives, and to redefine negative, painful, or frightening experience is part of what makes it so compelling. Play is therefore not necessarily the opposite of conflict, although many forms of play contain within them structures to avoid or resolve disagreement. Instead, play often creates artificial antagonism[33] and exposes its players to risk and danger. The undercurrents of conflict and danger in play give it the ability to manage contentious realities.[34]

The intrinsic qualities of play that account for its ubiquity include its ability to generate pleasure while managing risk and exploring confrontation. These qualities call for further interrogation, since they are part of the dangers of play and they form the basis of the so-called dark or edge elements of play. Any claim to investigate play via martial arts therefore needs to contend with martial arts' ever-present other: interpersonal violence. Martial arts, as we'll see, relies on components of violence while altering their meaning. As such, violence is both the ground of martial arts training and its opposite. It's worth inquiring into how martial arts differentiate themselves from violence and why this difference is important.

Good Game: How Kinetic Play Differs from Violence

A while back, Guro Dan Inosanto brought his pradal serey, Cambodian kickboxing, instructor, Kru Omrey, to the academy. Kru Omrey presented a demonstration by a few of his competition fighters. One of them, a young guy with a sweet, childish face that belied his status as a high-level sport fighter, spoke regretfully of the conflict between Cambodian and Thailand and its

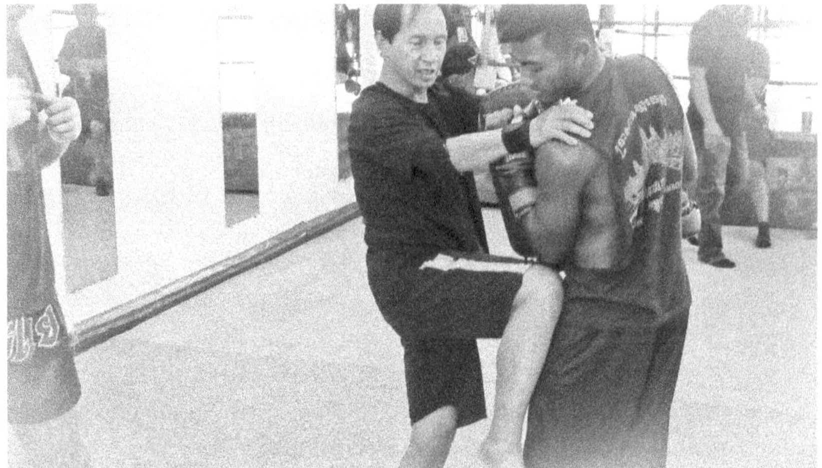

FIGURE I.2 Kru Omry and his student.
Photograph courtesy of Tim Becherer.

accompanying missed opportunities for competition between muay Thai and pradal serey fighters.

"I just want peace," he said. "So I can fight."

We laughed. He smiled, embarrassed.

"In the ring," he clarified. "So I can fight in the ring."

His audience smiled. Not because we didn't know what he meant, but because we did.

Pradal serey is a rough sport. Like muay Thai, it combines powerful kicks with the punches of Western boxing while incorporating knee and elbow strikes. It also consists of a relentless forward pressure, so that a Cambodian kickboxer uses these knees and elbow strikes to mow an opponent down.

And yet pradal serey, like other sport fight idioms, centers on controlling and regulating violence, not indulging in it. After all, the young fighter didn't long to fight a Thai boxer to wreak revenge for their countries' disputes. He wanted to go up against a Thai fighter so they could challenge one another's abilities, surmount their differences, and treat one another as equals. He wanted to see how their training systems held up when put alongside one another. His desire focused on interpersonal competition and not on the destruction of his opponent's will.

The use of the term "fight" in the young kickboxer's description is both casual and revealing. This term seems to contradict my insistence that martial arts and violence are fundamentally different. Indeed, the use of the term "fight" in and alongside such less equivocal sport terms such as "match,"

FIGURE I.3 Like muay Thai, pradal serey makes extensive use of elbow strikes. Photograph courtesy of Tim Becherer.

"bout," or "game" suggests that competitive martial arts blur the lines between play and violence, and that this is part of their appeal.[35]

However, even in real-world confrontation, a fight is radically different from other forms of violence such as an assault or an ambush. A fight implies a conflict between equals. Fighting suggests intention. The term fight, when it comes to conflict, rather than sport, refers to a confrontation that two individuals with opposing intentions or goals enter into knowingly. As sociologists have long insisted, a fight, by definition, hinges on consent whereas violence obliterates consent.[36]

Thus, you may fight or you may get into a fight. You may be drawn into one or find that a conflict escalates into a fight. But you don't get fighted at or fighted upon. The term fight refers to ruptures in a relationship, as in "we're not speaking to one another after that last fight," but also to the more beneficial, healthy conflict that characterizes ongoing interactions, as in "we had a fight about it but we worked it out." Fighting, in this sense, lines up with philosopher Erin Manning's argument about the reciprocal nature of touch: because touch implies intention, I can impose my touch upon you but I can never force you to receive that touch.[37]

The consent that accompanies fighting may, of course, be fraught. A schoolchild who fights to protect himself from bullying, a teenager who scraps to maintain her social status, a young man who fights so he can keep his head up in a neighborhood that would tear him down: these are instances of coerced action. And yet they are radically different from an assault, a one-sided attack.

Within sport fighting as within real-world conflict, consent may be fraught. The structure of sport training in most of its forms consists of encouraging an athlete past his perceived limitations. Athletic training encourages ignoring the voice in our heads that says "I can't do this," replacing it with the voice of a coach or trainer that insists that we can. This is typically an empowering experience for an athlete and yet it brings with it the risk of injury. Moreover, as sport becomes more professionalized, the decision to participate or to decline becomes more complex. When a fighter or other athlete can stand to make money off of a particular match, her participation is not linked only to the individual decision to play or to not play. When his participation operates as a spectacle, his obligation to provide the fans with a good show can override his concerns for his own well-being or that of his opponent.[38]

However, constrained choices are still choices. The verb "to fight" evokes decision-making, even if those decisions are made under duress. For that reason, as we'll see, the use of the term "fight" in self-defense training is strategic. The term fight in sport evokes the central paradox of martial arts training: its practice can make an adherent more focused, calmer, and even more peaceful. The young kickboxer's statement was, therefore, less tangled up than it appeared. It is entirely possible to want peace so we can fight.

Their Humanity is Heightened: Intersubjectivity and Martial Arts Practice

My friend Cristina is not, primarily, a martial artist. She's an architect who plays music and runs for exercise. Recently she began a once-weekly boxing class, and, like so many of us, got the sport fight bug. When describing the allure of boxing, she commented on the good-natured, accepting attitude of her boxing coaches, reflecting that "their humanity is heightened" by the brutality of their sport.[39]

Cristina's observation is reflected in martial artists' accounts of their practice as conquering violence through exploring its elements. The effort it takes to simultaneously engage and control aggression during a sparring match indicates the extent to which martial arts and violence differ as well as suggesting where they intersect. The intense control required of a sport fighter is an example of the balancing point achieved: if a fighter is not aggressive enough, he'll get steamrolled. If a fighter is too aggressive, she'll take foolish risks. Sport fighters comment on this paradox with some regularity: boxer Brandon Rios said in the lead-up to his bout with Manny Pacquiao, "if I go in there mad, I'll get knocked out." Muhammad Ali was known for taunting his opponents in order to get them riled up so they lost track of their game plan. The very possibility that a sport fight can unleash uncontrolled aggression signals their intersection.

Fight sports thus engage the very risks they provide the opportunity to overcome. Martial arts, in this sense, explore violence, structuring and ideally transcending it. Loïc Wacquant, in his ethnography of boxing, calls this phenomenon the social regulation of violence.[40] The simultaneous foray into and distance from brutality that combat sport allows, the disinterest of the effective sport fighter, and the impermeability of the skilled contender to aggression, pain, and fear combine to externalize violence rather than foster it.

The difference between how combative sport looks and how it feels has negative consequences as well as positive ones. The ability of combative play to build community leads to an underexamination of the violent undercurrents of sports such as American football, where winning is privileged over interaction and where athletes are excused when they indulge in off-field violence. Combative play's simulation of violence can also lead to a recurrent illusion that any and all martial arts training prepares its practitioners for real-world violence. Physical play neither automatically reduces violence nor does it necessarily equip us for encountering violence. Play and violence meet under particular conditions and diverge under others, the specifics of which I explore in this book.

My suggestion here is that sport fighting and especially its live training practices bring us into radically interpersonal encounters that require us to contend with fundamental differences and similarities between human beings. We witness vulnerabilities that are similar despite disparities in age, gender, size, skill set, or training background. We also confront our fundamental differences: that our agendas diverge, as do our intentions, strategies, and tactics. When we participate in live training—sparring, grappling, or padded assailant self-defense trainings—we learn to read another person's behavior, anticipating it by identifying the shift of weight that precedes a kick or the twitch of a shoulder that telegraphs a punch. We confront the basic unknowability of other human beings and learn methods through which that obscurity becomes decipherable, if not fully understandable.

Through this interchange of radical difference, sport fighting brings us into an encounter with risk. It gives us methods for managing the unpredictability of confrontation. Just as psychologist Mihaly Csikszentmihalyi argues that alternative sports such as bungee jumping and rock-climbing are about not courting risk but managing it through the activation of skill,[41] fight sports are not about courting violence but about managing it through expertise.

Martial arts, therefore, are a staging ground less for violence than for disagreement. This kind of confrontation brings with it the possibility for violence, as it is a negotiation that can fail and spiral out of control.[42] The extraordinary thing, to my mind, is not that it sometimes falters but that it works at all. Although it doesn't do so automatically, sport fight training can provide a space in which disagreement is managed with respect, civility, and kindness.

"I Love these People": Oppositional Civility and Confrontational Play

It's a quiet Saturday morning at the Inosanto Academy of Martial Arts. The training space is cavernous, reminiscent of the auto body shop it once was. Today's muay Thai class is small, but its pace is swift.

Kru Bill lets us know we're about to spar.[43] My hand shakes as I put in my mouth guard. Queasiness crawls its way up my torso. I resort to tactical breathing—slow inhale, hold, slow exhale—to quiet my anxiety.

I square off against my partner. We touch gloves and circle. She throws a quick jab, a diagnostic. I throw one back. Her movement is compact and precise, her kicks powerful. I land a few shots. She lands more. But even as her strikes come at me, my fear exists in another world. The queasiness is gone. In its place is a brisk clarity.

Kru calls time. Without a break, we start another round. My next partner is, in another context, my instructor. He knows I can fight hard, if not consistently well. He comes at me, swift, powerful, yet detached. His strikes land hard enough to hurt, not hard enough to injure. My dropped guard, slow footwork, and tendency to hover inside the pocket catch me out. I give up on restraint and duck under my opponent's reach just as Kru calls time again.

My opponents and I touch gloves and hug as we step off the mat. I'm elated even as sweat pours into my eyes and I struggle for breath. "I love these people," I think. Then I pull myself up short. I barely know these people. And we had just been trying to kick each other in the head.

Martial arts, especially its live training elements, are fundamentally about disagreement. If my opponent is trying to punch me and I'm trying to take him down, we disagree on a fundamental level as to what we want from that encounter. And yet when we spar, we cooperate as to the terms of the encounter: how hard we're sparring, how fast we're moving. We begin by touching gloves and end by shaking hands or hugging, and usually, we mean it. The decision to engage in this planned confrontation rests upon our initial cooperation. Even in the most intense competitions, the presence of the opponent enables a contender's victory.[44]

Martial arts are not unique in providing the grounds for exploring disagreement: many games are oppositional in their structure. Indeed, game theorist Roger Caillois in his taxonomy of play gives agonistic games their own category and treats sedentary strategy games, such as chess, as combative ones.[45] Even nonconfrontational play can incorporate mockery and inversions of order. Kinetic play, however, is particularly good at enacting disagreement because it is so immersive and its effects are so immediate. These forms of play, because of their exploration of risk through encounters with other people, involve a mobilization of trust that, paradoxically, is greater than that which develops in safer arenas.[46]

This alignment of risk, confrontation, and trust means that kinetic play can model disagreement with respect. It can act as an exercise in what philosopher Erin Manning calls "dis-sensus," and can provide an on-the-ground opportunity to model political theorist William Connolly's ideal of agonistic respect.[47] The possibility of disagreement with respect facilitates the ability of fight sports, with their simulation of combat, to create a powerful sense of community. They generate a sense of commonality because they create opportunities for developing and engaging oppositional civility.

Civility can carry anti-progressive connotations. For example, as David Palumbo-Liu points out,[48] the concept can be used to squash dissent; civility, in this context, discourages debate and squelches nonmainstream political positions. Palumbo-Liu quotes poet June Jordan on the roots of polite behavior in the maintenance of the status quo. The cry to "come together as a nation" that followed Donald Trump's election is a large-scale version of this urge: a claim that dissent is inherently divisive and that unity requires its participants to ignore their differences and swallow their disagreement.[49] Even political opposition movements sometimes insist that solidarity must come at the sacrifice of debate. For instance, the planning for the first Women's March on Washington was rife with accusations that discussions of intersectionality needed to be sidelined until after a certain (indeterminate) milestone had been achieved. Unity, in both these instances, one emerging from the political Right and one from the Left, was positioned at odds with opposition, debate, and dissent. Civility appears in these instances as the mechanism through which unity can be achieved.

At the same time, however, global right-wing populism has given rise to a politics of disrespect. The conservative populism through which individuals express their dissatisfaction with global economic inequality not through solidarity but through the scapegoating of vulnerable communities—immigrants, people of color, refugees, women, gay and transgender people—sheds a different light on the detriments and promises of civility. An overt lack of caring, if not outright cruelty, is taken as a necessity in a time of precarity.[50] A backlash against political correctness is celebrated as honesty.

In response to this valorization of vitriol, poster artist Shepard Fairey, known for his Hope and Change images of Barack Obama, produced a series of Women's March posters and launched an organization called Make America Smart Again in order to offset the rewarding of "uncivil and disgusting behavior" that, he maintained, the election of Donald Trump initiated.[51] Fairey argues that the mechanisms of democracy and specifically the creation of public policy require a degree of civility, expressing concern that the election of Donald Trump rewarded incivility.[52] Fairey went on to say that "when the status quo is fearful and scapegoating, then the most punk rock you can be is finding common ground with your fellow human beings,"[53] suggesting the possibility that radical respect can engage—rather than override—differences, diversity, and disagreement.

FIGURE I.4 Artist Shepard Fairey created poster art following the 2016 election in the hopes that his images would cultivate civility in the face of disrespect.

Artwork by Shepard Fairey and Delphine Diallo, commissioned by and in collaboration with Amplifier.org.

Fairey's alignment of civility with punk rock is not incidental. A radical civility, as opposed to a cautious one, hinges on a similar relationship to risk as that explored in the mosh pit:[54] a readiness to collide while watching out for an opponent's well-being; a willingness to stumble and fall; and a trust that the same person who sent you spinning will help you up. It's also similar to the exploration that happens on the mat and even in the ring: an inclination to take up opposing positions and explore their limits while recognizing that there are parameters for engagement that need to be respected in order to keep the exchange going.

Fights sports and other forms of kinetic play can therefore operate as powerful metaphors for and lived lessons in disagreement with respect. Fight sports, when practiced with respect and approached with clarity of intention, can model a behavior that is both diminished and increasingly necessary in today's political climate. The rise of right-wing populism around the globe suggests that many of the world's largest and presumably strongest democracies have become increasingly unable to contend with diversity of identity and position. We have become unable to withstand, it seems, the back-and-forth, the contention, the opposition, and the power-sharing that are necessary to democracy.

Civility, in the sense of Palumbo-Liu's critique, is courteous; it is safe. It is a preservation of the status quo via a masking of conflict. A kick to the ribs is neither courteous nor safe. It is not comforting. It may, however, be an honest act of communication and not a violation of will. It may be the result of positions taken up in opposition but rooted in regard. A respectful kick to the head shows that it is possible to delve into dissent and explore opposition with esteem and care.

Oppositional civility does not mean that everyone needs to be nice all the time, nor does it mean that everyone needs to get along. Instead, oppositional civility represents a politics of discomfort, a willing off-balancing, but one in which the codes of respect endure through the most intense moments of unease. Oppositional civility is a politics of confrontation, trust, risk, and cooperation.

Oppositional civility aligns with the agenda of what political theorist Chantal Mouffe calls agonistic democracy.[55] Mouffe argues that agonistic confrontation is a condition of pluralistic democracy.[56] While agonistics is an ideal that has the potential to move a society closer to pluralistic democracy, oppositional civility comprises sets of practices and attitudes toward practice. Oppositional civility happens on a quotidian level, allowing individuals to live out social and political ideals within the cultural and historical situation that they're situated in. Oppositional civility is also the effect generated by sets of practices dedicated to respectful disagreement. It bears a definite resemblance to the oppositional pedagogy invoked by Judith Halberstam.[57] Oppositional civility is, potentially, ongoing.

Oppositional civility does not mean all points of view are equally valid, just as the act of sparring does not mean that all fighters are equal in skill. Acts of respectful disagreement point out the flaws in a position without violating the will of the person presenting them, much as sparring is a reminder to be open to failure and the teaching and learning that can result from it.[58] Oppositional civility allows for an honest inquiry into the strengths and weaknesses of an argument just as the act of sparring allows for an honest investigation of the components of a fighter's game. Oppositional civility, like sparring, rests on a confrontation with the capacities and vulnerabilities of another human being, which signals our fundamental commonalities and our radical differences. A punch to the face, delivered not in animosity but as a reminder that our guard was down, is an evidence-based claim. There are few alternative facts on the mat or in the ring.

I am not arguing for a utopian interpretation of martial arts and other oppositional sports. Play does not automatically give us the tools we need to disagree with respect and to learn from disagreement. Martial arts, and even more so other confrontational sports (such as American football), often fail to create oppositional civility just as they fail to generate the strength of character and goodwill that they are reputed to cultivate. Kinetic play can easily model unchecked confrontation rather than managed disagreement. As we'll see, this is particularly true when games become commercialized and standardized, and when institutional concerns such as prestige and money outweigh the experience of the participants. Instead of arguing that we can play our way to a better, more just, and more equal world, I am suggesting that how people play in a particular social and historical context reveals much about how they interact and how they would like to interact. Playing gives us an opportunity to imagine other ways to live beyond the ones right in front of us.[59]

The ability of martial arts to heal and to mitigate aggression is not a given. Instead, these potentials must be actively cultivated.[60] Such considerations can provide a way of examining games and sports more generally for their interpersonal potential and, hence, for their politics. But it can also extend outward as a metaphor for understanding the human exchange that characterizes politics on the macro-scale, a move from the investigations of the personal-as-political to the interpersonal-as-political.

As is probably already evident, I do not make a distinction here between martial arts and combat sports. A stereotypical assumption is that Eastern martial arts work on principles of energy transfer and the deflection of energy whereas Western fight sports, such as boxing and Greco-Roman wrestling, do not. This is not the case: boxing teaches skills of evasion, whether that's the head- and handwork and angling of a skill infighter or the dynamic footwork of the skilled outfighter. Similarly, all grappling arts, including Greco-Roman styles, require an understanding of the differential physics that obtain when two bodies come into contact than when the two bodies are separate, relying on sensitivity to determine when and how an opponent is going to move. On the flip side, many Eastern arts deploy "hard style" training elements such as the techniques required to produce a stronger kick or a more effective punch. The rigorous training methods of, for instance, Chinese kung fu align with—more than they differ from—those of a serious boxing gym.

My sense of the transformative possibility of martial arts lies not in practices such as meditation and breathing exercises that allow a practitioner to overcome the presumed violence of their practice or through forms that abstract violence into aesthetics, but through fight sports that turn violence into a game. The changes I sensed in myself, the transformation other fighters speak of, and the sense of community I have witnessed in numerous training settings suggests a reveling in the tangible, brutal components of fight sport: the "good pain" of holding the Thai pads for a strong kicker, the dull ache of an opponent's glove on my cheek, the gasping for air to get through an untimed round of sparring.

My central claim here is that these properties emerge out of the practices that inhere in martial arts training. As such, I suggest that immediate, tangible undertakings, especially those that are repeated and that are shared with others, bring about particular habits and ways of being in the world that align with larger political, and even economic, propositions. As theorists of practice suggest,[61] we enact social relationships in much of what we do on a quotidian level. We practice ways of being in the world and ways of interacting with each other. We learn to value particular actions and particular outcomes over others. We learn to focus on outcome or process, an attention that structures our daily lives. Seen within the framework of arts and humanities disciplines such as performance studies, theater studies, dance studies, and musicology, where we've suggested that forms of representation not only reflect but also contribute to social reality, it is no great leap of logic to suggest that forms of recreation likewise enact social reality.

This is not simply a theoretical claim. Martial arts practitioners and self-defense advocates reflect on how their training empowered them in other arenas of their life. Educators, coaches, and parents debate the merits of sport competition for children, questioning what precisely we are teaching our youth when they compete in, for example, AYSO matches: Are they learning the grit and fortitude that comes with competitive sport? Or are they learning that winning is all that matters? Students and administrators question the central role of sports to high school and college life, asking what it says about education when a school week leads up to Friday's big game and when our movements across a college campus are structured by the position of its football field. Journalists and public health workers raise questions regarding the increasing marginalization and fragmentation of kinetic leisure, considering what values the American worker enacts when she knows that she is expected to answer emails even as she runs on the treadmill. These are questions that are actively being debated in contemporary American society and, to a lesser extent, throughout the English-speaking world. They are addressed as issues of educational policy, of cultural attitudes toward games and sports, and of the structure and routines of daily life.

It is my hope that a discussion of the multiple connotations of play and its relationship to mastery, failure, and intersubjective exchange will help to connect such seemingly disparate concerns as the role of respectful disagreement in civic life and a public health crisis around insufficient exercise. Likewise, I suggest that examining issues such as the pleasures of risk and the ways in which shared vulnerability can generate an experience of community links reflections on the inequalities of a neoliberal economic system with considerations of an increasingly mediated public sphere. Play, despites its intrinsic value, opens out to larger concerns regarding the structure of society. In order to realize the value of play, we need to account for its dynamic and fanciful nature while recognizing its significance in enacting social relationships. To fully understand how we interact, we need to take play seriously.

1

No Hard Feelings

WHY MARTIAL ARTS DOESN'T MEAN WHAT VIOLENCE MEANS

IN A DECEMBER 2013 UFC 168 match, Judo player and mixed martial arts competitor Ronda Rousey went up against submission wrestler Miesha Tate. Tate survived the first round with Rousey, an accomplishment no other fighter had achieved until that point, emerging from the intense encounter with only a cut above her eyebrow. Early in the second round, Tate advanced on Rousey, preparing to strike. Rousey flipped her with one of her characteristic judo throws, isolating Tate's arm in the aftermath of that moment of instability. As Rousey leaned back into an arm bar, Tate tapped, ceding the match. When Tate stood, she offered Rousey her hand. Rousey refused the handshake and turned away.

The crowd erupted into shouts and boos that didn't die down even when the winner came out for her post-match interview. Sports pages, martial arts publications, and blogs couldn't stop referencing the refused handshake. Even now, years later, should you Google "Ronda Rousey Miesha Tate," an image of Rousey turning away from Tate's outstretched hand is one of the top five images to appear. Rousey's subsequent refusal to touch gloves pre-match with Holly Holm, the fighter who bested her, seemed to justify the spate of post-match trolling leveled at the defeated champion.

In both instances, however, Rousey played the game by the rules. She followed the referee's instructions and adhered to the requirements of the sport, avoiding eye gouges, groin strikes, dynamic attacks to the joints, head butts, and air chokes. She gave the officials and the crowd the "good, clean fight" that was requested. And yet the refusal of mere gestures prompted an outcry.

Why do we accept the bloody spectacle of sport fighting but decry the fighter who rejects its protocol? Why do we encourage trash-talking but call out the contender who refuses a handshake? As Rousey vs. Tate and a long line of similar grudge matches suggest, real-life antagonism makes for an enticing lead-up to an athletic competition, especially one where the contestants hit each other. There's something titillating about the idea that a sport fight, beyond its decorum, under the rules, has a touch of the real to it. At the same time, as the outcry over etiquette breaches suggest, there's something appalling about the idea that combat sport is actual violence.

The uproar that followed these instances of nonsporting behavior pertains to the refusal of gestures, such as handshakes and fist bumps, small in themselves but rich in significance. These gestures take on an importance far beyond their minor role in bracketing a sport fight. They function as symbols, signals as to the meaning of what happens in the ring, and frames, temporal indications that what happens there begins on command and ends when the referee calls it. Although trash-talking intentionally blurs the line between the game and life beyond it, viewers crave the reassurance that what happens in the ring stays in the ring. We want martial arts competition to be "real," and yet we also want to know that it's not. Symbolism and framing devices take on a particular urgency when players accumulate points and wins through inflicting intentional injury. Paradoxically, the importance of such gestures and the rigor with which they're maintained indicate just how different sport fighting is from violence.

The English word etiquette comes from the French *étiquette*, meaning "tag" or "label."[1] This etymology suggests that meaning gets applied onto an activity via particular gestures. Gestures attach meaning to an action. Viewed this way, it's not surprising that when the stakes are high, labels take on a particular importance.

Fight sport conventions operate in just such a way. They signal that what happens in the ring or the cage or on the mat is a test of skill, and not an attempt to devalue another human being. Etiquette separates combat sport from "real" life. They remind the participants and the audience that the event is a competition that both participants agree to participate in even, and perhaps especially, when people get hurt. No hard feelings, as the saying goes.

Etiquette, with its inbuilt symbolism and framing, signals the participants' agreement to what follows, the acceptance of some dangers and not others, a contract that is freely accepted. A meme that circulated the Internet a year or so ago brings this point home. On the top half of the rectangular image is a picture of two men, sweaty, shirtless, their faces bloodied, and black MMA gloves covering their knuckles. Their hands clasped in a handshake, they embrace, smiling. Under them is text: "Good game." In the lower half is a picture of a soccer player sitting on the pitch, clutching an injured shin. The caption there reads: "Ow, you kicked me."

Martial artists and martial arts fans circulated this image to indicate how tough martial artists are in contrast to other athletes. After all, we get kicked repeatedly and still smile and hug our opponents while everyone else, including other athletes, can't handle a single strike. They complain when someone kicks or hits them, whereas we just take it and move on.

This meme misses fundamental points about the differences between sport fighting and other interactions. I'm as willing as anyone else to take kicks and punches on the mat. I'm as unwilling to be kicked or punched off the mat, including on a soccer pitch, should I ever end up on one. Getting hit outside the martial arts context is not what most people have signed up for. In hitting, an aggressor is typically doing something that their target has elected not to do in order to spare another person injury and humiliation. They're cheating, in a particularly unpleasant way, using utterly quotidian ethical behavior against another person. One of the things that's terrible about violence is this imbalance in ethics: one person chooses to do something that another has, intentionally or implicitly, removed from their repertoire of options. An aggressor renders the encounter inherently unfair because of one person's desire for even-handedness and the other's disregard for the same. That's why getting punched after a game of tennis is nothing like getting hit in a boxing match. Getting kicked in soccer is nothing like getting kicked in muay Thai.[2]

While all sports have codes, conventions, and symbolism, and all have the potential to erupt into violence, martial arts constitute a special case. Physical confrontation isn't just a possibility; it's the form the sport takes. In martial arts, we alter the function of violence—hitting is about outgaming our opponent rather than destroying their sense of self[3]—while keeping elements of its form—kicks, punches, elbow strikes, takedowns. Maintaining this difference between form and function is crucial to fight sports.

Thoughts on the Real: Sport Fighting versus Violence

Two years ago, at a self-defense special training, I participated in a padded assailant workshop, a class in which an instructor acts as the aggressor in various role-play scenarios, dressed in body armor so defenders can land palm strikes, elbows strikes, and gouges, attacking such normally fragile targets as the eyes, the throat, and the groin. In the pre-class introduction, I identified myself as someone interested in sport fighting, rather than primarily in self-defense. Seeing my lightweight, fingerless gloves and shin guards, the instructor took sport fighting to mean mixed martial arts specifically and said,

FIGURE I.1 Sports such as Shooto and Mixed Martial Arts allow more strikes than traditional martial arts and Western boxing.
Source: Collection Commons License.

"MMA is about as close as you're going to get to a real fight. But you still don't gouge the eyes, break the eardrum, and kick the groin."

She had a point. Sports such as MMA and Japanese Shooto, referred to as no-holds-barred or no-rules fighting, allow more attacks than other martial arts; they therefore walk a finer line between sport and violence than more rule-bound, traditional martial arts. But they do, in fact, bar some holds. They have rules, conventions that dictate who can do what, when, and in what way.[4] A sport with no rules would not only be unmanageably dangerous; it also, as we'll see, wouldn't be a sport. Rules make the game.

Because of this difference between the intentional limits imposed by sport fighting and the expanded possibilities of violent confrontation in the world beyond the mat, martial arts stands in a troubled relationship to what it is labeled the "real." In martial arts parlance, "real" typically refers to nonconsensual conflict in the world outside the cage, the ring, or the gym. On one level, boxing matches, mixed martial arts fights, and karate tournaments are perfectly real; they are real sport fights. On another level, none of these are real because they do not approximate the conditions of violent conflict in terms of space, timing, number of opponents, mindset of the participants, or the meaning of the encounter. The question of the real is why combat sport tends to be both condemned and dismissed. It's condemned because it's too real: that's just people bashing the hell out of each other. It's condemned because it's not real enough: a UFC match doesn't involve people pulling out knives and swinging baseball bats.

Violence is far messier, more mean-spirited, and more bizarre than anything we encounter on the mat. Aggressors typically strike when their targets are in a compromised position—tired, distracted, lost, or drunk—and, often, violence is motivated primarily by narratives in the mind of the aggressor rather than by outside events. It mimics the normal interactions of daily life while twisting them to a cruel end. Violence happens with one person's consent and awareness in direct opposition to the consent of another.

Violence is context- and logic-destroying. Sport fighting, by contrast, relies on a very specific context and uses a specific logic as its structure. Martial arts enhance a practitioner's sense of self, rather than attempting to destroy one (although more totalitarian teaching methods can damage an aspirant's sense of self-worth in order to build it back up again). Martial arts structure and organize violent actions, offering them a different meaning.

Most sport fighters are careful to differentiate between what happens in the cage or in the ring and on the street.[5] Some have used their ring or cage skills in self-defense, while others have brought violence out of the ring to use their skills against nonconsenting people, including their intimate partners.[6] Some writers who comment on martial arts, especially those who discuss modern sport fighting, argue that full-contact, minimal rule sport fighting is delving into the heart of violence.[7]

Martial arts writers who compare a ring fight to a "real" fight refer to a very specific kind of violence. They're recalling (or imagining) a scenario where someone feels slighted by the actions of another, challenging them to step out of their vehicle after a nearly missed collision or out of a bar after a perceived infraction. They recall (imagine) standing off and circling as a crowd gathers to watch the fight. They are not imagining themselves arriving home late at night when an assailant hits them in the back of the head. They are not expecting an acquaintance to become infuriated and race at them with a baseball bat. They are not envisioning someone on a subway platform lashing out for no apparent reason.

In other words, when they think of "real" conflict they are thinking of a fight—a mutually consensual, clearly designated confrontation rather than of the kind of violence in which one person tries to eradicate another person's will. This kind of fighting is a test of tenacity, ferocity, and skill; like a sport fight, it bears little resemblance to being attacked at random. It's also a performance, an improvised, violent enactment staged for those who gather to watch. There is a contract, albeit a murky one, that is sometimes broken without consequence.

Self-defense instructors call this kind of confrontation the challenge fight and sociologists designate them simply as "fights," contrasting them with violence, in order to signal their participatory nature.[8] This is not to say, of course, that challenge fights are not dangerous. Replete with the risks of a sport fight, such as the danger of a concussion, they offer none of its protections: no mats or ropes, no protective gear, no ringside physician, and no officials with any real authority. Although participants agree to fight, far too often that agreement is conscripted, rendering the fight less-than-consensual. As in other forms of violence, one person typically drives the interaction while the other responds to the aggressor's script.

The parallels that do exist are not an indication that sport fighting is, or replicates, real-world violence. Instead, they suggest that some real-world confrontation mimics athletic competition. As I suggest in the next chapter, these conflicts operate as a kind of edge play that muddies lines between game and reality, blurring the consent that is so crucial to sport fighting. Despite these clear distinctions between violence and fighting, it is important to acknowledge that combat sport participants walk a fine line between intention and aggression, between violence and play.

Walking a Line: Fighting and Aggression

About six months after I started training, I broke my finger in a sparring match. What I thought was a jammed finger turned out to be a spiral fracture, requiring surgery, pins, and a cast. The cast came off to a healed bone and atrophied muscles in my hands and arms. I practiced physiotherapy exercises until I could almost make a full fist. I wasn't supposed to spar until I had full range of motion.

I held off for weeks. Then I did a little isolation sparring, delimiting the interaction and restricting which body part does what. Once that happened, I had the bug. When time came to spar, I couldn't bring myself to sit out. Each person I paired up with, I reminded them of the hand injury and we made vague plans about fighting one-handed. Then we started and both hands flew. Even wrapped in a glove, the slightly open fist reminded me. Somehow, I managed not to make impact with that vulnerable left hand.

I pair off with Vincent. He's as intense as me but with more control and a lot more skill. He's more adept, technically. His punches are more precise and, hence, more powerful; his kicks are more accurate. He's got a better repertoire of tactics and a stronger sense of strategy. He moves his head and his feet constantly in a perfect rendition of a broken rhythm, making him hard to hit. While I've been recovering from injury, he's been training.

And I'm about to fight him one-handed.

We touch gloves and step in. I keep trying to duck in under his reach. His head moves all over. I feint, he bobs, I feint in a different direction, he bobs again, I throw a punch, he bobs.

I don't just eat the punches the way I did a few months ago. In that sense, I've learned to be a moving target too. But I'm dancing around all over the place, like I'm pretending to be a boxer. It wears me out. As I get worn out, I take more shots. Every strike that lands, I get angrier and more frustrated. I move in to strike. I have enough time to think, I'm telegraphing. I don't have enough time to tighten my strike. Vincent blocks and hits.

I'm afraid. Afraid because Vincent is the better fighter. Afraid because I've held my own with him before and will feel my failure intensely if I can't do so now. Afraid for the dreary fact of my injury. The fear–aggression–tunnel vision loop gets tighter as I get tired. Out of nowhere, I feel impact. Vincent's fist hits my face at the jaw, my head turns, and I stumble backward. I'm cognizant enough to identify the strike as a right hook. I hear our instructor, Sifu Alain, say, "nice," with a degree of enthusiasm that tells me I'm not being weak in reeling from the strike.

Everything goes black. For a moment, I wonder, did I get knocked out? But my body's dashing forward; my feet move underneath me. It's an out-of-body experience; a self is lagging behind somewhere. I feel a surge of anger but I'm not sure where it's coming from. From behind me, I hear a voice.

"Don't get mad," Alain says. "Keep your cool."

I drop back in my body, into real time. It's just a sparring match. It's just the gym, people in pairs, throwing punches. Just Vincent moving in front of me, striking, blocking, and bobbing. That's all.

I have been angry plenty of times. I have been so furious that the chemical cocktail in my bloodstream turned everything around me shimmery and metallic. But this is the first time I've understood the meaning of the term blind rage. In that moment, it became clear to me that to sport fight requires moving beyond anger. It means getting to the point that being hit means nothing: no insult perceived, no anger provoked.

Writing about play in the animal kingdom and the evolution of meaning-making, anthropologist Gregory Bateson suggests that combat play signals an awareness of the difference between sign and meaning among animals. When dogs play, for instance, they crash into each other, they take each other to the ground, and they place their teeth on vulnerable throats and underbellies. Dogs do this with dogs that they like; they don't play this way with dogs they have grievances with. Crucially, both dogs recognize this behavior as play. This, Bateson suggests, indicates that dogs recognize "the sign as a signal . . . which can be trusted, distrusted, falsified, denied, amplified, corrected."[9] Bateson points out that animal play includes meta-communication, the inclusion of information whose sole function is to frame an action. Animal play is full of meta-statements. The canine play bow is a clear example: it's a gesture whose meaning, "this is play," refers solely to the nature of the interaction.

In addition, animal play includes actions for which the sign and its meaning diverge. When a dog places her teeth on another dog's neck in play, she refers to a bite without invoking the meaning of a bite. As Bateson puts it, "the playful nip denotes the bite, but it does not denote what would be denoted by the bite."[10] This distinction, Bateson argues, is fundamental to play and symbolic logic alike. He goes on to suggest that symbolic reasoning is, therefore, not specific to humans.

When an animal places her teeth on another animal's throat, however, she mimics a bite. She doesn't actually bite; she just signals that she could. The other animal accepts this mock bite as part of the play. The movement mechanics of a real bite (sudden adherence, with the teeth landing rapidly, a pause to sink the teeth, and a swift pulling of skin) are entirely different from a simulated one (deliberate placing of the teeth on the target zone with no adherence, no sinking of the teeth, and no pulling). This is a difference not just of degree but also of kind. The distinction may look subtle to us, but it feels completely different to both animals.

Human fight sport relies on a related distinction between sign and meaning as animal play. Seen in this light, the importance of etiquette makes a lot more sense. The framing gestures of a sport fight, whether a bow, a handshake, a

FIGURE 1.2 This does not mean what a bite would mean.
Source: Collection Commons License.

touch of the gloves, or fist bump, operate as meta-communicative statements. They are play markers. When two boxers touch gloves, the only meaning the gesture carries pertains to the action that is about to occur—"this is a match"—and the relationship between the two participants: "I recognize you as my opponent."

In sport fighting, what follows the play marker is simulated combat. And yet unlike in animal play, the attacks are real. In animal play, the movement mechanics of the nip and the bite are markedly different. In sport fighting, the punch is a real punch; the kick is a real kick. Except for the exclusion of certain strikes (and, sometimes, the exclusion of noncorporeal weapons), the movement mechanics are subtly, rather than significantly, different from what we would use in a violent encounter. But the kicks and punches, as hard and direct as they are, don't mean what a "real" kick or a "real" punch means.

Hitting on the mat or in the ring carries an entirely different set of meanings than hitting in the context of real-world interactions. Conversely, as sports sociologist Alex Channon points out in an essay on mixed-sex martial arts training,[11] when it comes to sport fighting, meanings are inverted so that to refrain from hitting or to hit too lightly implies an opponent is not skilled enough to handle a strike. To not hit, in the martial arts context, is to withhold respect whereas in the real world, to hit is to withdraw respect. Hitting off the mat means "I'm angry and I want to hurt you," whereas on the mat it means, "I think you can handle a challenge."

This is one of the hardest lessons of sparring. Beginners often treat sparring as a do-or-die challenge match. They seethe in anger or walk away in tears. I understand why they react this way; I wish I could say my reaction in that round with Vincent was an aberration. But I struggle to contain my emotion whenever I'm encountering someone else's fists. Fighters far more skilled than I occasionally find themselves losing their cool or facing someone who sets them off.

We speak of violence as meaningless. It rarely is. Violence is replete with meaning. Violence rests on an association of form and function. A strike to the face, in the world outside the academy or the fight gym, is not just a random violent act; it is a rebuke, an aggressive correction to a perceived infraction. Strangling is a potentially fatal attack, but also an attempt to establish control. Grabbing the wrist or arm is a less lethal version the same message. A kick, at least in North America, is typically an act of spite or frustration.

The heavy signification of real-world violence is one of the things that makes sport fighting so difficult. A punch received competitively plays with signification. Although it doesn't convey the disrespect of a punch in violence, it carries some of its connotations: "I have bested you." In sport fighting, unlike in violent conflict, we best someone by respecting their value as an athlete and as a person, not by trying to take away their self worth.

However, a punch delivered to a trash-talking opponent comes dangerously close to carrying the meaning of a punch outside the ring: "I will best you" quickly becomes "I will silence you," a meaning that aligns with an aggressive rebuke. It's a fine line, and the narrower it is, the higher tempers can rise and the more tightly the conventions in place need to be observed. This is why trash-talking is both dangerous as well as, for some viewers, exciting.

Before I trained in martial arts, I marveled at canine combat play. Imagine, I would say, if we goofed around by miming shots to each other's faces. Now, I marvel at human combat play. Other animals play fight by signaling an attack; we actually attack and change the meaning in the process. Unlike the play bites of animals, a punch in the ring or on the mat doesn't just reference a real punch. It lands with the same (or, more likely, greater) force than the strike of a person who's actually mad at you.[12] But it doesn't mean what a real punch means. Except that it sort of means what a real punch means. The thinness of this line is what's exciting.

Taming Violence: The Art in Martial Art

In a Brazilian jiu jitsu class, the guest instructor has us skip our usual free rolling in favor of self-defense work. We run through a drill in which one person, the aggressor, lowers his or head and charges straight at the torso of the defender. The defender hooks her arm above the neck of the aggressor, drops her weight into a modified wrestling sprawl, and walks her feet backward, taking the aggressor facedown to the ground. The defender initiates a few strikes, gets up, and escapes.

Knowing the attack is coming, I feel a nauseous sheen utterly unlike the anticipation that leads up to a sparring match. A sickening dread combines with a surge of angry intention. Fortunately, knowing that all I have to do is shoot my arm over the aggressor's neck and drop my weight overrides my fear.

After a few rounds of the drill the counter attack comes automatically. It shifts my gears. Something strange happens when I arch my hand around the aggressor's neck. Once he is down and I am striking, euphoria kicks in, faster and harder than in a sparring match. As I go to stand up, a skip comes into my step; I dance around like it is a round of boxing.

Art plays with the distinction between form and function.[13] Martial arts, including combat sport, explore the space between violence and sport, and thus explore the differences between form and function. This difference is why the "real" is a point of concern for martial arts and a reason why drills like the one I've described get invented: to address a gap between violence and competition. Although this difference between martial arts and real-world violence is cause for concern, debate, and even dismissal of some martial arts practices, it is also unavoidable if martial arts are going to manage violence rather than cultivate it.

It's because of the ability of martial arts to externalize and structure conflict and aggression that we see them as arts. This play between form and function is at the root of this distinction. Sports, like arts, engage a relationship between form and function. Sports are often based on military strategy, even if the reference to warfare has long been forgotten. Similarly, sports are often structured around utilitarian efforts such as running and throwing. The meaning of these activities are subtly (or substantially) altered.

This distinction between form and function, between sign and meaning, is fundamental to the ability of martial arts to organize and externalize violence. Sociologist Loïc Wacquant, in his ethnography of boxing, refers to this process as "domesticating violence" and as the "social regulation of violence."[14] Combat sports tame violence through practicing its form, stripping away its conventional meanings, and replacing them with new ones. Aggressive actions are externalized, removed from emotion, and depersonalized. This delinking between action and meaning becomes effective through constant practice: we strike, we take punches, we work deflections and evasions with someone's fist coming at our faces. The components of violence take on new meanings through sport.

As the arts show us, however, in playing with meaning and altering function, we also play with form. Control is a key element of good sport fighting: the ability to get hit and respond, get hit and re-evaluate, get hit and circle around. Good sport fighters use the strike of an opponent as a gauge of their strategy and their tactics; they appraise their decision-making and they move on. This level of aplomb, this reduction of conflict to its mechanical components, is what makes these sports what they are: it's what makes them watchable, for one thing, and the control is part of what makes us able to actually see what's going on.[15] It's also what makes them enjoyable to do.

Our state of mind is also utterly different when on the mat (or in the ring) and when attacked on the street. For many of us, in sparring, a perversely happy fear precedes the event. I experience, in the run-up to sparring, a funny kind of anxiety that urges me forward instead of warning me to get out: shaky hands, dry mouth, the jumpy-stomach feeling that gets referred to as butterflies. A desire to turn away that doesn't let me turn away. As in stage fright, I wouldn't forgive myself if I passed up the opportunity it presents.

Violence, by contrast, brings with it a sickly rush that accompanies the sudden, unexpected explosion of a normal interaction into conflict. Time slows. Color washes away and contrast brightens, as the world turns a silvery black and white. In my experience, fear, in those moments, is not anticipatory. It is the sickening realization that I will do what needs to be done.

This isn't specific to me. Those who write about self-defense talk about the OODA loop: Observe-Orient-Decide-Act.[16] A violent attack puts the defender at a fundamental disadvantage: the aggressor is already at the act stage, while the defender is still observing and orienting. This allows an aggressor to write the script for violence and it puts the defender in a position where she merely reacts rather than decides upon a strategic response. This also allows the aggressor to think of himself as a subject and the intended victim as an object.

This is a key point at which sport fighting and self-defense diverge. In sport fighting, both contenders begin at the act stage. An additional, crucial difference between sport fighting and violence means that an aggressor, unlike a sport fighter, has a script in his head that he is confident will remain unaltered.[17] Sport fighters, by contrast, know from the outset that even if they have an overall strategy, the script is constantly rewritten by the actions and reactions of each contender. Actions can be read but intentions are, more often than not, opaque.

Playing with Fire

Here's another way in which we know that sport fighting and violence differ: because sport fighting sometimes turns into violence. When it does, it's gone wrong. And we all know it.

In 1962, welterweight boxer Emile Griffith beat opponent Benny Paret in the ring so badly that Paret died from his injuries. At the weigh-in, Paret had taunted Griffith, a closeted bisexual man, with homophobic slurs, calling him *maricon* (faggot) and, depending on the account, either grabbing his buttocks, miming sexual intercourse behind him, or both. Paret's trainers laughed and egged him on.

Once in the ring, during the twelfth round, Griffith rope-trapped Paret and struck him with repeated upper cuts. Paret went limp. He remained on his feet during the onslaught but it's likely that this was because the ropes supported his weight. His eyes closed even as he took punches. He was carried out on a stretcher and never regained consciousness.[18]

While the public blamed Griffith, the referee, and Paret's manager, as well as the sport of boxing, it seems clear in retrospect that the lead-in to this fight rubbed at and smudged the fine line between sport and violence. Trash-talking always carries the risk of turning the fight real, but when one contender attacks another's identity, particularly when that identity is already threatened, the risks are particularly high. Paret's incursion from trash-talking into harassment suggested the reuniting of form and function. And the consequences were deadly.[19]

Boxing, like more apparently wholesome sports such as American football, is dangerous: contenders accumulate points and wins by injuring one another. This means that the risk of serious damage is high. The dangers are heightened by professional boxing's status as a commercial enterprise. If ring fighting were mere blood sport, however, no one would have been shocked or outraged by Paret's death. The story wouldn't have carried forward, recounted to reveal the sweet science's dark shadows. When a gladiator died in the coliseum, the ancient Romans didn't stop the tournament; there was no public outcry, no discussion as to whether such a practice should exist. The death was the point.

When we sport fight, we play with fire. Typically, this expression means courting disaster and taking unnecessary risks. If you play with fire, you'll get burned, is a common variant of the saying. If no one played with fire, it's true that there would be fewer burns. We also wouldn't have cooking, we wouldn't be able to forge metal, and we wouldn't have combustion engines. If we didn't play with fire, we wouldn't be human.

Just as the solution to arson, accidental house fires, and wildfires is not to eradicate fire but to manage it, so, too, is this the case with human aggression. Violence can be useful, especially when it's the defensive kind, especially when it allows us to protect ourselves and others. Aggression, like play, endures across species and across time. We needn't think of aggression as a baseline or natural state to recognize that conflict is recurrent.[20] Because it is persistent, violence needs domestication quite badly.

Why Etiquette in Martial Arts Feels "Real"

Considering that sport fighting explores the line between violence and competition, taking the form of confrontation while awarding it a different function, it makes sense that codes and conventions of respect would be crucially important. In martial arts, etiquette is not surface dressing. Rather, etiquette and respect have tangible effects in martial arts, as the tragic account of Emile Griffith and Benny Paret indicates.

It's easy to see, in the link between ethics and etiquette, an argument in favor of traditional martial arts and against modern sport fighting. After all, traditional martial arts practice codes of respect, traditional martial arts include a great deal of etiquette, and traditional martial arts put all sorts of brackets around fighting. But at least one sociological study found that college students who practiced Western boxing became less aggressive after training; another suggested that a fair and caring coach, who models respect in training practices is more influential than the style of martial art practiced.[21] Loïc Wacquant corroborates such an assessment with his reflections on the relationship between the respectful, disciplined nature of the boxing gym at which he trained and the supportive environment it produced.[22]

Correlation does not equal causality, of course. But correlation can be an indication of causality in the presence of a plausible explanation.[23] It may not be that etiquette produces a respectful fighter, but that respectful fighters practice good etiquette. From a practice-theory perspective, the chicken-or-egg question doesn't matter. Practicing oppositional civility doesn't just mean putting a frame around an interaction; it consists of rehearsing relationships and modeling them. Respect isn't just a trait we have—it's something we live.

While it's easy to think of etiquette as a cover for something, a mask that shields real emotions, etiquette is also a way of practicing our regard for others, reminding ourselves of it on a regular basis until we internalize it. Etiquette can, in Pierre Bourdieu's terms, become part of our habitus so we live out our respect for others and it feels like a real part of who we are.[24] Gestures, as Carrie Noland points out, can present us with new sensations to feel.[25] This connection between what we do and what we feel is, I suspect, the underlying reason for the elaborate codes of respect in traditional martial arts; the integration of behavior into a sense of self as well as into interpersonal interaction allows oppositional civility to extend into agonistic, respectful community.

Given that martial arts interrogates the human propensity for violence, however, it would be surprising if we just threw in a few gestures of respect and left it at that. Indeed, martial arts, including modern sport fight systems, draw on features common to other games as a way of managing the human propensity toward violence. Games and other forms of play allow us to contend with unpleasant aspects of ourselves, such as our potential for deception and betrayal. As such, games require specific spaces and particular parameters for play. They also require an agreement as to what kind of game is being played.

2

The Magic Ring

HOW COMBAT SPORT TRANSFORMS MEANING THROUGH SPACE AND MOVEMENT

UCLA'S JEET KUNE Do Club is training in the Yates Gym. I'm holding the Thai pads for a partner. Like me, my partner struggles with the distinctive flip of the hip, the lift and turn of the heel of the standing leg, and the inward rotation of the kicking leg that constitutes a muay Thai kick.

Vincent, who is leading the session today, comes over to demonstrate. I turn toward him and hold the heavy Thai pads to the side of my body at a ninety-degree angle, preparing for the impact of his kick. He switches his feet and *thunk*! His shin meets the pad. It lifts me slightly off the ground and stumbled backward. For an instant, I fly.

I stand still, staring at Vincent. My mouth is hanging open, ever so slightly.

"You okay?" he asks.

I finally find the words for what I'm thinking.

"How'd you do that?" I ask.

Vincent smiles, and wriggles his fingers, invoking the image of a comic-book villain. "Magic," he says.

In evoking the idea of magic, Vincent was teasing me and saving face for me at once. Magic is typically what we *don't* talk about in martial arts, at least not while we're practicing them. Practitioners of combat sports are fond of saying there is no magic. By this, they mean both that there is no technique that works in all situations and that there are no techniques that are learned without effort. Magic is associated with the humiliations you see on YouTube videos where someone claims to be able to knock people out with just his thoughts and ends up being hit in the face. It's because of "magic" that some think martial arts, or traditional martial arts, or the arts that they don't study, are nonsense. Sport fighters say there is no magic to counteract the conventional association of martial arts with the sword epic *wuxia* films

FIGURE 2.1 Receiving heavy Thai kicks on the training pads requires its own skills.
Photograph courtesy of Augustus John Roe.

in which actors swing on wires to fight in the air. Magic gets called fancy if you're feeling kind and bullshido if you're not.[1]

The idea of magic has a different meaning altogether when it comes to theories of play. Game theorists Katie Salen and Eric Zimmerman suggest that magic refers to "the transformation of meaning within the game," which allows players to create a new reality.[2] Martial arts, in this sense, clearly mobilize a kind of magic. As we've seen, martial arts use the components of violence, but its strikes and its takedowns carry a different meaning. A kick in the outside world means "I am frustrated," while in the instance I've described, the hard kick to the Thai pads meant "I'll show you this so you can figure it out."[3]

In addition to altering the meaning of punches, kicks, and takedowns, martial art practices refine these elements. Violent action is often banal—and, fortunately, unsophisticated. An untrained kick or punch is typically big and, even if powerful, sloppy. Martial arts practices hone these movements, tightening them up, making them more direct, faster, sharper, and crisper. Whether those are straight-from-the-midline karate strikes, the vertical chain punches of wing chun, or the horizontal punches that initiate from a high guard typical of modern boxing and kickboxing, they all involve a refinement of movement.

FIGURE 2.2 The muay Thai round kick offers a particularly vivid example of body mechanics and synchronization.
Photograph courtesy of Mich Yap.

Some of these movements, like a muay Thai kick, are so utterly unlike the actions included in a garden-variety flare-up that they need to be learned component by component.[4] A muay Thai kick requires rehearsing a series of individually difficult movements—lifting and twisting a heel, rotating one hip in as the other turns out—until they are no longer awkward. A Thai kick gets its power and speed from the heel, hips, legs, and upper body working together to form a powerful whole. It's a study in body mechanics, the coming together of several well-honed parts of a process.

For a lot of martial artists—and even more so for those outside the practice—this is not what gets called "magic." Movements that appear magic are those that are subtle: the one-inch punch, where an apparent flick of the wrist sends an opponent flying back; the kotegaeshi, where a three-quarter turn of the wrist takes an opponent to the ground. Effortless throws often appear magical, although their fluency is predicated upon physics: throwing an opponent in the direction where she has no base of support is more effective than throwing her in a direction where she can keep her feet under her. These tend to be the maneuvers that get dismissed out of hand until you see them or, better yet, feel them in practice. Pressure points seem like kung fu magic until you're the one whose nerve clusters get set off.

Physical play often includes drilling skills outside the context of the game: we get good at baseball by playing catch in the park. As Guro Dan Inosanto likes to say, there are no tires on the field in a football game. There are likewise no jump ropes in the boxing ring. This constitutes a difference between kinetic and sedentary games: we learn to play chess by playing chess, not by drilling chess-related skills; we get better at playing poker by playing poker. For physical games, by contrast, we hone our understanding of biomechanics and our tactical responses, our speed, our sensitivity, and our balance, in order to refine the components of the game.

Magic also carries the connotation of sleight of hand. Sparring, in particular, is an opportunity to explore magic in the quotidian sense of the art of misdirection. Sparring, like a magician's show, relies on tactics designed to direct another person's attention so he sees what you want him to see rather than what you're actually doing. Sparring hinges on getting an opponent to think you're doing one thing while doing another: aiming high to hit low; throwing a jab to solicit a catch or parry that opens the opponent's jaw to your hook. This is the basis of the chess game with which sparring is so frequently compared (and which I discuss in more detail in the next chapter). This is play in the sense of playing a game of strategy as well as in that secondary but crucial sense: "don't play me" and "played for a fool." Magic and trickery go hand in hand.

Sacred Playgrounds and Gyms of One's Own: How Space Creates Meaning

The Inosanto Academy is a converted auto-body repair shop. Pillars run in rows throughout the space. Yoga mats are wrapped around them with electrical tape to minimize the risk of injury when students run into the pillars, accidently strike them with weapons, or accidentally throw a training partner into them. A massive folding door on runners opens the training mat to the outside world. Where cars once sat on lifts, heavy bags and wooden dummies line the floor.

My daughter illustrated the magic of the space for me. From the time she was three and quit karate because she found it boring, she had asked to train at the Inosanto Academy. When she was finally able to join the academy's Little Dragons class, I brought her in to observe. She spent much of the class not looking at the students but at the walls. Every few minutes, she would stage whisper, "Hey Mom! Look! There's Bruce Lee," as she spotted yet another image of the long-dead master, preserved, like James Dean, in eternal youth.

Like a novice boxer pacing in front of the gym before deciding whether to go in, it took me weeks to work up the resolve to inquire about training at the Inosanto Academy. After close to two years of practice of jeet kune do and Filipino martial arts, I had to muster my courage to even ask about a membership. Part of me wondered if I might have to prove my worth before I was allowed to train there. Could I really just walk in off the street and start training? Eddie, who worked the front desk at the time, was clearly puzzled; he took my apprehension for fear of hard training. "Don't worry," he said. "We're not a fighter's gym."

Defeat, injury, and exhaustion weren't my concern, however. Nor was I star-struck. Bruce Lee was an icon in my childhood, but I don't idolize him. Admittedly, I was intimidated by the prospect of training under a master as accomplished as Guro Dan Inosanto. The high level of his students and his instructors prompted a certain level of apprehension. But that wasn't the whole picture. After all, I had studied bharata natyam with a rigorous instructor in India and modern dance in all sorts of studios from small town to professional; I knew how to muddle through a class.

The intimidation I felt had to do with the space, the kind of transformation that people had undergone there, the kind of ordinary miracles it staged. I am not the first person to have noticed this: Anna, my sometimes instructor and sometimes training partner, recalls standing outside The Way of No Way Academy before her first class, pretending she was just there to watch. Boxers and other sport fighters' stories recount that lingering indecision, that conjuring of fortitude to step over the threshold into a new kind of experience; it is not simply a fear of the rigors and the dangers that lie within, because the outside world is also replete with risks. Entering the space of fight sports involves a decision to enter an alternate dimension of experience. To walk through the door is to agree to be changed. This is why judo players speak of stepping onto the mat, both literally as in stepping into training and competition, and metaphorically as in facing a challenge.[5] That's why stepping into the ring is a trope and perhaps even a cliché.

Nearly everyone who writes about martial arts describes the space in which it happens. In part, that's because of a room-of-one's-own phenomenon: a would-be fighter needs a space to train and an instructor needs a place to teach. Finding the right space can present the sort of practical challenge with the deeply emotional and professional implications that Virginia Woolf identifies in the struggles of women writers in *A Room of One's Own*. The space to work, to practice, to play isn't just about a physical place; it signals the opportunity it provides. Sometimes it's the struggles around creating and maintaining the space that mark it out as special.

Martial artist and memoirist Susan Schorn describes the efforts required to maintain a women-only karate dojo in Austin, Texas.[6] She describes the work demanded to revitalize a neglected space and the search for a new site for the school as an emotional and not solely practical undertaking. Schorn links the physical maintenance of the space, the structural, electrical, and plumbing work, to the self-defense training provided by the dojo: these tasks were means of problem-solving in dangerous circumstances. Working on a space turns it into a home for the art and the community that trains there. (This, and not just practical necessity, is also why maintaining the space is so often part of martial arts training, and why cleaning and organizing a space appears so frequently in movie training montages.)

Likewise, Loïc Wacquant invokes the many ways in which the Woodlawn boxing gym operated as a separate world for its members, "an island of order and virtue" in an otherwise desperately impoverished, dilapidated, and dangerous neighborhood.[7] Ruled over by a strict and paternal coach, Woodlawn required particular actions of its members and prohibited others. These requirements, Wacquant suggests, together with the continual, daily practices of boxing, require of the boxers a monastic existence while giving them the sense of community that enabled them to survive in an environment fraught with unemployment, alcoholism and other addiction, violence, and homelessness.[8] Like Schorn, Wacquant discusses the struggles to maintain a training space, describing an ailing infrastructure but one in which the space never felt run-down. Maintaining the space contributed to the devotion it elicited.

Naturalist, poet, and author Diane Ackerman, following Johan Huizinga, calls the space established through focused play the "sacred playground." Game theorists such as Salen and Zimmerman call it the "magic circle," and performance theorist and theater director and performance studies progenitor Richard Schechner invokes the metaphor of the net. Game theorists debate which is the most appropriate metaphor, but for our purposes, whether it's a frame, a circle, a bubble, a membrane, a zone, or a net doesn't so much matter. What's most important is that focused play happens in a place that distinguishes itself from ordinarily life, physically and in the imagination; what Ackerman calls "deep play" occurs in a space rich with meaning and marked by experience.[9]

In this sense, the ring, cage, gym, dojo, or academy becomes a spatial palimpsest marked by the efforts of those who have come before. Martial artists make direct reference to space when they distinguish sport or art from real-world violence: they speak of what happens on the mat (or in the ring) versus what happens on the street. While referring to real-world violence as "the street" is problematic, given that most violence happens in the home, this expression nonetheless serves an important function. It differentiates play from self-defense, sport from self-protection. In this context, a physical space that acts as the boundaries of play—the magic ring—discriminates between martial arts and violence.

Ackerman's insights about the magic space created by play align with historian and philosopher Michel de Certeau's understanding of the difference between spaces and places. For de Certeau a place is a physical, often institutionally marked off, site whereas a space is a practiced place.[10] A space comes into being through what people do there. Practice, training, and activity are what give the magic circle and the sacred playground its significance for people who play there.

Fight sports carry a different meaning than violence by virtue of the spaces in which they take place, spaces that conjure up a history of practice. At the same time, the converse is true: the space is transformed by the structured, controlled, and consensual fighting that takes place within it. Through the

FIGURE 2.3 Boxing rings such as this one at the world-famous Gleason's Gym have become iconic because of the training that has taken place there.

Photograph by Carlos Pacheco (Flickr: Boxing Ring) [CC BY-SA 2.0 (https://creativecommons.org/licenses/by-sa/2.0)].

efforts of fighters, trainees, coaches, cornermen and cornerwomen, referees, and judges, it becomes a magic circle and not a site of mindless bloodshed. The actions that de Certeau describes as practices create a space of stability, consistency, safety, and reliable sociality that contrasts to the violent actions mobilized in the training.

Deep Play and Sweat-Soaked Matts

I'm on my way to my first-ever jeet kune do class, held in UCLA's Wooden Center, its recreational gym. The gym buzzes with a kind of activity that is foreign to me. People walk or run on treadmills. Students pedal stationary bicycles and lift weights. The dance studios and yoga rooms are not visible, so the climbing wall offers the only comfort of familiarity.

I head upstairs and into the Blue Room, named for the wrestling mats that line the floors and walls of the space. The space has a comforting smell that reminds me of yoga mats; only months later do I realize it's the smell of sweat-infused plastic. Along with forty UCLA students, I sign in and wait for a signal of what to do. Alain and Paul call us out onto the mats, Paul boisterous and commanding, Alain, agile and light-hearted.

The class opens with footwork: step and slide, slide and step, push shuffle, forward, back, side to side. We practice boxing head movement: slip left, slip right, sway back, bob and weave. My arms ache with the effort of keeping my hands in a tight guard, utterly unfamiliar from my (lapsed) kung fu practice of midline punches and defense. My left hip burns from the orthodox boxing stance; we don't change leads and my body rebels at this lack of symmetry.

Alain teaches a lap sao, wing chun's pulling wrist or forearm grab, then shows how it could move into a takedown driven by a grappler's figure-of-four. My partner, Royce, and I are in the back corner of the room, struggling to understand the complexities of the takedown. Alain comes up, demonstrates on Royce. When he asks if I could see it, his enthusiasm is such that I say yes, even though I couldn't. He asks if I want to feel it and I agree. He pulls my wrist so I lurch forward. As I pull back to regain my balance, he snakes his hand around my arm, torques it, and steps backward, taking me to the floor. The elegance of the movement, the idea that wing chun could transform into wrestling and that one person could veer between training systems so fluidly: these factors come together to create my devotion to jeet kune do.

The lap sao into a figure-of-four takedown sparked my love not just of particular movements, their elegance and their shape, but also of an entire art. I walked out of that class elated and went back each week religiously; I began adding martial arts classes so that eventually, I was in the Blue Room nearly every day. The specifics of the movement and the feel of a space came together so that the transition between the grab and the takedown sparked my love for an art and my love of the art prompted my devotion to a space. What seemed to be a generic space became marked, slowly and without my realizing it, with all I had learned there. I can't remember how the Blue Room looked to me before I trained in it. I only know that it changed.

High-risk and high-attention activities don't just change our relationship to the space of practice. They also change our relationship to time. Ackerman identifies the melting away of the world in focused activities as deep time, a temporal alteration, a compression, speeding up, or slowing down that accompanies deep play's state of immersion. This fading away of the world and the collapsing of time is a common experience in martial arts training. Face off against an opponent, even in the congenial environment of the gym, and outside concerns drift off. Texts and emails, dishes and shopping lists, to-dos, pick-up times, Facebook conversations, applications, and writing deadlines cease to exist. Even a drill, rather than live sparring, can have this effect where focus on a partner and the action at hand is complete. Partially, of course, this is negatively defined, as even a drill carries the risk of failure: minor failures such as struggling with the drill and adversely affecting a partner's experience, and major failures such as getting hit.

In order for an intense experience to feel satisfying, it requires that focus turn inward, away from outside distractions and toward the task at hand. This condition aligns with what phenomenologists call transcendence, a state in which intention seamlessly yields action. Phenomenologists suggest that this state of seamless realized intention is one of mastery and that we know ourselves *as* selves because of this experience.

On the flip side of the experience of mastery is immanence, a sense of being stuck within a body that fails to execute our commands. Immanence, especially for the applied phenomenologists, is the state in which we fail to realize our intentions and our bodies refuse to act as the extension of our wills. Most phenomenologists see immanence as moments where our sense of self, our status as a subject, is threatened. However, Greg Downey argues that immanence is necessary to the learning process; Vivian Sobchack maintains that immanence can produce a new awareness of the body, and that one person's immanence is another's transcendence.[11]

Just as phenomenologists focus on mastery as it constitutes a self, psychologist Csikszentmihalyi investigates how the autotelic, or flow state, enables a person to become "more of a unique individual, less predictable, possessed of rarer skills."[12] To do so, he highlights the autotelic state, in which attention is fully focused on an activity at hand. Csikszentmihalyi notes that the flow state is produced when challenges and abilities line up, producing neither the boredom of too little stimuli or the anxiety of too much. In the flow state, our capacities are challenged but not quite beyond the point that we can't handle them. Because an activity that produces an autotelic state sometimes does so by pushing us to the edge of our capacities, the flow state sometimes arises from experiences that are not all that enjoyable at the time.[13]

Like sparring. The flow state comes about when our abilities are tested. Being tested is not always pleasant, especially when the challenge comes in the form of someone else's fists. As Csikszentmihalyi indicates, some encounters with another human being's oppositional intention appear, in retrospect, as truly happy memories. (Others, for me anyway, remain tinged with unpleasantness; I suspect these are the ones in which the challenges outstripped my abilities, resulting in anxiety.) Csikszentmihalyi's argument goes a long ways toward explaining why, in the pursuit of play, we can go to great lengths and expose ourselves to risk, danger, and distress.

It is not surprising that play produces an autotelic state since, as Csikszentmihalyi points out, games, sports, and art are designed to induce flow. However, the flow state as the balance of ability and challenge explains how we can find pleasure, empowerment, and unity within play that seems, from the outside, antagonistic, brutal, and painful. Such an insight is, of course, not limited to martial arts. All sorts of games, from board games to American football, stage artificial disagreement and some do so via physical risk. In all these cases, however, play is an invitation to enter the flow state, one in which we can intentionally choose to let the outside world slip away.

On the flip side of the association of martial arts training with unchecked violence is their association with spirituality. Just as there is a tendency to break martial arts down into traditional versus modern and refined versus brutal, there's a tendency to perceive martial arts as spiritual versus worldly. Eastern arts such as tai chi chu'an and ba gua tend to be characterized as refined and spiritual, whereas Western boxing is depicted as brutal and corporeal.[14] Such divisions suggest an Orientalist nostalgia, imagining of a way of fighting that is respectful and controlled, one that relies on ancient wisdoms and reveals fundamental truths, in contrast to the gritty reality of day-to-day life. These associations deny the rough practicality of many Asian and ancient traditions and the thoughtfulness and the sustained practice of the Western or modern ones. (They also ignore the long history of practices such as boxing and Greco-Roman wrestling.)

Of course, many practitioners have learned a great deal about themselves and others, taming their furies and conquering their fears through traditional Asian arts. However, the taming of violence through its reduction to energy exchange is not specific to Eastern martial arts. Brutally deep play through combative competition is not specific to Western arts. It's a mixed bag either way.

Martial arts—including the most modern, the most hybrid, the most competitive—induce an intense focus. The deep play of sparring and grappling create an altered sense of time and space. They bring us into a state of profound, intense immersion. They do so because of, not in spite of, the risk of physical injury, emotional despair, and possible loss of dignity. In the case of modern martial arts, intense focus happens in a space that stinks of sweat rather than being perfumed by incense, and that reverberates with the noise of fists hitting heavy bags rather than resonating with the sound of gongs and bells. However, these spaces inspire a dedication and a sense of community such that Loïc Wacquant's labeling of the boxing gym as monastic is not incidental.[15] The more athletic and the more esoteric martial arts come together in that they develop an enhanced sense of self through mastery and induce a flow state, a compression of time, and a devotion to particular spaces.

I wonder if the accelerated pace of the modern world and the pressures of an unstable late capitalism leave us so scattered that the experience of intense focus seems extraordinary to us. We are so used to multitasking, splitting our focus, doing many things at once, that when we finally are able to concentrate, we have to label it. We see it as extraordinary. We call it spiritual. We call it magic. But perhaps magic is simply the state of heightened attention that allows, in Susan Foster's terms, the delight of "creating the new and creating anew."[16]

Taking Play to Its Edge

Dark play, as director and performance studies scholar Richard Schechner describes it, is a state of play where some or all of the players don't know they are playing.[17] For Schechner, dark play isn't merely dangerous—many kinds of play can be perilous—it is the kind of play that takes place even though players feel "insecure, threatened, harassed, and abused."[18] Schechner's view of play has to more to do with the state of the prankster rather than the pranked, although he also includes instances in which play breaks the metacommunicative frame, "this is play," so that all players may lose sight of the game until after the fact.[19] As we've seen, other commentators insist that play can only exist as play when it is voluntary and consensual.

Within the context of martial arts, "brink play," which pushes at the boundary of consent and occupies an ambiguous state between ludic and cruel, requires some attention. Brink play, as a condition in which cruelty is mobilized in the interest of a future deepening of experience, appears in hierarchical training methods where a master or senior student insists that a trainee submit to difficult ordeals in order to pass a test of devotion. Brink play is characterized by actions that instead of signaling "this is play" raise the question, "is this play?"[20] Abusive training methods that present a trial by fire that a novice must pass to enter into the realm of the serious student are not specific to martial arts: fraternity hazings, medical internships, and even some ballet schools have these elements to them.

Martial arts training intersects with brink play in its history. Martial arts, when they relocate to new environments, often involved a master or senior students fighting in the world beyond the mat to demonstrate their skills. Older martial artists describe the process of establishing karate in the United States as one in which each effort to open a school was met with fight challenges. Author and martial artist Choon-Ok Harmon describes her efforts to launch a kuk sool won school in the United States as replete with challenges from locals to test her fight skills.[21] Bruce Lee famously developed his jeet kune do style by getting into fights with the martial arts-trained gangs of Hong Kong.

Unlicensed sport fights, where rules are likely to be much more expandable and an unruly crowd may have an influence on the terms of engagement for the fighters, likewise veer close to brink play. Street fights, or challenge fights, have an element of edge play to them since, as we've seen, they typically begin as consensual when two people agree to fight while others stand around watching and, presumably, looking out for them. That these are usually designated as fair fights, based on the participant's age, gender, size, and fight history; that they consist of two and only two participants (at least at first); and that they happen at a designated place and time, often separate from the original grievance; sets them up as the distorted mirror image of sport fighting.[22]

There are also more benevolent forms of brink play that intentionally take play off the mat and into the world, framing themselves *as* play and resting upon consent. My training partners and I have been known to sneak up on each other to test our awareness. We throw punches and kicks at each other as a kind of greeting. We joint-lock one another when the opportunity presents itself. One of my instructors mimed kneeing me in the face as I bent down to pick up a kali stick. In kali class, a common expression of affection, or even greeting, is an unexpected tap with the stick on the shoulder. Brazilian jiu jitsu practitioners show affection by posing for photos in chokeholds.

Other martial artists report the same thing. Susan Schorn describes her paroxysm of laughter when her training partner punched at her face as she walked out of the dojo changing room.[23] Greg Downey describes capoeira as a trickster's art, one in which trainees learn a constant state of vigilance from their classmates sneaking up on them, trying to catch each other out in moments of inattention.[24] For capoeiristas, Downey suggests, this is a serious game, one in which players remind each other that danger is everywhere. Given capoeiristas' tendency toward sarcastic comments in the songs of the roda and their proclivity toward practical jokes outside of it, these kinds of tests are also a form of brink play.

In contrast to street scrappers, most sport fighters generally see a firm division between what happens in the ring and what one does outside it. Fighters are praised for "leaving it in the octagon" (or in the ring or on the mat).[25] There's a good reason for this: martial arts already walks the line between sport and violence, competition and aggression, form and function. An intentional subversion of that line means a return to violence. As Christopher Matthews has argued, it is important to examine the "worst moments of the best fights" to recognize both violence in sports and the physical damage that athletes risk.[26] This is, after all, the danger of sport fighting: that its play can turn toward its edge and its players can exceed the parameters of acceptable confrontation, resulting in long-term consequences inflicted on the body of their opponents.

Much like the relationship of art and life, sport can mimic life and life can mimic sport. The seepage from fighting to violence beyond the ring occurs in a particularly spectacular way when it comes to modern fight sports. This may be tied to their excessive attention on winning. As we'll see in chapter 7, the idea that winning matters more than a well-played game dominates much professional and high-level amateur athletics. Just as football players sometimes put ethics to one side in order to bring their team to victory, so, too, do commercial sport fighters learn to concern themselves with winning rather than with playing with respect. At the same time, however, the ubiquity of the rogue martial arts student stock character in martial arts novels and films suggest that such figures predate modern commercial fight sports. Or at least that people have considered this possibility for quite some time.

Combative play thus sets up and blurs lines between competition and violence. There are some sparring matches so intense they feel, in the moment, almost identical to a real combative conflict. It feels so engaging and so intense and, sometimes, so painful that we find ourselves thinking we'd do anything to survive it, even as we know we wouldn't. As much as we use metaphors of play and sport to describe martial arts, we also use metaphors of real-world conflict. The most obvious of these is the use of the word "fight." Even if we accept that fights are defined by consent, they are also characterized by conflict.

Just as comedy is often about situations that are not inherently funny, games often simulate situations in which we wouldn't want to find ourselves, creating a sense of anxiety and threat, in order to figure out what our options are. Seen in this light, the apparently violent elements of martial arts and other physical games make a lot more sense. This doesn't mean that play is a rehearsal for real life, however. Rather, play is itself a real situation, where we make decisions under simulated or artificial duress. For all the reasons we've seen, play is a different kind of real situation than that which appears in a nonplay world.

Because martial arts and other games can slip so easily from play to nonplay, they encourage a consideration not just of individual mastery but also of interpersonal interaction. The magic of play happens not only through space and movement but also through its ability to bring people into artificial confrontations that allow opportunities for problem-solving. Competition is one means of, in Csikszentmihalyi's terms, creating complexity.[27] And yet when competition becomes an end in itself, it tends to heighten animosity and decrease enjoyment, suggesting a need to balance competition and cooperation.

3

Chess with Cardio

FINDING THE MEETING POINT IN SPORT FIGHTING

You have to respond to what's there. You can't force it.

—GURO DANIEL LONERO

Boards don't hit back.

—BRUCE LEE IN *Enter the Dragon*

IN FEBRUARY 2014 George Zimmerman, the acquitted killer of Trayvon Martin, tried to recuperate his public image by volunteering to participate in a "celebrity" boxing match. Sports writers and civil rights advocates alike opposed the venture, pointing out that such an event would aggrandize Zimmerman and put money in his pocket. Zimmerman's claim to box as a hobby, having "been in training" prior to his confrontation with Martin, belied his claim that he killed the teenager in self-defense. Since Zimmerman insisted that a scuffle with an adolescent left him so out of his depth that he resorted to a lethal gunshot, a public boxing match would confirm that his acquittal was based on a lie.

A twitchy excitement accompanied the criticism, however. The idea that a boxing match would give Zimmerman his just deserts floated around the media and the Internet. Rapper DMX stepped forward to face off against Zimmerman in the ring and deliver punishment, promising to break "every rule in boxing to . . . fuck him up right."[1] This threat made a brutal sense: evading justice in the courts, Zimmerman would get his comeuppance in the ring.

If the event had gone forward, however, DMX wouldn't have gotten to break every rule in boxing to wreak vengeance upon Zimmerman. Rule-breaking—at least any that the referee saw—would mean warnings, point loss, and eventual disqualification. For the fight to take place, DMX would have had to adhere to the codes of boxing, weighing in alongside his opponent, allowing the inspection of his gloves pre-match, walking into the center of the ring at the same time as Zimmerman, and agreeing when the referee said, "gentlemen, I want a good, clean fight." They would touch gloves to start the match, break when called, return to their corners on command, and offer a gesture of respect at the match's end.[2]

Viewing a boxing match as an opportunity to inflict punishment misses a central point about what boxing—or any competitive martial art—is and what it means. While trash-talking and grudge matches are common in combat sports, even the most modern and commercial martial arts distinguish between sport and unchecked violence. They do this, as we've seen, through gestures of respect and other markers that define the activity as competition and not violence, as well as by delineating a space that is separate from everyday life. They also do this through rules. Rules establish the conventions and the parameters of play and confirm the dignity of the contenders, positioning them as athletes, not as mindless scrappers. Rules make provisions for the well-being of the participants as they partake in a dangerous sport. On a more fundamental level, however, rules make the game.[3]

If martial arts are described through metaphors of play, they are even more frequently associated with games. Whereas battlefield arts like ninjitsu and Filipino martial arts use unequivocal terms such as "enemy," sport fighters are known as contenders, opponents, and competitors. We describe competition in terms of matches and bouts. We talk about someone's skill sets in terms of their game: she has a good ground game, or his defensive game is weak but he moves so fast that it's not a problem.

Martial arts are often specifically compared with chess. Brazilian jiu jitsu practitioners, for example, call their sport "chess with cardio." Because of its highly technical nature, its complexity, its disallowing of strikes, and its slower pace of movement relative to boxing and kickboxing, jiu jitsu's gamelike nature is evident: a player needs an overarching strategy, made up of both offensive and defensive tactics; participants make moves to set up options down the line, thinking several moves ahead even as opponents' responses change the agenda. Boxers and kickboxers speak of baiting and faking, setting up an opponent to respond in particular way in order to launch the intended offensive that undergirds the game plan, all the while recognizing that the plan may need to change at any time.[4]

Chess consists of a series of moves and countermoves, some offered as bait to initiate a response, others a set-up for the execution of a maneuver later. Chess is a back-and-forward dance in which a player keeps in mind an agenda while responding to the counterposing strategy of an opponent. Like

FIGURE 3.1 Brazilian jiu jitsu requires anticipating an opponent's defensive actions.
Photograph courtesy of Patrick Becker.

martial arts, chess is simultaneously a form of recreation (old men playing under the trees in the park); a game with well-defined parameters (players in a chess club calculating a next move); and a sport that emphasizes excellence and striving for perfection (young men in suits seated at a table on a raised stage). Chess, like sport fighting, is competitive: individual participants confront each other and play to win. Indeed, the pleasure of playing chess lies in this competitive interaction. Yet chess, like martial arts, is subtly cooperative. Players unite in their agreement to play, even as they struggle against one another. The consent of one occasions the victory of the other. A team, visible and otherwise, stands in the wings when the two players face off; both chess and martial arts are practiced in communities where players train one another, testing out moves and strategies, exploring them in cooperative yet challenging environments before taking them into competition.[5]

Chess, as a metaphor for and parallel practice to martial arts, reveals the tensions in combative games between rule-bound competition, interpersonal interaction, and the drive for perfection,[6] suggesting a nuanced relationship between play, games, and sports. Play is the most open-ended of the three, being exploratory and focused on experience rather than on a goal. Games are a subset of play, a defined activity that contrasts with more ambiguous and experimental modes of play. Games, as philosopher Bernard Suits suggests, divide further into open and closed games.[7] Open games have no "inherent goal whose achievement ends the game," whereas closed games have a clear objective the achievement of which results in winning the game.[8]

In games, the act of playing, with its concomitant pleasures, is usually just as important as its outcome (winning or losing). Although games and sports both generate enjoyment through competitive confrontation, sports emphasize the outcome of competition over and above its pleasures. Sports, with their emphasis on achievement, their clear designation of winners and losers, and the disdain frequently attached to losing, imply that winning matters more than playing. Sport, as Henning Eichberg points out, is therefore situated "in a complex way between work and play."[9]

The Long Way Around: Inefficient Means in Play and Sport

Games present a problem to be solved and they typically involve a confrontation, either with another player or an obstacle.[10] A game requires that its players use particular tactics to solve this central problem and that they avoid others. The inclusion of specific options and the exclusion of others constitute the rules of the game. Within the game, these rules are absolute: to break them is to cheat, to be disqualified, or to have failed to play. From outside the game, the rules are anything but absolute. Indeed, if we remove the rules from the context of the game, they become illogical: soccer players edge a ball across a field with their feet, when they could pick it up and throw it. Despite their contingent and arbitrary nature, rules are crucial to the activity. If the soccer player's use of her feet when her hands could do a better job is illogical, the player picking up the ball and running across the field is preposterous. If she holds the ball (unless she's the goalie), she's no longer playing soccer; she's doing something else.

The rules of a game demand the deliberate selection of what Suits calls inefficient methods. The soccer player would, in all likelihood, get the ball into the goal faster if she used her hands, especially if the other players didn't expect her to do so. That she chooses to not use her hands, and continues to do so throughout the play, is precisely what makes the game enjoyable. So, as Suits points out, we agree to run around a racetrack although we would get to the finish line quicker if we ran across the middle of the field.[11] We play monopoly, gradually accruing play money from movements on the board, when we could just reach over and grab a handful of cash from the bank. We circle our opponent, punching, kicking, and looking for a takedown, when we could incapacitate him by smashing his trachea. An action that in the outside world makes sense nullifies the game. A game without rules isn't simply dangerous; it's not a game at all.

Combat arts, of all kinds, traditional and modern, involve the selection of less efficient over more efficient means of fighting. Martial arts involve bringing physical force to bear upon another human being. At the same time, martial arts put limits on what we do in these planned confrontations with others. The selection of intentionally inefficient means is the source of two central, contradictory confusions around martial arts: one, that martial arts represent a mere indulgence in violence, and, two, that martial arts don't work in situations of real violence. Thinking about martial arts as games helps address these two critiques, which have a grain of truth to them but which overlook the basic assumptions of most martial arts.

If sport fighting were simply a matter of brutality on display, the contest would come down to who gouged the eyes or struck the groin first. We would allow contestants to head butt, to apply air as well as blood chokes, and to kick an opponent when down. If sport fighting were violence, contenders could grab chairs from the stands and hit each other, we would praise them for their cleverness when they brought additional fighters with them into the ring, and people wouldn't still talk about Mike Tyson biting off Evander Holyfield's ear nearly twenty years after the fact.

On the flip side, as the numerous examples of those who've used martial arts in self-defense suggest—from the elderly British ex-featherweight boxer who felled a neighbor who attacked him to the merchant marine who put a knife-wielding assailant to sleep with a triangle choke[12]—the narrowed options of the ring develop a mastery over combative movement that give their operator an advantage in a violent encounter. Getting good at games requires enhanced capability within the requirements for less efficiency. So, for instance, when UFC fighter Leslie Smith came to the aid of a friend who was sexually harassed outside a club, the aggressor threw a punch at her but, when he realized he was facing a superior fighter, he deployed what for him was maximum efficiency: hair pulling, scratching, and attempting to bite. Smith off-balanced him with a double-leg takedown, got him in a rear choke, then switched to elbow strikes to protect her recent knee surgery.[13] Her deliberate selection of less efficient means was still more effective than the aggressor's attempt at maximum efficacy.

Practice with intentionally less efficient means doesn't preclude the possibility of using more efficient means when it's necessary. Presumably a track star could flee an explosion faster than someone who has only ever run to catch a bus, even though the former had trained herself to run in large circles not in a straight, continuous line. Likewise, sport fighters and traditional martial artists have proven more than capable of defending themselves using highly efficient means—eye strikes, throat shots, and kicks to the groin—as well as intentionally less efficient ones.

A key difference between sport-oriented martial arts and aesthetic ones is the permissible degree of efficiency. Modern sport fighting involves a higher degree of effectiveness in a combative encounter, but it still rules out the most efficient means. When viewers and promoters talk about mixed martial arts as being closer to a "real" fight, this is what they're referring to: MMA allows for more options than tae kwon do, for instance, in that it permits punches to the face as well as elbow and knee strikes, takedowns, and joint-locks. It doesn't include all possible attacks.

Suits depicts this contrast with an illustration. In its foreground is a boxer, gloved up and in a fighting stance. An arrow sticks (improbably) through his head. In the background, an archer peers haughtily into the distance as he drops his own gloves in a trashcan. Underneath the image is an epigram: "It is impossible to win a game and at the same time break one of its rules."[14] This sketch signals the importance of restricted means in fighting games. The obvious way to victory, in combat with another human being, is to introduce a variable the opponent hasn't thought of. To cheat, in effect. In violence, an aggressor "cheats" by breaking the social contract and initiating the attack. In self-defense, the most desirable means are the most efficient. Self-defense, in Suits's terms, is therefore "technical"; it is about availing oneself of the most effective means to hand (although, as we'll see, self-defense training uses elements of games).

In a game, as Suits indicates, the means are nonultimate; they are not binding outside the game. They are also typically subordinated to real-world concerns. So, for instance, a rule in sport fighting may specify that a round lasts three, five, or ten minutes; however, a round will stop when a contender is seriously injured, taps, or is knocked out. A round will also end if a fire breaks out or a water main ruptures in the arena. In self-defense, however, the restrictions are ultimate; they are not subordinated to rules outside the encounter. The goal is to hurt or cause injury as efficiently as possible with only an ultimate (legal and ethical) rule attached: do no more harm than needed in order to escape.

In sport fighting, one does more harm than *necessary*—there is no good reason for a sport fighter to kick or punch the opponent that appears before her. At the same time, a sport fighter in a match does less harm than *possible*: she doesn't grab flesh, break eardrums, or smash a bottle over her opponent's head. Rules are in place to protect the competitors, certainly, but safety is not the full explanation. After all, we allow the intentional inflicting of concussions as part of the rules of most fight sports. We accept that contenders will break bones, split skin, and tear ligaments. We accept that, rarely, a competitor may even die in the ring. While safety is certainly a consideration and officials in sport fighting clearly take their job seriously, safety is not primary, otherwise we'd abolish sport fighting as well as other dangerous sports like American football, ice hockey, horseback riding, and downhill skiing. Instead, we have rules in sport fighting so that we can have sport fighting; we have rules so there is a game to play.[15]

The Reluctant Victor and Competitive Pleasure

Rules give us the game, but they also enhance pleasure by requiring a balance between playing and winning. Games with too few rules result in too easy a victory.[16] A victory that comes too swiftly generates little pleasure. Even in closed games, which are goal-oriented, process still matters: playing matters at least as much as winning. There is, as Bernard DeKoven maintains, a difference between playing to win and having to win,[17] with the former enriching the experience of play and the latter being solely about outcome.[18] Games, then, consist of a tension between the desire to play and the desire to win. Game theorists call the enjoyment generated by this pull between playing and winning competitive pleasure.

For Suits, competitive pleasure arises not only from the players attempting to defeat one another, but also from the difference between the cooperative and antagonistic aspects of the game.[19] Players agree on the fact of competition but they disagree as to its desired outcome. They come together to oppose one another. This explains one of the central paradoxes of sport fighting: the sincere appreciation and affection with which competitors often conclude a match. Whether we've won or lost, in most cases we've experienced competitive pleasure and, often, with it a feeling of affection toward our competitor.[20]

To illustrate the importance of competitive pleasure and the ability of the game to supersede its outcome, play theorists such as Suits, DeKoven, and Caillois reflect on a common practice in which the more skilled player offers strategic advice to the beginner or assumes a disadvantageous start to slow her victory. Suits refers to this practice—when a more accomplished player intentionally places obstacles in his own way in order to slow the process of defeating the opponent—as the paradox of the reluctant victor.[21] If we assume that the goal is to win, this behavior is senseless. But it is pointless only if we assume that the purpose is winning and we forget that the game is in the playing.

This intentional placing of obstacles in order to improve the quality of the game happens a lot in sparring. Sparring differs from competition fighting in that playing the game, keeping it going, is more important than winning.[22] Sparring brings with it no designated winner. It usually becomes obvious whether one person or another is the better fighter, but sparring has no clear outcome. Although sparring can be fiercely combative, and even dangerous, it remains an open game to competition fighting's closed one.[23]

In sparring, unlike in competition fighting, players are not necessarily well matched. Although hierarchies exist in most martial arts classes in terms of who trains with who, with senior students gravitating to one another or, more simply, participants selecting training partners they are comfortable with, sparring partners can vary depending on the class, its personnel, and the opportunities provided. When opponents are not well matched, an intentional scaling back becomes necessary. This is especially the case in gyms or academies where martial artists train in a range of different arts: you never know what training background your opponent has, what's in his tool box, or what tricks he may pull out and it can take careful observation to figure this out.

The paradox of the reluctant victor explains the importance, in martial arts, of weight classes and separation by age, gender, style, and rank (pro versus amateur; novice, beginner, advanced categories; white-belt only competitions). The argument for such restrictions is safety, but in the gym we train with people of different sizes, ages, and genders; in some gyms, participants fight as hard as competitors in the ring. Competitions such as absolute grappling, where there are no weight classes and no division by rank, rely on a different commonality: a high level of skill. Contenders in absolute grappling are capable enough that they can assume they will meet a worthy opponent, against whom there is no need to scale back, regardless of other differences.

Fairness is another explanation for division within competition and this, to an extent, is closer to the point. However, although we tend to believe that sports are played on a level playing field, they are not:[24] players have different access to training and different resources for competition depending on their race, gender, socioeconomic status, and the sheer luck of finding the right opportunity at the right time. Internationally, athletes receive different training based on the economic status of their country and region of origin.[25]

Moreover, researchers have identified two hundred genetic traits that provide an advantage in elite sport.[26] Some sports require that participants modify their bodies in profound ways to participate, requiring extreme weight loss (gymnastics) or extreme weight gain (Sumo wrestling, American football). In some sports, height confers an advantage (basketball, running, swimming), while in others a diminutive stature is preferable (gymnastics, jockeying). Nearly all sports favor young adults over older ones. The racial integration of professional and collegiate sports, Title IX requirements, and adaptive athletics have all improved access to sports, but efforts remain incomplete and excellence at sports depends on opportunity and not solely ability. Certainly, many athletes, coaches, and referees concern themselves with equity and their interest in sporting behavior is sincere. But given the many imbalances in sport and in wider society, sports are a long way from being fair.

Categories of competition don't rectify imbalanced or unfair circumstances, although they can create points of entry for those who have had their abilities questioned or challenged. They do, however, allow players to give it their all. By addressing obvious, perceived advantages, competition categories can foster a situation where no one need play the role of the reluctant victor. As Roger Caillois points out, categories of competition represent an effort, in agonistic games, to isolate a single factor by which success can be measured.[27] Ideally these restrictions maximize competitive pleasure, although they often repeat discriminatory patterns of their larger society.[28] These distinctions are often about enhancing spectatorial pleasure as well; as sociologist Francisco Duina points out, viewers who enjoy competition are drawn to the idea of a close match among peers so much that they favor competitions where the athletes look alike.[29]

The complex negotiations required to create a satisfying competition illustrates how much combative play relies on a negotiation of difference between two people. Although competition entails besting another contender, it also illuminates, in a particularly vivid way, the power of another person's will. Sustaining the game entails gauging where someone else stands—evaluating their intensity as well as their skill and fitness levels—and figuring out how they want to play; it involves rising to their level, challenging them and attempting to circumvent their strategies. In the case of sparring, rather than ring fighting, it demands challenging them while not running roughshod over them (if they are less skilled) or getting overwhelmed by them (if they are more skilled). I call this physical encounter between two people's wills the meeting point. Philosophers call it intersubjectivity.

Finding the Meeting Point: Intersubjectivity and Competitive Pleasure in Sparring

I'm sparring with a new student. We're in a fast-paced class that I don't attend regularly. The other students are more advanced and some are competitors. Because of this and because the new student is the only other woman in the class and about my size, we seem like a good match. In many ways, we are. She's not a novice; her punches are strong and her kicks are crisp. She picks up movement quickly.

She hasn't done much live training, however. When we begin sparring, it's hard to find a place where we might meet. I throw a punch; she throws one at exactly the same time and we clash in the middle. I throw a kick and she throws one simultaneously. It's a common occurrence in sparring, this mirroring of movement, but this is the first time I've seen someone do it so rapidly, where she echoes what I do as I do it. Mimicry is second-nature—and rapid-fire—for her.

Because she's new, I move at about 50 percent speed and 30 percent force. If I focused on winning, I would overwhelm her with a blitz of punches and kicks, outpacing her so she could no longer mimic. That would be unsporting and, besides, it would defeat the purpose of the game. My goal is to figure out how I might communicate with her in a competitive way, determining what I can learn from her and she from me. It's a debate, not a screaming match.

Later in the class, I'm stand off against the instructor. He's a former competitor. Long and lean, he footwork is brisk and his movement sharp. He's got a precision to his strikes that I can only dream about.

We touch gloves and circle. I step in and he taps the top of my head, following up with a few strikes. I go to kick and he stop-kicks my thigh before my foot even leaves the ground. I try to kick with the other leg; he's out of range, and I'm kicking air. I step in again, he taps me again. When I spar with someone skilled, it feels like he knows what I'm going to do before I do it. With this guy, it feels like he knows what I'm going to do before I come up with the idea.

He realizes this. He begins coaching me. The sparring match has tapered into a series of drills. I'm dismayed. I've failed, not because I couldn't win the match—that would be unlikely—but because my lack of skill meant that he could find no other way to communicate with me other than teaching.

Both of these instances involved a negotiation typical of sparring, a coming together that gets figured out in the process of it happening. Once you've determined that the interaction will happen, you have to figure out the specifics of how it comes into being. This carries with it the possibility of disappointment—not so much that one contender will "lose" the bout but that the two contenders will fail to fully realize the encounter, the game will fail to happen, and the two players will be left puzzled as to how to interact. As we'll see, coming out of the round as the inferior fighter after completing it is not necessarily a failure. Failure consists of stopping the game partway through: retreating from the match in fear, collapsing from exhaustion, or a collapsing of the match into explicit teaching. Keeping the game going is a success.

In sparring, competitors need to figure out *how* to keep the play going. This negotiation begins with the fundamentals. Sparring can involve anything from noncontact stalking and striking, looking for ins without landing punches; to light contact, touching the opponent at the target zones; to full contact, competition-level force. So the first thing that has to happen is that partners have to decide how hard they want to play. Do they want this to be training for the ring? Or to feel like it? Or do they want to have the space to explore without the anxiety that comes with being hit hard in the face?

When partners figure out how to deal with each other's energy—match it, diffuse it, or meet it with its opposite—they are figuring out how to maintain the game. Tactics such as calculating the abilities and preferences an opponent has, figuring out whether to try to match an opponent's speed, or bait

FIGURE 3.2 Sparring is as much about reading intention as it is about technical skill.
Photograph courtesy of Patrick Becker.

her low to get her to drop a tight guard, are ways not just of surviving an encounter without injury (ideally) but also of figuring out how to interact.

Maintaining the game also requires working with the physical attributes of the opponent. When working with a larger opponent, I try to stay conscious of the fact that his blows are likely to land harder than mine while taking advantage of the larger target he presents. When I move from sparring with a larger opponent to working with a smaller one, my opponent seems completely inaccessible. Although I can hit his head easier, there's much less opportunity to land a strike, especially if he's got a tight guard. We switch again, I'm back with a different taller opponent, and it feels like she's looming over me.

Finding the meeting point also means deciphering an opponent's signature moves, preparing for her favorite attacks, and figuring out her preferred defenses. It means scanning for indications of their training—Does he come from a traditional karate background? Has she practiced mostly grappling and will she be looking to take me down?—and figuring out what the traces of that training suggest. Will that side kick be followed by a spinning backfist? Does that high guard and upright torso mean hard Thai kicks will follow?

The need to find the meeting point, to locate the point at which the conversation will start, and to be continually responsive, is one of the reasons why it's notoriously hard to work with enthusiastic beginners: they're difficult to read. It's why it's hard to fight an excitable, awkward opponent. It's almost easier to fight someone really good—because their movement is legible and their patterns recognizable—than it is to fight someone whose lack of skill makes them unpredictable.[30] The need to find the meeting point is why professional fighters study each other before a match and they still come out stalking. They're trying to decode out the opponent's strategy and tactics, but they are also trying to find the place where they'll meet. The meeting point sets the stage for much of what follows.

This is part of why grudge matches hold so much appeal: the contenders know where the meeting point will happen. At least they think they do. When they get out, they'll get straight to business. Or they try and get faked out by a changed game plan, a new strategy, or an unfamiliar tactic.

This process of cooperatively developing the means through which competition can occur is similar to what philosophers call intersubjectivity. Phenomenology, broadly defined, is the study of perception and experience. As we've seen, phenomenologists suggest that we know who we are through the experience of transcendence, our body's seamless execution of our will, the ability of our bodies to act as an extension of our intention. For phenomenologists concerned with intention, we know ourselves *as* selves by the apparently effortless mastery we experience as we pick up a pencil and write down our thoughts, walk across the room to turn on a light, or hammer in a nail that has come loose. Mastery makes us a self, a subject.

When we extend ourselves into space and execute our will, what happens when we come into contact with another human being? Other people don't simply acquiesce to our intentions. Other people can foil our exercise of mastery. Or, as Bruce Lee's character says in *Enter the Dragon*, "boards don't hit back."

It's precisely because boards don't hit back and people do that martial arts, and other competitive activities, are both pleasurable and challenging. One of the hardest stages in martial arts training involves moving from working with objects (heavy bags, focus mitts, Thai pads, wooden dummies) to working with human beings. A similar challenge arises when we move from working with compliant partners to resistant ones. That's because other people rarely agree to be the mere recipients of our will.

This insight is, of course, not restricted to fight sports. In love and friendship, in collaborative work and play beyond the mat or the ring of combat sports, other people exercise their will, which causes us to reappraise and refigure our strategies. Because of this quandary created by other people's will, phenomenologists, beginning with Edmund Husserl, emphasized intersubjectivity as well as experience, intention, and mastery. Intersubjectivity, in its most general sense, entails putting ourselves in someone else's place.[31] It consists of realizing that another person's basic frames of reference are similar to our own (left, right, up, down, front, back) and that they exercise their intentionality in similar ways. It also means recognizing that they do something different with this information.

Philosopher Erin Manning investigates intersubjectivity through movement, taking tango as her primary example.[32] She argues that the coming together of people through physical touch allows individuals to experience difference and disagreement as well as harmony, proposing a politics of intersubjectivity. Consensus, Manning suggests, is not necessarily the same thing as agreement; consensus can mean managing and benefiting from disagreement. Cooperation is often about managing difference, dissent, and opposition. For Manning, disagreement, friendship, and touch are mutually constituted. Intersubjectivity and touch erode a fixed division between one individual and another.

Sports ethnographer Henning Eichberg makes a related argument about games. He suggests that games erode "the dualism between object and subject,"[33] maintaining that when we play a game, the game plays us as well. Play, for Eichberg, unravels a subject–object boundary and dismantles the idea of an autonomous individual bending the world to his or her will. Because games bring us into an interaction with another human being that is simultaneously cooperative and competitive, it gives us the opportunity to practice disagreement without conflict.[34]

Sparring, as a form of competitive play, provides opportunities for intersubjective exchange. Sparring brings us into confrontation with other human beings, reminding us, in direct and sometimes painful ways, that we are not simply individuals carrying out our own agenda. The oppositional force of another human being is a potent reminder that the world does not bend to our will. Indeed, following on Eichberg's assessment, it's not just the game that plays us; our opponent plays us as well, in at least three senses: exercising a fluid, responsive, mastery; working out the game with it; and tricking us in order to win.

When Manning speaks of touch as intention and as something that is always, by its nature, dual and reciprocal, I find myself thinking of a core insight of the grappling arts: once we touch, we are no longer separate entities. We have a created a different shape than when our bodies stood across the room from one another. On a literal, biomechanical level, we form a temporarily conjoined whole:[35] our center of gravity changes and our points of balance shift when we touch. Each of us moves according to our own agenda, but we are more successful when we realize that when our bodies come together, they create a new shape that can be moved according to different principles than that which guide a single, moving body.

FIGURE 3.3 Once we touch, we are no longer separate entities.
Source: Collective Commons By Schnuffel2002 [CC BY-SA 3.0 (https://creativecommons.org/licenses/by-sa/3.0)].

Controlled opposition reminds us that we are not alone in the world.[36] It reminds us of this in a visceral and sometimes painful way, but remind us it does. Indeed, sparring illustrates that even when human interaction is not harmonious, it can still be managed, sometimes so both sides are satisfied. And yet it also teaches us about how hard it is to understand another person's intent. Coming into contact with others can be euphoric but it can also be painful, challenging, and infuriating. Sparring illustrates this complexity of human interaction.

Sparring, with its opportunities to investigate oppositional intent in a structured way and its understanding that two opposing forces can easily become one, offers an entry into understanding the complex and fraught nature of human interaction. In this regard, sparring is a lot like friendship:[37] both require reading another person, both demand trust, and both signal how to teach and learn at the same time. In friendship and in sparring, often you walk away thinking, "that was amazing." But you also have to accept that people get hurt. You have to be all right with ending up close to tears. Frequently, you come out of it with a list of the things you could have done differently.

The intentions of sparring are, typically, sincere: to teach, to learn, to challenge and be challenged. But sparring differs in an important sense from friendship in that it hinges upon deception. Sparring teaches us how to respond to trickery, bending an interaction to our will while recognizing that efforts to do so are incomplete. It is most comparable to those friendships where we achieve intimacy through banter and jocular one-upmanship. It gives us a way of navigating (artificial) disagreement. It teaches us, in a relatively safe environment, how to manage deceit.

The profound intersubjectivity of live martial arts training explains the appeal of intense training, indicating why training partners who play rough, sparring and grappling hard, sometimes do so with great affection. It may be that deep, intense play, as Diane Ackerman suggests, has a kind of magic to it. Intense experience, by definition, marks out its participants as different, special, outside the routine;[38] when it's shared, these kind of distinctive experiences create a powerful bond.[39]

Sparring partners, like friends, have to figure out how to oppose one another without causing damage. In sparring, unlike in friendship, a degree of managed hurting is necessary and even desirable. But ideally, sparring partners learn to hurt without injuring, riding a fine line between inflicting pain and causing damage. I have trained with sparring partners who balance this brilliantly; during the match, I find myself getting beaten up (the people who have this control are usually highly skilled so they're almost always able to best me); I feel the pain of impact, body strikes leave me groaning and gasping for air, face strikes land with a thud. My cheeks sting after the round. But I walk away from the match uninjured.

I have also sparred with partners who lack this ability; although more skilled than me technically and strategically, they lack this control and, with them, I frequently leave the round injured in some way or other. Or they do. Every once in a while, I've come across a sparring partner who cheats, ups the ante, or exploits a partner's good will. But more often an overly aggressive sparring partner means no harm. She just can't access the meeting point—at least not in this particular instance.

Finding the meeting point—an encounter with physical intersubjectivity—takes on a particular urgency in a world where much of our interaction can happen without our physical selves present. If finding the meeting point requires an encounter with the will and the subjectivity of another human being, then the lack of a physical encounter can make it easier to objectify, dismiss, and otherwise diminish other people. This seems to happen in trolling, where an aggressor belittles and sometimes threatens another individual online but without direct, physical confrontation. It is telling that trolls mask their identities, through false names and misleading images, hiding their physical selves. This may be an attempt to avoid legal consequences, but even trolls whose behavior is not legally actionable disguise themselves.

I suspect the larger fear is of confrontation: while trolls provoke written tension they conspicuously avoid the physical conflict they threaten. For example, a few years ago, the hash tag #MasculinitySoFragile prompted presumably male trolls to call out women for their supposed weakness, insisting that they would assert their dominance through a challenge match in the ring. Missing the irony that this defensive response confirmed the validity of the hashtag, these trolls were apparently shocked into silence when women fighters responded with a virtual shrug and an acceptance of the challenge. One troll went so far as to arrange a challenge fight with a retired female MMA competitor, but never showed up for the match. These retreats occurred no doubt because of (legitimate) fear of injury, as result of an encounter with a more skilled fighter. The greater injury posed by a loss on the mat would be the psychic one, however. This is particularly likely in a cultural context in which toxic masculinity teaches men to foreground their competencies and to doubt women's physical and cognitive abilities. Conversely, the lack of exposure to those capacities amplifies a sense of superiority, at least in part because without the constant reminder of the abilities of other human beings, we can grow in our imagination to superhuman stature. It's easy to envision ourselves as undefeated in contests we never participate in.

Sparring and other physical games don't automatically make us more respectful, compassionate, or aware of the consequences of our actions. Clearly, sports, including recreational and competition fighting, often fail to render participants tranquil and more respectful; they can even, depending on the gym, render a participant more aggressive. The clearest example of this lies in team sports, where affection and compassion extend from one teammate to another but players engage in cruel and vicious behavior toward those beyond the team. All too often, empathy only extends to those in an immediate circle.

However, combat sport, when handled with an appropriate degree of care and respect, teaches us about our own capacity for violence and defensive aggression as well as how to modulate it. It reminds us that we need to manage our aggressive tendencies precisely because we can inflict damage on other people. It also signals our limitations; it shows us that we can get hurt or injured. It reminds us that other people can surprise us and that it can be hard to gauge what someone is capable of just from looking at them.

Finding the meeting point is only the first step in allowing artificial disagreement to teach us about human interaction. The steps beyond that require exploring what, in the physical encounter, enables us to feel affection and respect for our training partners. It entails understanding what intersubjectivity provides and why it's important. It demands the reflection to look at a moment where we've found the meeting point and being ready to ask not just "what can I do better?" but also "what did that show me about myself?" What did it teach me about how I interact with others, what did it reveal in someone else that surprised me? It is not enough to recognize the interdependence that play evokes; it is also necessary to understand our own vulnerability and to confront our capacity for failure.

4

What's There to Lose? Vulnerability in Combat Sport

ONE SATURDAY AFTERNOON, we closed a jeet kune do class with rounds of sparring. It was early on in my fight training and, when I sparred, my performance followed an alternating pattern of success and failure. One day I was on top of my game, swift to decipher my opponent's code, to provide a response, and even to anticipate upcoming moves. The next, I struggled to make sense of an encounter that moved too fast and provided too many complexities for me to even make sense of what was going on, let alone to stay ahead of the interaction.

This particular session was an off day; the sparring matches led me into spectacular confrontations with my inadequacies as a fighter. I flailed, playing catch-up to my partner's decisions: walking into punches, taking fakes and feints for the real thing, getting distracted at the highline and finding myself on the receiving end of a sweep kick. I found myself hit without understanding why and outsmarted at every turn. Not only did I fail to keep up with the more advanced students, I couldn't maintain my expected level of fighting.

When I got home, I explained this to my family. Having trouble finding the words to describe this low-level misery and self-doubt, I was reduced to vagaries of self-deprecation. My daughter, who was three at the time, looked up from her lunch, extended her palms wearily, and said "You suck *again*?"

I'd been here before. I'd been here enough that my young child knew the crude vernacular for it. The elation that followed a good sparring session was equaled by the gloom that followed a bad one.

This kind of dismay is not specific to me. I have heard instructors speak of sparring matches that reduced them to tears. My coach and training partner Anna speaks of sparring sessions that "stay with you." My instructor Sifu Alain describes sparring sessions that left him thinking, why do I do this to myself? Fellow students respond to tough sparring sessions with the same self-deprecation my daughter heard from me.

Self-doubt is part of the learning process. This is as true in martial arts as elsewhere. In martial arts, however, and especially in live practice, this collision with inadequacy is forceful and pronounced. It's one reason why rates of attrition in martial arts training are high: when sparring starts, students drop out. The risk of injury is part of the misgivings that sparring generates, but the emotional risks carry weight too: I have heard senior students refer to feeling defeated by sparring.

Training reduces the emotional impact of a fight, but it doesn't obliterate it. Professionals handle strikes to the face and kicks to the head with remarkable aplomb but they are not immune to moments when the implications of failure kick in. When a punch knocks a boxer to the ground, a dazed, sorrowful look sometimes crosses his face. It's different from the resigned disappointment on the face of someone who has lost a match. This is much more basic, a sense of fundamental loss, a feeling of dismay.

Because of its unpredictable nature, sparring produces a rollercoaster ride of emotion: fear, anger, elation, uncertainty, and satisfaction. Sparring prompts a fighter to confront these emotions directly and to determine how feelings relate to tactic, strategy, accomplishment, and skill. Although sparring looks like a confrontation with another human being—and it is, obviously—it is also a process of inquiry into oneself and one's own responses to pressure and stimuli.

For this reason, kickboxer Benny "The Jet" Urquidez speaks of sparring as "turning yourself inside out." In an improvised lecture on sparring offered to a group of students,[1] Urquidez briefly mentions physical pain, but he moves swiftly to the emotional duress that accompanies a partner's heavy strikes: "It's not that they're kicking hard; they're kicking those buttons, they're touching them. It brings up the wounds." For a fighter to learn from sparring, Urquidez suggests, she must be willing not only to analyze her own game and that of others but also to open up her interior, emotional world so that she can figure out what she is sensitive to and why. Urquidez maintains that sparring exposes us to emotions many of us have spent a lifetime suppressing.

Urquidez thus refers to sparring as "learning to look at your truth," arguing that its purpose "is to be able to bring it forward, what you're feeling . . . and learn how to heal it." He calls this process "woundology." He suggests that sparring puts us in a position where we have to confront ourselves through our confrontation with others. Urquidez's commentary evokes the paradoxes that constitute sparring: sparring is a confrontation with another human being that serves as a form of self-reflection; it consists of masking emotion externally but, to be executed most successfully, requires delving into emotion. It demands being closed to an opponent but exposed—turned inside out—to oneself.

As we've seen, a central difference between fighting and violence is the ability of fighters to differentiate sign from meaning: a strike to the face in sparring doesn't mean what a strike to the face means off the mat. So far, however, I have spoken about this separation as a thing and not as a process. While a sport fight relies on a separation of sign and meaning, this detachment doesn't happen easily or automatically. It also doesn't transfer seamlessly from the conventions of the ring to the interior life of the fighter. It is a struggle, one that every fighter, at every level, contends with: how to confront the sting of blows to the face, the dull ache of body shots, the stifling pressure of an opponent's weight and remain unfazed.

The famed "no ego" promoted in combat sport and traditional martial arts alike emerges out this ability to confront physical limitations and emotional turmoil while remaining unaffected. When sport fighters speak of inhabiting the eye of the storm, they refer to an ability to operate rationally within the unpredictability of a raw encounter with another person's intention. However, they also refer to their capacity to manage a complex inner world of physical sensation and emotional response while executing a strategy and adapting that strategy to rapidly changing circumstances.

This process is not only about acquiring skill to reduce error, although getting hit fewer times per round certainly helps a fighter stay calm. Most martial artists insist that dedicated practitioners should avoid situations where they succeed in every round and match. If we're serious about the training process, we continually expose ourselves to the strikes, takedowns, and submissions of better fighters. Skill provides only incomplete protection against physical pain and emotional anguish as rigorous training pushes a fighter to the limits of her skill—limits that are, ideally, continually expanding.

Exploring the realm outside the boundaries of mastery means an inquiry into unpredictability. While plenty of fighters would deny their own limitations and disavow this emotional maelstrom, others make its exploration central to their practice. Investigating these limitations means confronting vulnerability. Vulnerability forms a fundamental baseline for the other elements of sport fighting and to physical play in general: without vulnerability, nothing is at risk; without vulnerability, competitive pleasure is incomplete, and failure is an impossibility. Without vulnerability, there can be no trust, as trust only exists when something at stake.

Rethinking Vulnerability, Limitation, and Trust

The standard definition of vulnerability is susceptible to harm. Indeed, the root of the word vulnerable is *vulnus*, the Latin word for wound. As such, vulnerability is typically associated with weakness.[2] It is socially distributed, associated with the very young, the elderly, women, the poor, and the disabled.[3] Normative-bodied cisgender men are typically thought of—and often portrayed in film, television, and literature—as invulnerable. The standard representation of people of color simultaneously evokes both vulnerability and invulnerability, as when popular portrayals condemn African Americans to a permanent victim status while also representing them as unstoppable criminals.[4] Vulnerability within this framework occupies a double negative status: it both an inferior state, to be avoided, and it comprises an absence of something (strength, agency, mastery) rather than a presence.

However, feminist philosophers, notably Judith Butler and Erinn Gilson, have challenged the idea of vulnerability as a negative condition. Gilson and Bulter note that vulnerability is an inherent condition of being alive. At the same time, they point to the ways in which vulnerability is "induced" through social, political, and economic circumstances rather than through the inherent state of having one kind of body or another.[5] Gilson suggests that we think of vulnerability as the ability to be affected and as open to experience.[6] Butler speaks of vulnerability as tied to receptivity and responsiveness.[7]

In thinking about vulnerability, then, I contrast it with limitation. Limitation, as I'm using the term here, is a physical condition that sets parameters around ability.[8] Vulnerability comprises exposure to that limitation. A limitation means nothing if it is never encountered. Our need to breathe air, a limitation, doesn't render us vulnerable until we're underwater, at high altitude, or living in a neighborhood with poor air quality. Following the lead of Butler and Gilson, I'm also taking this idea of vulnerability a step further to mean a state of awareness that arises when limitation meets conscious acknowledgment.

Far from being a condition that can or ought to be avoided, limitations inhere in having a body. All animals experience vulnerability by virtue of their corporeality. Moreover, sentience and susceptibility to pain arise out of movement; in the absence of movement, there is no evolutionary need for a pain response. Conversely, without pain, movement would be a greater detriment than an advantage. Limitations therefore are not only a condition of being alive but of moving through the world.

Humans' upright posture offers us a great deal of mobility in our limbs. This mobility comes with inherent weaknesses: the possibility of joints moving in directions that are not favorable, causing pain and injury. This mobility, a capability, goes hand in hand with a limitation. Joint-locking, as a practice that exploits the simultaneous mobility and restriction of joint movement, can constitute an investigation of vulnerability.

A wound is a tangible marker of limitations. Vulnerability, as I understand it here, is not identical to wounding or the ability to be wounded per se. Rather, vulnerability lines up with Urquidez's woundology: the acknowledgment, the consideration, and the study of our susceptibility to harm. Woundology and vulnerability open limitation out to a greater understanding of ourselves and our interactions with others. As Judith Butler points out, vulnerability can operate as a way of being exposed and agentic at the same time.[9] Turned inside out, in other words.

Erinn Gilson argues that an ethics of vulnerability can enhance our accountability.[10] A relationship between vulnerability and accountability explains the central paradox of martial arts training: that knowing how to fight can make you less likely to fight. Part of this paradox lies in confidence: those who know how to fight are less likely to be targeted, and thus are less likely to need their fight skills. Those who fight recreationally or competitively don't need to put themselves into violent situations to test their knowledge; they have ample opportunity to experiment in consensual circumstances. In addition, however, fight training forms a powerful reminder of vulnerability. Fight sports teach us that anyone can lose a fight and anyone can win one; they show us that strikes hurt regardless of who they come from;[11] and they signal that fundamental limitations unite us more than differences of shape, size, gender, and age separate us.

It's a truism that sport fighting requires trust. There's a tangible material reality behind this truism. When two people come into rough physical contact, trust, like respect for the parameters of engagement, is necessary to not only reduce the risk of injury but also to facilitate the cooperation that sustains the interaction. A fighter needs to trust herself, her sparring partners, her coach, and the rules of the gym, academy, or dojo where she trains. Trust assumes vulnerability in that to trust includes acknowledging the possibility of both injury and positive change. Trust is also a conscious decision to be open to that change.

As we've seen, fight sports differ from violence because fighting is consensual.[12] Like other forms of consent, this agreement is specific and contingent: when we decide to fight we accept certain kinds of actions—punches to the face are okay; eye gouges are not—and certain degrees of intensity: a brisk pace is good, running a partner down is not. Consent is the internal side of the equation: what we're willing to do and what we're not willing to do; the external side is trust: the presentation of our vulnerability to another human being and our conviction that our partner will stick to the parameters we expect. In consenting to an activity, we trust our partner to respect our boundaries as well as trusting ourselves (or the rules or a present authority figure) to enforce those boundaries. While sparring partners, like other people, sometimes violate trust, more don't. For a consideration of play as a confrontation with both limitation and aggression, the situations where sparring partners respect one another's boundaries form the more interesting case.

We trust our sparring partners to understand the difference between hurting and injuring: hurting us enough that we learn but not inflecting the injury that would impede our continued training.[13] We trust our partners and ourselves to maintain a consistent level of intensity. We trust that partners will bring a different degree of care to a drill, where we are letting them land a shot on us, and a sparring match where we make our best efforts to prevent those shots from landing. We trust our partners to adhere to codes of etiquette and to respect the rules. We trust ourselves enough to know we can handle the interaction and, ideally, to set our own boundaries, although in the heat of the sparring moment, that is admittedly difficult.

Recreational sport fighting, as a practice that requires trust, can encourage its adherents to "turn themselves inside out," exposing themselves not only to pain but also to change, reflection, and care. This process operates, in martial arts, in a paradoxical and counterintuitive way, through practices that hurt without injury (ideally) but sometimes do cause injury. This is not to say that sparring is not dangerous (it is), that it can't be the ground for the expression of grievances as well as of cooperation (it can be), or that participants don't break the rules they agree to (they do).

Rather than arguing that sparring always renders us calmer and less violent, then, I suggest that reflection and introspection, particularly the process that Urquidez calls turning yourself inside out, can shift sparring and other competitive practices away from a fixation on winning and the potential violence that can entail. In the presence of introspection, sparring and other competitive activities can prompt an exploration of vulnerability and responsibility. As such, the physical consideration of vulnerability can operate as part of a skill set that fosters oppositional civility.

Vulnerability as the Ground of (Alternative) Play

Recently, in a Brazilian jiu jitsu class, I found myself marveling at what we were doing. Grappling, in itself, is not extraordinary. People have participated in ground fighting for a long time across many cultures. Plenty of people have practiced styles of fighting where the aim isn't to hit but to subdue.

The confrontation of two bodies through touch offers a lot of movement possibilities and sets up interesting limitations of the kind that are central to games. Wrestling accords with play among other mammals where the goal is to tussle, rather than fight: a clear way of distinguishing play from violence is by avoiding strikes (or bites in the case of nonhumans).[14] Grappling, like other combat sports, walks a line but it's a broader one, on which it's easier to stay on the side of collegiality and comfort.

Jiu jitsu, in its various forms (Japanese, Brazilian, Can-Ryu) doesn't just involve practitioners manipulating each other's bodies. Instead, jiu jitsu investigates the most basic and most fundamentally human limitations we have: our exposed neck and our joint mobility.[15] Brazilian jiu jitsu, unlike Greco-Roman wrestling, doesn't depending on pinning: in competition, a BJJ player on his back may still acquire the points necessary to win the match. In friendly sparring, a BJJ player on her back may find the submission that prompts her partner to tap out.[16]

Jiu jitsu thus finds possibility within the limitations of the human body, taking primary human frailties, our brain's need for blood supply, the exposure of the neck and its blood vessels, and the capacity of our joints to move in some directions and not others, and building a game around it.[17] The only elements of the body more vulnerable are the eyes, the airways, and the groin, and allowing eye gouges, throat smashes, and groin strikes would end a wrestling game pretty quickly. Sport jiu jitsu focuses on human limitations that are fundamental, but can be guarded against well enough that an attempt to attack them can be thwarted and the game can continue. As such, BJJ takes human limitations, turns them into an exploration of vulnerability, and constructs its game accordingly.

All martial arts, in some sense, trade in human limitations. Fight sports construct themselves around such frailties: our noses can break, under our chins lie knock-out points, shots to the liver and kidney stun us, and kicks to the thigh inhibit our movement. As we've seen, sparring, in particular, engages human emotional vulnerability and the messiness of interior experience. Sparring presents as a problem to be solved both the many ways in which human bodies can experience injury and in which emotion can throw off strategy.

Martial arts are not alone in this consideration of vulnerability. Most alternative or "extreme" sports contend with human limitations.[18] Free diving, for example, explores the limits of human lung capacity: it explores the line between the human ability to swim and the human inability to breath underwater.[19] Rock-climbing (largely) foregoes horizontal movement, which humans excel at, in favor of vertical movement, which humans find considerably

FIGURE 4.1 Brazilian jiu jitsu explores human limitations through chokeholds. Photograph courtesy of Patrick Becker.

harder. Skydiving and bungee jumping confront the fundamental condition that humans do not fly.

By contrast, conventional sports play to human strengths, confronting but usually aiming to overcome vulnerability.[20] Humans are very good at throwing, for example, because of our upright stature.[21] We're also quite good at the rotational kicking of sports like soccer. Like a lot of other mammals, we can run pretty well and we can learn to swim with ease and speed.

The danger, for conventional sport, is that human frailties get ignored and suppressed in the interest of the sport. Indeed, so focused is conventional sport on capability that vulnerabilities are ignored until they force their way into the collective consciousness of players, coaches, and viewers. The danger for alternative sports—and this is something that is generally more widely acknowledged—is that they play with vulnerability, which emerges from physical limitations.[22]

The Ultimate Fight Technique: Martial Arts as a Search for Invulnerability

There is a certain irony in writing about vulnerability as a martial artist. The pleasure of martial arts training lies not only in the immediacy of its practice but also in the traces it leaves on the body. I take enjoyment in sensing the strength and mobility of my back and shoulders as I sit to write. I walk with a lightness and quickness in my feet that could turn heavy and grounded should I need to use the power of gravity to execute a strike (or, more likely, to move a large, unwieldy object). The quickness of my physical reactions and my visual perception please me. The joy of combat sport lies at least in part in this transformation of an ordinary body into a system of rapid responses.

Martial arts doesn't just craft a body whose vulnerabilities are reduced through the strength, mobility, and stamina that extend physical limitations; these practices include ideas and theories that reveal a desire to reduce vulnerability. The media and online incarnations of the martial arts world are peppered with websites, books, and blogs with titles such as "Ultimate Martial Arts" and "Attack Proof." Martial arts magazines, websites, and YouTube videos promise undefeatable techniques and sing the praises of one ultimate fighting system or another. Individual fighters are held up as undefeatable, although few athletes can inhabit that category for long. The fight stance of arts ranging from Western boxing to wing chun kung fu to Filipino stick fighting are built around protecting target zones: creating a smaller or narrowed target, guarding the face, the throat, and the ribs simultaneously with the hands or the weapons.[23]

Competitive martial arts accustom a practitioner to fear and pain, so fighters acquire the aplomb under pressure that Loïc Wacquant calls a studied disinterest.[24] In the traditional Chinese martial arts, trainees engage in a more pronounced search for invulnerability through Iron Warrior training, striking their fists against sand bags and ball bearings and receiving blows with iron bars to the chest. Learning to withstand impact is sometimes referred to as conditioning. Identifying it as such associates acclimating to pain with other acquired physical attributes like enhanced cardiovascular function. This neutralizes the emotional impact of punches and kicks. It robs strikes of their emotional power so that receiving body shots and thigh kicks becomes just another taxing exercise, like running another mile when you're gasping for breath. This is one means through which sign and referent get separated. In addition, conditioning the body in this way separates limitation from vulnerability; the limitation of target zones on the body remains the same, but the perception of them differs.

Sparring manages emotional response and sometimes suppresses it. Taking a hit to the face while staying the course requires squelching feelings of fear and anger. Professional boxers comment on this struggle to maintain their equilibrium and manage their responses.[25] This emotional control extends to the intentional manipulation integral to the fight game. Boxers engineer opponent's emotions through their actions inside and beyond the ring;

FIGURE 4.2 Boxers learn to register threat of a punch as mere stimulus. Photography courtesy of Martin Agius AMIPP ASIFGP.

Muhammad Ali was nearly as famous for his creative, lyrical take on trash-talking and its ability to incite his opponent's reactions as he was for his deft footwork and impeccable timing. This ability to manipulate an opponent's responses while remaining unaffected means privileging the rational over the emotional, an effort in the direction of invulnerability and one that arguably allows the development of the killer instinct for which professional fighters are praised.

Competition-level sport fighters are praised for the relentless pursuit of victory that allows them to dispatch with an opponent swiftly and efficiently. While fighters who intentionally and permanently injure their opponents are maligned, so too are those who take too much care with their opponents. Fighters who lose their drive to win at all costs, as Manny Pacquiao was reported to have done after permanently injuring opponent Antonio Magarito, are criticized for taking on a role that in commercial combat sport belongs to game officials, not to players.[26] A competition fight displaces concern for physical and emotional well-being from the individual to the structure of the game. Along the way, a competition fighter is expected to bracket their own vulnerability and that of others.

Vulnerable on the Attack: Lessons from the Sweet Science

I once had a neighbor who tried to convince me that Western boxing was a soft-style martial art. He was being contrary in that way that young men in San Francisco in the 1990s often were. But some truth lies behind this hyperbolic statement. Boxing is not, in fact, a soft-style martial art; it does not depend on using an opponent's force against them. It is, however, also not what it is reputed to be, mere brutality on display. Like other martial arts, boxing relies on discipline, skill, and technical accomplishment.[27] Much of its technique is about evasion, on being a moving target that's hard to hit; deflecting punches only as much as required to diminish their force; breaking rhythm to throw off an opponent; and building a strategy around all those elements.[28] Boxing contains built-in tactics designed to lure an opponent into behaving in a way that gets used against him. In this limited sense, perhaps, boxing shares elements with soft-style arts in that it works with the inherent vulnerabilities that attach to any aggressive effort.[29]

My first jeet kune do class began with drills from Western boxing. Sifu Alain introduced the class to JKD via boxing footwork: step and slide, slide and step, and push shuffle, to the front, back, left, and right. We worked head movement: slip left, slip right, sway back, duck, bob and weave. Then blocks: catch, parry, hook cover. We worked these evasions well before we moved on to striking.

Before I trained in jeet kune do, I had learned wing chun kung fu. Wing chun focuses almost exclusively on the attack, targeting the vulnerable points at the centerline and trapping the hands that come up to protect them. Evasion comes in the form of angling off the centerline and through hand trapping. But, as my wing chun instructor would say, the purpose is to hit. Because of this, my first encounter with boxing confused me: Why all this attention to evasion? Why not just work the attack and deal with interceptions as they come? Why the preoccupation with reacting rather than initiating the interaction?

I figured out a few months later why boxers train this responsiveness.

Three months after my first jeet kune do class, I gloved up and got on the mat to spar. JKD is cast in Bruce Lee's experimental approach, focused on the tenet to take what is useful, discard what is useless, and make it one's own. Sparring, with its emphasis on application rather than abstract knowledge and its demand for full personal commitment to the act at hand, is fundamental to such a questioning approach. In practice, JKD sparring resembles MMA. Anything, within reason, goes: shots to the face, kicks anywhere except

FIGURE 4.3 Wing chun kung fu emphasizes hand trapping.

the most vulnerable targets, takedowns, chokeholds, and joint-locks. Bruce Lee's central principles included the use of all fight ranges—weapons, kicks, punches, hand trapping, and grappling—and the use of whatever you can from whatever you know.

First, I face off against Joseph, a skilled fighter from Hong Kong who's at least twenty years younger than me. Joseph is swift, light on his feet, and highly tactical. I come at Joseph fast and direct, throwing multiple jabs and the occasional cross. He circles, just out of range. Calling up my wing chun training, I try to trap his hands but he evades. I keep charging; he keeps evading. One solid hook of mine gets through, Joseph's expression surprised and a bit impressed. But far more of Joseph's shots connect than mine.

After that first session, Sifu Alain seemed pleased. "Nice sparring," he said.

After the second, he said, "It's good that you're aggressive, but . . ."

After the third, he said, "When you're so aggressive, there's a lot that you miss."

The fourth time, he gloved up and went a round with me.

Alain is a former competitive kickboxer and sparring partner to professionals. Small and fast, he can really move, his footwork brisk and light, his punches snapping like the end of a whip and landing with sudden, unexpected power. He angles off the centerline with crisp precision, his movement reminiscent of the Filipino martial arts in which he's trained. He's got an intensity that calls up his competition days. But he's also a stunt actor and he makes a show of his fakes and his feints, revealing that a trick is in store, but that reveal only makes it harder to figure out what the trick is. It's like an actor's improvisation exercise in which I get hit when I get the storyline wrong.

Alain adjusts to the level of his partner, but he never scales it back completely. Despite the differences in our skill levels, he has never stopped a round of sparring to coach me. Once the round begins, we're in. His strikes are perfect: heavy, hard, and painful. In the moment they are devastating, but the only injuries I've sustained sparring with him have been bruises.

This first time I sparred with him, it was a Saturday morning and there were just few of us in class. I had sparred with Vincent, who is compact and focused, precise in shots that he has minimal interest in pulling. This was only my second time sparring with him and I had yet to learn how to manage his intensity and my own. I took a lot of shots to the face, thinking, oh, that was a little scary. Alain stepped in to spar with me. My cheeks still stinging from the last round, I thought, "He's my teacher; he'll have to go easy on me."

Then again maybe not.

I step in to strike and get hit with a solid hook. I advance again. And get hit. A surge of anger follows. Aware of it, I can't seem to push it back. The equation works quickly: pain-fear-anger; fear-anger; fear-pain; pain-anger. I swing harder and faster. I rush Alain and he traps me in a headlock. I try to remember what boxers do when they end up like this, attacking his ribs, pummeling him with swift upper cuts to the body and charging him backward toward the wall. He releases me, breaking the stalemate. For a moment, I'm gratified at getting out of a tight spot. Until I swing at him, he lands a strike, and I start to think that pressuring him to release me wasn't such a good idea after all.

My breath becomes ragged and my fighting sloppier. In between gasping for breath, a thought occurs to me, slowly but inexorably. This is not just about a difference in skill. I'm erring repeatedly, making mistakes that were avoidable. He had set me up to come face to face with the limitations in my skill set. There was something specific that I didn't understand. And I was running into that something as I stepped into his punches.

We square off; I swing at him but he gets to me first. "You okay?" he asks. I nod, gesture: keep going. A few more back and forths: I attack, he hits, I eat another punch. Eventually, Alain calls time, we hug, and I collapse on the mat, gasping for breath.

As I work to slow my breath and get my heart rate back to something resembling normal, that thought comes back to me: there's something I'm missing here.

"You have to stop being on the attack all the time," Alain says. "It makes you so easy to hit."

That was it: the realization that ferocity, in itself, was insufficient protection against a trained opponent. More than that, it was the paradoxical understanding that a skilled opponent could use my intention against me, knowing what to do with that aggression. Understanding that my response to any stimulus was to hit made my responses transparent to a skilled fighter like Alain; it presented him with a clear battle strategy, as if I had handed over the keys to the vault of my consciousness.

As Urquidez suggests, sparring is a truth meter that shows up flaws and strengths, effective decisions and faulty ones in bright, shining relief. Contact sparring reveals fundamental truths quickly: anger gets in the way, aggression is a flash in the pan that unsettles a skilled partner for only a moment, and fear is a second opponent who lingers at the edge of the mat. Sparring demands a continual reflection on our own abilities and limitations as well as the quality of our decisions.

Coach Kathy Long, kickboxing champion and instructor at the Inosanto Academy, echoed Alain's sentiment with a more specific reflection on human body mechanics. Every time your hands leave your body, she says, you've created possibilities for your opponent. Conversely, any time your opponent's hands or feet move toward you, all sorts of things open up. A strike, she says, is a gift; it creates opportunity. Coach Kathy's remark indicates that it's not just aggressive intention that makes a fighter vulnerable. Physical limitations get exposed at the movement level. Hands held close to the face are available for protection. Hands that leave the face to strike render the face and the body open for counterattack.

The effort spent on avoidance and deflection in modern sport fighting arts, such as boxing and kickboxing, emerges out of this condition: that it is impossible to attack without opening oneself to counterattack. Skilled fighters use this condition to advantage: letting an opponent drive the interaction, or letting them think they're doing so, allows their aggressive overtures to open them to counterattack.[30] Conversely, launching an attack requires an awareness of vulnerability, which is why boxers keep their guard up on one side as they strike with the other. It's also for this reason that self-defense systems can teach purely defensive maneuvers such as a palm heel strike to the face: such attacks rely on the forward motion of an aggressor to acquire their force. It is difficult to chase someone and land a palm heel strike with accuracy.

Given the cultural association of vulnerability with weakness, in daily life we tend to think of force and limitation as at odds. Sport fighting indicates that aggression and vulnerability accompany each other rather than counterposing one another. Sparring therefore doesn't just reveal emotions we'd rather avoid, it also brings us into direct confrontation with the inherent limitations of intended actions: any maneuver can be intercepted or countered by the efforts of another.

One of the central paradoxes of martial arts training is that its effort to create predictability where there is disorder remains incomplete. Although skilled fighters have an almost uncanny ability to predict an opponent's actions, reading intention in small movements, in facial expressions, and eye movements, they also know, through experience, the limits of such ability. Accomplished fighters get hit, kicked, and taken down even by those with fewer skills. Professional boxers get hit hundreds of times per match. There is, in fact, no point where we become invincible. Sparring is a powerful and poignant reminder of this fact. That's why some trainees and even some systems avoid sparring. Conversely, that's why some fighters decry martial systems that avoid live training. In this sense, fight training evokes vulnerability as much as it does mastery.

As we'll see, fight sports, in a fundamental way, rely on failure as much as they aim for success. All sports and many games expose us to unpredictability of various kinds: luck, physical conditions of time and space, the elements of natural and built environments. Vulnerability feels heightened in combat sport because the unpredictability we're exposed to takes form as the will of another human being. That's why deciding to spar requires bravery, even in a gym that tends toward sparring light and where partners are respectful. It's why combat sport matches are referred to in hyperbolic terms, like the fight of the century or ultimate fighting, and why fighters are described as those who've risked everything.

A confrontation with another human being produces a raw, fundamental realization: we are made up of flesh that opens, bones that break, and ligaments that tear. When we undertake a live practice that puts our skills to the test, we stake our physical integrity. I've broken digits, have bruised ribs more times than I can keep track of, received black eyes, and popped an elbow ligament that mysteriously dropped back into place. My training partners have torn knee ligaments and shoulder rotators. They've sprained ankles, developed tendonitis, and suffered broken noses.

A peculiar pride attaches to these injuries. Nearly every martial arts memoir provides a list of injuries as an emblem of sincerity and dedication. Injury, of course, can be debilitating—injuries end careers as well as presenting obstacles that are overcome—but the happenstance approach that martial artists take to injury suggests a familiarity with confronting limitations and managing them. To get injured, to heal, and to get back on the mat means a willingness to contend with vulnerability. This is the literal version of the woundology that Urquidez describes: a reflection on physical limitation (as well as on emotional and mental ones). That confrontation with vulnerability becomes, paradoxically, a source of confidence.

Treating injury as incidental can go too far, so that the body of the athlete becomes expendable. When injury renders an athlete disposable, it is no longer an opportunity for pondering vulnerability. Instead, it becomes a search for the less vulnerable, run by the machine of competition and not by the individual practitioner.[31] When athletes are objectified and their individual well-being sacrificed to the mechanics of competition, their sport becomes an attempt to circumvent human vulnerability rather than to contend with it. This is a real and immediate risk of formal, institutionalized, and commercialized competition.

Vulnerability in itself is ethically neutral. The vulnerability of others demands little; to accept the injury or death of others asks nothing of us, especially if we are not exposed to material reality of that pain.[32] Indeed, the vulnerability of others can easily become an abstraction. To come face to face with our own vulnerability, however, can destabilize our sense of ourselves as fully separate from others and wholly in command of our circumstances. Confrontational play, at its worst, can teach us to disregard the pain of others. At its best, it can signal the many ways in which vulnerability is relational, dependent on other people and circumstances.

Nothing's Going to Happen to Me: The Politics of Vulnerability

As we've seen, in contemporary American society we think of vulnerability as socially distributed. We're led to believe that vulnerability is a condition, a state of being that unequivocally belongs to some people and categorically circumvents others. We are led to believe that the vulnerability of women, for instance, is unconditional and inherent, a production of natural limitations. Young, white, cis gender, heterosexual men, by contrast, are encouraged, through everything from the practices of sports to the content of safety advice, to think of themselves as immune to harm. Women are taught to think of themselves as helpless before men's violence, while men are taught that they are impervious to the violent intentions of women.

This creates a tautology: women are discouraged from fighting in the face of men's violence, thereby offering men the invulnerability that we are told is inherent. If, as I've suggested, vulnerability consists of the experience of a limitation, white cis gender men are, in this sense, invulnerable in relation to (most) women: our society spares them exposure to their physical limitations by the cultural prohibition on women responding to men's violence in kind.

While the tautology is apparent, its components, at first glance, still appear natural. For instance, we're told that men attack women because men's physical limitations are fewer than women's; because men are statistically larger than women, we are told, they are stronger and can therefore easily overpower any woman they encounter. There are obvious gaps in this logic: not all men are larger than all women, not only small women are attacked, and large women don't attack small men in numbers anything like the numbers in which men of all sizes attack women of all sizes.[33]

In addition, Western industrial societies create another tautology in defining strength as what normative men are good at,[34] designing sports and work activities around, for instance, the upper body more than the lower body and around short-burst strength rather than endurance.[35] The sexual dimorphism we're told is a hallmark of our species becomes mapped onto the body through gender-specific workout regimens and fad diets.[36] Men who target women exploit gendered codes of behavior through which women are taught to be polite and accommodating rather than firm and direct, and in which men are encouraged to be charming and allowed to demand emotional labor of women.

Such cultural constructions of the body and of behavior set the stage for men's violence against women, but men who attack women don't simply rely on cultural codes of behavior to avoid confronting women's physical force directly. Instead, men who attack women manage their crimes, socially and physically, to shield their own physical limitations. They render their targets vulnerable by manipulating circumstances, choosing as victims those who are very young, very old, disabled, exhausted, sick, drunk, unconscious, or in a situation of emotional, institutional, or financial dependence. Men who attack women reduce the risk of exposing themselves to a woman's power by how they initiate violence: men's attacks on women typically involve an approach from the side or behind; they involve rushing the target, closing the distance quickly so that the defender has little time to process what is happening, let alone to respond; they involve knocking the target to the ground, making it difficult (although not impossible) for her to effectively use her arms and legs. They thus exploit the inherent limitations of all humans—we all age, need sleep, fall ill, and need other people, and we all have a limited number of weapons on our body—rather than those that are specific to women. Far from being an inherent result of men's and women's physiology, then, men's violence against women is carefully constructed to minimize risk for the assailant and to create a temporarily invulnerability through its parameters.

In spite of this, well-meaning but underinformed feminist mothers and strict patriarchs alike teach boys about sexual consent via recourse to men's ostensible invulnerability. I am always dismayed when I come across think pieces by mothers asserting that they teach their boys about consent by reminding them that "they could easily overpower any girl or women and they must be sure never to use this advantage." If we take Gilson's suggestion seriously, that a denial of invulnerability supports a culture of oppression, we can see that this effort at consent education undercuts its own intention by failing to remind boys and young men of their vulnerability and, thus, their accountability. When we teach boys that women under threat will deliver no immediate, physical consequences, we add to the societal condition in which most sexual violence goes unpunished. It's easy to feel invulnerable when your limits are never tested, and it's easy to push boundaries when you think you're invulnerable. Indeed, the sheer arrogance of using one of the most vulnerable parts of the body as a weapon can only happen in a culture that denies vulnerability even when it comes in such obvious form as a pair of testicles.[37]

It's worth considering whether a culture of date rape would change if, instead of hearing how vulnerable girls are, boys were reminded of their own vulnerability, that they have eyes that can be gouged, ears that can be torn, collarbones that can be shattered, and a groin that is considerably more fragile than that of a women.[38] Boys (and girls) could be taught that an attack on someone perceived as conditionally weak—someone smaller, younger, older, or disabled—offers legal and ethical license to the defender to respond with brutal force. It might be helpful if boys were reminded that a person at risk of violence is under no obligation to fight fair and that the very definition of a fair fight, in this society anyway, favors a larger person. Following Martha McCaughey's suggestions, what if, instead of teaching boys about consent by coaching them in their power and agency, we sent them to watch a full contact women's self-defense class where they saw women and teenage girls in live fights, gouging eyes, palm striking noses and chins, kneeing groins, and ax kicking faces?[39]

The dangers of young men perceiving themselves as invulnerable extend beyond what they might do—or attempt to do—to women. In stark contrast to the perceived wisdom about women's vulnerability, young men are the group most likely to encounter violence at the hands of strangers and are the most likely targets of robbery, assault, and homicide.[40] Young men frequently assert that "nothing will happen to me" as a justification for exposure to danger, such as traveling alone, being out late, and moving through desolate spaces. Young men's exposure to violence also arises from a society that doesn't teach boys and men skills for deescalating conflict. Although the causes for the violence young men experience are complex, including the perception of men's violence against men as consensual and young men's proclivity toward unmanaged risk-taking, men's perception of themselves as invulnerable contributes to difficulties with risk assessment.

The race politics of vulnerability are more complex yet. As Erinn Gilson and Sara Ahmed note, those who are feared are less likely to be seen as vulnerable. The traits that are valued in white men as markers of power—loudness, confident gestures, and definitive statements—appear as threatening when deployed by people of color. Because African Americans are repeatedly represented to and by white America as dangerous, vigilantes and police officers alike regularly shoot and kill black youth even when they are in a vulnerable positions, such as stuck by the side of the road with a broken-down car late at night. The simultaneous perceived physical vulnerability and invulnerability of black men becomes a justification for violence against them—as in, for instance, the killing of Eric Garnier. Garnier's girth was, on the one hand, the justification for the force police officers used against him: large and imposing, he seemed fearsome. At the same time, his obesity identified him as supposedly more fragile than an average-size person: his weight, not the officer's assault, was given as the reason why he stopped breathing and died, with the officer's strangling dismissed as nearly incidental.

Both the denial of vulnerability and its overemphasis, then, have serious political consequences. As Martha McCaughey has so powerfully argued, the assumption that women are physically vulnerable and men are invincible fuels the mechanisms of a sexist society.[41] The racial distribution of vulnerability subjects thousands to police brutality and unnecessary death. The assumption that vulnerability is nationally distributed has serious environmental and public policy implications, as we too easily accept devastation and conflict in the developing world. In the Western capitalist countries, especially in the United States, we assume that our infrastructure and our geographical positioning will spare us the worst of climate change, even as fires rage across the Midwest and ever-worsening hurricanes flood New York City and New Orleans.

Physical play, when handled with intention and respect, can encourage a reconsideration of vulnerability. Women find combative play empowering not only because of the skills it imparts but also because they learn in a direct and immediate way that they are not as vulnerable as they've been taught;

they are likewise reminded that men are not invincible. Conversely, cisgender, normative-bodied men learn to respect the skills and power of women and smaller men as they learn their own bodies' limitations. This observation about gender carries over to other forms of difference as people enter into combative play with those of different ages, sizes, ethnicities, and abilities and understand the extent to which our vulnerabilities unite us.[42] Such an understanding goes some way toward explaining the camaraderie that develops in fight gyms and other spaces of physical play.

It would be naïve to suggest that we could spar our way to a more equitable world, to more compassionate policing, or to a cleaner planet. Physical play can be an opportunity to reflect on vulnerability, but it can also provide an opportunity to deny it. As we've seen, a real danger exists with martial arts training, as with team sports, that combative play may cross over into violence. More commonly, the inquiry into vulnerability that accompanies sparring can take form merely as a personal investigation that begins and ends with the self.

And yet we can see instances where play opens up opportunities for the creation of community. There is a reason, for instance, that the community policing initiatives that have showed success in reducing police brutality include sports activities and other forms of physical recreation. Despite the prevalence of sexist, homophobic, and transphobic rhetoric and action in commercialized fight sport, martial arts practice has been embraced in social justice movements including feminism, black power, and gay rights. Community dance initiatives sometimes include contact improvisation as a means of allowing underserved and threatened populations ways of interacting dynamically. Similarly, peace-building initiatives rely upon interactions through sports.

In order for physical play to cultivate accountability, it needs to provide opportunities to reflect on and work through vulnerability rather than to deny it. Since experience typically takes on a political and ethical significance in the presence of reflection, kinetic play to needs to include opportunities for reflection if it is going to encourage us to rethink vulnerability. Part of this reflection involves a consideration of risk. Physical play can enhance our understanding of risk and can signal a need to comprehend and to manage risk, rather than avoid it entirely. Understanding danger is particularly important in a society that increasingly has a skewed perception of risk. Risk, like vulnerability, deserves sustained attention.

5

On the Line

THE PLEASURE OF RISK VERSUS THE CULTURE OF FEAR

Nothing ventured, nothing gained.

—CHAUCER

IT'S AN EVENING class and I'm sparring with David. He's from Hong Kong, studying at UCLA for the year and picking up some training along the way. Tall and slender, he has a remarkable reach. He's also fast getting his punches out and snapping them back. But my shorter stature isn't the disadvantage I thought it would be; I can get in and under his arm length, striking his body with swift, heavy blows, then retreat. I take a few shots to the face here and there, but overall my game plan seems to work: I come up and under, I land something, and I get out.

Then I throw a strike from farther out and our forearms meet as he blocks. This is the perfect set-up for a lap sao, the yanking wrist grab that ideally throws an opponent off balance. It works. David stumbles forward and I use the opportunity to land a strike. My fingerless MMA gloves allow my hands the freedom to take hold of David's forearm and pull him. I start curating my attacks around my search for a lap sao, taking some satisfaction as I off-balance my taller opponent.

Experienced fighters call this going to the well too many times. I'm about to find out why.

My hand reaches for David's forearm, acting of its own accord, like a swerve I notice too late to turn out of. I lap sao even as I sense that something is wrong. David jerks forward but my left ring finger torques, moving in the opposite direction. I hear a quiet snap and a metallic, queasy feeling washes over me.

I finish the round, less bold than before. Alain calls time and David asks if I'm okay. I tell him I jammed my finger, although I suspect the damage is worse.

After a few rounds with other partners, where I spar one-handed, I take off my gloves. My left ring finger sits at an odd angle to my hand, veering at an acute angle where it used to stand straight.

That injury led to my first sparring-induced emergency medical visit. It included an X-ray that showed one part of the bone completely separated from the other, and a visit with an orthopedist who identified it as a spiral fracture: a surgery that required pins and a cast to return the finger to its normal function followed.

Walking around with an arm in a bright green cast inspires questions. The most typical one was, of course, "what happened?" Responses varied in a way that echoes the social distribution of vulnerability I've explored in the previous chapter. Older women would give a sympathetic look and ask what had happened *to* me. Strangers' expressions were more suspicious, casting me as a victim, as they glanced skeptically at my partner;[1] others seemed to see me as an aggressor, scanning my partner's face and even that of our child for evidence of impact injury.

Young men, generally, saw something quite different. Their questions invoked not my vulnerability but my agency. They would glance at the cast and ask what I *did*. Some would be even more precise: "Did you break it doing something fun?" One man commiserated with me about the dangers of MMA gloves and another, as we pushed our kids on the swings, called his wife over to meet the boxer on the playground.

The strangest question I got, by far, however, was: Are you going to stop training? That threw me every time. No, I answered swiftly, but not so quickly that I managed to ask them why they assumed I would. Because when I thought about it, it was a strange question. Runners don't stop running when they twist an ankle, dancers don't stop dancing when they tear a knee ligament, and boarders don't stop snowboarding when they break a wrist. Maybe some do. But many more don't.

That I got injured on another person's body likely had something to do with the alarm the injury caused. I've gotten injured dancing and rock-climbing and have never seen the look of dismay that accompanied the admission that I broke a digit sparring. That the danger came from another person's body cast the injury in a light that made it seem higher risk than an activity where I encountered injury via the environment or my own body. I also suspect the injury's source in an unpredictable interaction with another human being prompted the enthusiasm it generated.

As we've seen, martial artists, like other athletes and like dancers, have a cavalier relationship to injury, sometimes even taking a muted pride in contending with injury and recovering from it. These injuries, as well as the ways in which they get incorporated into the continuation of training, reveal a fundamental component of live training: it requires that we stake something. We put our bodies on the line. In other words, we take a risk.

As in the case of vulnerability, risk forms a baseline for play, especially physical play. Risk operates as a means of managing external circumstances, including dangerous ones. Acknowledging—rather than disavowing—risk offers benefits for ethics and politics. Attending to risk can offset a cultural predilection toward risk aversion and victim-blaming. Moreover, understanding the components of risk, as well as what danger is and what it is not, can be helpful as part of rethinking threat in a contemporary moment where economic risk is praised and its consequences disparaged.

Reflections on Risk, Vulnerability, and Danger

If, as I have suggested, a limitation is a condition and vulnerability is an awareness of that condition, risk takes the perception of vulnerability and puts it on the line of experience. Just as limitation and vulnerability differ, so too do risk and danger. Danger is not absolute; as anthropologist Mary Douglas illustrates, danger is socially constructed.[2] Danger, however, consists of conditions external to the self. Risk is experiential. Risk comprises coming into contact with danger. An action can turn out to be dangerous, but risk happens in the moments immediately before and in the moments of doing. It's not possible to risk something in retrospect.

Although risk and danger differ, risk-taking operates as a response to danger. As we'll see, risk-taking is often an attempt to control dangerous forces rather than to unleash them. High-risk play, in particular, involves efforts to mitigate dangers and reduce margins of error. For example, to illustrate a point about optimal experience and risk, Csikszentmihalyi quotes the philosopher Democritus on water as both generative and dangerous, with the remedy to water's danger being learning to swim. Taking a risk in this case means contending with danger. A possible solution to the danger of water could be avoidance. This would reduce risk in the short term. However, it introduces greater danger in the long term. (It also, of course, narrows a person's possibilities for pleasure.) Eschewing water as the solution to danger only works as long as water can be avoided; as soon as the encounter with water begins, the avoidance becomes more dangerous than the confrontation would have been.

Swimming represents an effort to contend with water's danger by facing it directly. Although swimming is a commonplace activity, it nonetheless involves an encounter with the limitations of the human body and the dangers of the environment. A creature that needs air to survive plunging into water is, despite its banality, an extraordinary thing; other land mammals swim, certainly, but many keep their heads above water. For a human to swim well, submersion—that is, confrontation with danger—has to happen directly. Swimming can vary from being low- to high risk depending on the conditions the swimmer faces, but it always involves some degree of risk. Activities such as scuba diving represent a further effort to bring danger under control in the interest of experience.

The seemingly paradoxical relationship between risk and danger is not specific to swimming. Other physical activities and practices involve a confrontation with danger, sometimes in more obvious ways. While conventional sport attempts to transcend danger by introducing order,[3] a willingness to engage both risk and vulnerability comprises alternative sport.[4] Surfing, for instance, plays with the power of the ocean, and rock-climbing explores the contradictory qualities of stone, at times unyielding, at others brittle. Skydiving works within the parameters established by gravity while also overcoming them.

In the case of martial arts, the danger contended with is human violence. As we've seen, martial arts and combat sport involve artificial, rule-bound reconstructions of violence that nonetheless include the physical consequences of violence. Sport fighting manages the danger posed by another person's oppositional intention, from physical techniques such as evasion and blocking to the rules and the etiquette that structure the interaction. Likewise, its training typically requires an ability to manage the normal responses to getting hit: fear and anger. This is another way in which sport fighting differs from real-world violence: fighting is to violence as risk is to danger. Such a distinction goes a long way toward understanding how we can simultaneously take good care of our partners at the same time that we kick, punch, off-balance, and submit them.

Martial arts and other forms of alternative play teach us how to manage danger through calculating risk. Identifying and isolating risk factors as well as practicing with them under contained circumstances allow a player to bring them under control. The ability to identify risk factors, however, works best when it's an individual decision made in a context of reflection. As we'll see, the more commercial and spectacular a sport, the more decisions about risk become external to the participants. Commercial, spectacularized sports simultaneously become risk-averse in regards to outcome while staking the safety and well being of athletes.

Just as contemporary postindustrial societies tend to represent vulnerability as socially distributed, so too do we position risk as more appropriate for some people than for others. For those we perceive as vulnerable risk-taking is to discouraged, whereas for those we perceive as invulnerable courting risk is celebrated as courageous. In contrast to this conventional treatment of risk, this chapter investigates risk as part of the flow, or autotelic state, drawing on feminist philosophy and self-defense literature to consider risk as a source of pleasure. Since reflection as to the consequences of our decisions can encourage accountability, this chapter examines the ethics and politics of risk. Attention to the pleasures of risk can, moreover, offset some of the investments of what sociologists have labeled a culture of fear.

Risk, Mastery, and the Fighter's Self

There's a frisson I get from sport fighters. I have struggled to identify what it is but when I'm around it, I recognize it immediately. The first time I noticed it was at the National Women's Martial Arts Federation conference and special training in 2015. The traditional martial artists I encountered radiated strength and a grounded confidence, but the sport fighters gave off an electrical charge. At first I thought I was reading the traces of full-contact sparring in the bodies of the sport fighters. The larger, more defined deltoids and biceps of someone whose practice demands a raised guard imply an experience with risk because they echo the threat of strikes to the face.

The physical traits made an impression in themselves, but that's not the whole story. They carried a charge because of what they meant, what the body had witnessed. The experimental nature of contact sparring and its intentional production of danger allow a participant to engage with risk.[5] Contending with risk, in turn, produces a sense of mastery and the distinctive focused and confident self that mastery produces.

Viewed one way, this seems obvious: sport fighters are tough because they get in the ring or on the mat and they fight. It doesn't matter that what happens in the ring is an athletic competition rather than unregulated violence. They expose themselves to conflict with other human beings on a regular basis. That toughens them; it signals their bravery and their resolve.

Such a commonsensical association does not, however, answer the question of why this would be so. Why doesn't exposure to danger unsettle rather than reinforce the sense of self? Why does exposure to danger in a controlled setting create this sense of confidence and control whereas exposure to danger in unmanaged circumstance often produces trauma? That the risks are freely chosen has much to do with the connection between risk and mastery. But it still raises the question of how, why, and under what circumstances risks can empower rather than distress. After all, the body and the brain only partially recognize a sport fight as sport; there are points when a fight feels a lot like violence. Often it is only the opening, the closing, and the aftermath that bring us back to a reminder that the opponent is not our enemy.[6] There are plenty of participants for whom sport fighting does feel traumatic, those who train to a point and then back off when training goes live.

Combat sport's function as play rests not so much on how and why it can feel like real violence but how and why it doesn't. In order to understand risk, the question becomes not only how sport fighting differentiates itself symbolically, but also experientially. The difference lies in the ability of sport fighting to expose adherents to risk while enabling them to mitigate danger. The experience of testing and being tested creates a capacity for handling danger through exposure to risk. The risk that fighters experience, far from being a reckless courting of danger, represents an opportunity to develop control and experience mastery. This ability to manage conditions outside oneself, particularly conditions created by another human being, creates a sense of accomplishment and, with it, an enhanced sense of self.

Following psychologist Mihaly Csikszentmihalyi, theorists of play have identified the state of immersion as flow. An investigation of the flow state and its relationship to risk, play, and intuition helps to explain how exposure to freely chosen, closely managed threat enhances rather than diminishes the self. Commentators on the flow state agree that risk becomes central to a state of full focus when it controls danger rather than courting it. Poet and naturalist Diane Ackerman suggests that when facing risk, we become "so thoroughly concerned with acting deftly, in order to be safe, that only reaction is possible, not analysis."[7] Ackerman does not put risk and safety in opposition, but instead points out how risk highlights our ability to evaluate circumstances and act accordingly. Risk, according to Ackerman, allows us to "scan, assess, and make constant minute decisions" through which danger gets recalibrated.[8] Risk fosters a constant adjustment of action in response to danger.

As we've seen, Csikszentmihalyi maintains that activities that put us in the flow state are ones in which we lose consciousness of the self as separate from the environment and our actions. He suggests that the flow experience involves a sense of control, typically lacking from daily life,[9] such that participants experience this sense of control even—and sometimes especially—when their actions involve a confrontation with danger. Some flow-state activities involve a deliberate exposure to threats beyond those of daily life, in which participants "deliberately place themselves in situations that lack the safety nets of civilized life."[10] He suggests that activities with "clear goals, stable rules, and challenges well matched to skills" override a potential threat to the self because they demand full attention to the task at hand, creating the enhanced state of focus that, he argues, enriches experience.[11] Csikszentmihalyi's examples include those placed under the heading of alternative play: hang gliding, rock-climbing, and deep sea diving. Clearly, sport fighting is another such arena through which participants achieve a state of flow or focus through exposure to unnecessary danger, hence its seeming opposition to "civilized life."[12]

Commentators on high-risk play take care to differentiate such activities from a pathological or reckless pursuit of danger for its own sake.[13] Enjoyment in alternative play comes not from the threats per se, but from a participant's ability to minimize them.[14] Moreover, participants do not so much contend with a lack of control; rather, they experience being in control through managed risk. Participants reduce what Csikszentmihalyi identifies as subjective dangers, human error, as opposed to the objective dangers produced by the environment. Risk players practice coming into contact with subjective dangers under controlled conditions. The point of training in these activities is to reduce the margin of error to "as close to zero as possible."[15] An encounter with risk therefore cultivates a very real ability to minimize danger in addition to producing a subjective sense of accomplishment.

Everyday life exposes us to of threats of varied magnitudes and types: accidents, interpersonal violence, illness, and injury of all kinds. In discussions of risk, the majority of these threats are overlooked. As we'll see, threats are not accurately perceived according to their magnitude or likelihood; instead, they are evaluated in terms of their alignment with or departure from the worldview of those who are doing the perceiving. Some of this denial of risk is necessary: we wouldn't be able to get through life if we considered every possible threat we might encounter. It is easier, if not fully accurate, to focus on highly visible dangers.

Those who participate in risk play see the managed risk of sport as minimal compared with the apparently unmanageable, uncontained risks of everyday life.[16] The sense of control experienced in high-risk activity contrasts with the vulnerability we experience when exposed to the unpredictability of quotidian life. Acquiring mastery via risk explains why those who intentionally take risks experience an enhancement of self and an expansion of their world. Conversely, it also sheds light on how and why those who avoid risk experience not safety but a constriction of their world and their sense of self.

At the same time, of course, risk-based play can create an *illusion* of control that causes a risk player to minimize or disregard objective dangers and to downplay subjective dangers. The illusion of control contrasts with the actual conditions of a player's life, as in the case of lifestyle athletes who neglect all aspects of conventional existence that don't pertain to training. The sense of mastery can also foster a dependence on high-risk, high-focus activities.[17] An ability to manage risk has the potential to teach us how to contend with danger in a range of contexts, but it does not do so automatically.

The relationship between risk and threat also indicates that risk does not operate in a vacuum. Risk teaches us about danger only if we are alert to the messages that it conveys. Risk produces feedback that reveals important messages about danger—messages that we are wise to heed if we seek the transformational, self- and world-enhancing experience Csikszentmihalyi discusses and, more importantly, if we wish to avoid disaster. Specifically, activities that provide instant feedback create opportunities in which a participant can gain an understanding of the acquired or temporary limitations that constitute subjective danger.

Getting Hit: The Paradoxical Pleasures of Instant Feedback

During the summer of 2016, I attended the annual Martial Arts Studies Conference in Cardiff, Wales. I gave an address at this event, in which I laid out some of the ideas that form the basis of this book. Afterward, the producer of Dojo TV, an online television station, asked me for an interview. In addition to producing videos on martial arts, Terry, Dojo TV's producer, is also father to an amateur martial arts competitor. His opening thought pertained to the experiential realities of sport fighting: "I was surprised to hear, in your keynote, that you enjoy being hit."

I do not, of course, enjoy being hit. Getting hit is painful. It's frustrating. It reveals my shortcomings. Worse than that, it's a distraction from the game plan that I thought would structure an interaction. More experienced fighters than I reflect on getting to a point where even a full-force strike registers as mere stimulus. I am not there yet. But even should I eventually reach this point, it's unlikely I'll ever enjoy a punch to the nose or a kick to the head.

My response clarified the difference between liking and valuing an experience. I spoke about the differences in meaning between fighting and violence and the ways in which a hit on the mat carries a meaning directly opposite to a hit in the outside world, issues I've addressed in the opening chapters of this book. I spoke of the negotiation between partners that take place in sparring, the adjustment to another person's temperament and skills that, following phenomenologists, I'm calling intersubjective. I also spoke about the ways in which a hit in sparring shows me the limitations of my game.

This ability to reveal limitations through feedback is central to live sparring. Sparring provides information in the form of another person's kicks, strikes, takedowns, joint-locks, or chokeholds. A key factor that distinguishes sparring from drills is its experimental nature, the ways in which it signals right away what works and what doesn't. Nearly everyone who spars values the information that lets them know whether or not their strategy works and whether their favorite maneuver is actually effective. Getting hit is a good way of accessing that information. Like our opponent's respect, the status of hitting as feedback shifts the meaning of a strike, in this case from reprimand to reality check.

In the case of sparring and other forms of interactive physical play, skill building requires risk-taking of some kind, even if what is staked is relatively minor. This is the source of the disputes between martial arts that use sparring and those that don't and those that rely on full-contact versus minimal-contact or touch sparring: we don't know what works until we test it. Testing requires getting feedback. Feedback can take many forms but physical sensation is a particularly effective indicator. It is only with continual and immediate feedback that we hone our responses under pressure.

As Csikszentmihalyi points out, the kind of feedback, in itself, may be, ultimately, unimportant.[18] Getting hit may well be painful but, on the mat, it doesn't much mean anything other than that my guard was down. By stepping onto the mat, I knowingly agree to getting hit, kicked, or caught in a submission. Csikszentmihalyi goes on to suggest, however, that feedback is enjoyable when it is "logically related to a goal in which one has invested psychic energy."[19] We learn to value, he says, some information more than others, on the basis of whether the information helps in the achievement of the goal. If my goal is to get through a round having landed a shot or two without getting hit, a strike to the face provides very important information indeed. Twisting my ankle on the mat could easily be as painful as a strike but it wouldn't convey relevant information (although it might suggest that my balance was off). Risk therefore relates to mastery not only by teaching us how to manage danger but also by providing the information it will take to achieve a goal.

Risk-taking provides the feedback that allows us to develop the intuitive understanding that characterizes expertise. As social psychologist Daniel Kahneman points out, experts can trust their intuition if the environment features regularities they've had ample opportunity to observe.[20] In order to develop this intuitive appraisal of a situation, a would-be expert needs "immediate and unambiguous feedback."[21] As Kahneman suggests, intuition, far

FIGURE 5.1 Getting hit provides instant feedback.
Source: US Navy photo by Mass Communication Specialist 2nd Class Elliott Fabrizio (public domain).

from being a mystical sixth sense is a rapid-fire thought process that mobilizes prior experience and provides swift judgments about a particular situation.

The ability to intuitively appraise danger takes on a critical importance when we consider that risk is not synonymous with danger but is, instead, a means of learning about and managing it. Expertise in danger management is a survival skill, one that most people acquire through life experience but one that is also, like vulnerability, socially distributed. Paradoxically, those considered vulnerable—women, the disabled, youth, and the elderly—are offered less opportunity for and are considered less capable of danger management. The poor and people of color receive mixed messages about danger management as their street smarts are acknowledged at the same time that they are blamed for the violence they encounter, as though it were a failure of risk management and not a product of the heightened threats of the environment, coming from both the expected sources (aggressive civilians) and from those who are supposed to provide protection (the police).

For those seen as less vulnerable—primarily white, cisgender, normative-bodied men—experimentation with risk is lauded. This is because we see them as less exposed to harm and therefore assume they have the freedom to play with risk. But it is also because we witness the less vulnerable exercising mastery: we regularly watch them playing team sports in arenas and on television, skateboarding in skate parks, and hang-gliding by ocean bluffs. We see the ostensibly less vulnerable expose themselves to unpredictability and emerge unscathed, reinforcing the idea of them as in control.

These concerns are, of course, also material. Marginalized populations have less access to lifestyle sports, those that emphasize the personal management of risk, as most of these sports are funded individually rather than being provided by schools, clubs, and other organizations. Team sports are available in low-income neighborhoods, but team sports are selective and tend to be restrictive based on body types and temperament. The funding for team sports, as for other activities, differs dramatically based on socioeconomic class, race, gender, and normative ability of the participants.[22]

Aligning risk play with conventional sport carries a certain logic given that risk produces pleasure through managing danger, not courting it. Pleasure comes not from the danger itself but the ability to control it. I've spent time articulating this idea because I think it is a large part of the enjoyment of high-risk activities. But it would be disingenuous to suppose that the pleasure only comes from surmounting danger, with no trace of satisfaction derived from the thrills provided by danger and the sense of bravery experienced as a result.[23]

In writing about women's access to public space, sociologists Shilpa Phadke, Sameera Khan, and Shilpa Ranade take a slightly different tack from theorists of play and the flow state.[24] In contrast to Csikszentmihalyi and Ackerman, Phadke et al. don't counter the metaphor of courting risk, but instead explore this figure of speech as a way of articulating the pleasures of risk. In their study of women's access to public space in Mumbai, India, they reject the conventional wisdom that women's risk-taking is a negative behavior to be avoided. In the process, they take seriously the metaphor of courting risk. They argue that the navigation of risk be seen literally as a courtship, "a pleasurable dance of forward and backward, of negotiation and choice," a relationship that is reciprocal and is characterized by the expectation of enjoyment.[25] Moreover, Phadke et al. argue for a close relationship between risk and access, pleasure, and even citizenship, maintaining that the ability to contend with risk represents freedom and maturity.[26]

Just as Phadke et al. suggest that we can revisit the idea of courting risk as a pleasurable dialogue, so too can we rethink playing with risk. Precluding risk-based play is not protection; it is restrictive. It produces not safety but an inability to manage danger. This is not to say that no restrictions should be applied to play and that no provisions should be made for players' safety.[27] On the contrary, the onus for safety is not only on the individual. Assuring that risk-taking happens in a situation where objective dangers are reduced to nil so that players can learn to manage what Csikszentmihalyi calls subjective dangers forms part of the responsibility of training institutions, schools, and municipalities. Providing the infrastructure for the intelligent management of danger belongs to society: the maintenance of roads, sidewalks, and bike paths, for instance, allow us to manage the inherent dangers that come with travel.

While some societies provide insufficient provision for safety in daily life—too few street lights or insufficient bike routes when it comes to play, provision for safety veers toward the excessive. Indeed, this is the argument made by psychologists and journalists who study children's play: contemporary societies have restricted children's opportunities for the exploration of risk in play. Led by but not exclusive to the United States, societies have moved toward an increased regulation of children's time, a standardization of playground equipment, and legal restrictions that prohibit children from exploring their environments. Psychologists have discovered that such restrictions produce not security but anxiety, not safety but recklessness.[28]

As in other instances, fight sports are not a simple solution to societal problems. Depending on how they are practiced and managed, combat sport can easily spin into a pursuit of danger, as in cases where fight gyms encourage unmanaged competition and brutal training methods. Likewise, the commercialization of fight sport can play into an outsourcing of risk, where fans watch players put their bodies on the line while living a curtailed life themselves. Instead, martial arts training, like other aspects of society, raise questions as to what facilitates an ability to handle danger, what constitutes excessive risk aversion, and what enables participants to develop the skills necessary to recognize objective dangers and minimize subjective ones.

A consideration of risk is important not only because managed risk-taking is necessary to individual psychological health but also because it facilitates interaction among people, creating a sense of community that can be hard to access otherwise in contemporary life. Controlled encounters with danger represented in the form of another person produce a particular kind of pleasure not because (or not only because) they are a way of letting off steam, but also because they rely on and generate trust. For example, Loïc Wacquant, in his ethnography of boxing, emphasizes the affection that regular sparring partners develop that is a direct result of "the risk that each takes with the other and in turn imposes upon the other."[29] Susan Schorn compares sparring partners to romantic partners, arguing that sparring relies upon a profound trust and a willingness to teach and learn. Earlier, I've suggested that sparring is like friendship in that it offers opportunities for intimacy and personal growth while also exposing participants to pain. Such comparisons, although counterintuitive, are not as unlikely as they might seem at first glance.

When we spar, we expose ourselves to harm at the hands of our sparring partners. We are continually reminded that what could (theoretically) happen isn't, in a respectful gym, happening: my training partner could break my arm when he gets me in an arm bar; instead he releases his grip. I could knock her out when I land a punch but instead I control its impact.[30]

Some commentators speak of submissions, joint-locks in particular, as a symbolic murder.[31] This seems to miss a central point, as a submission happens when one person signals her inability to escape the lock within the parameters of the rules of the game while the other acknowledges that signal by releasing the hold. Tapping out means acknowledging the superior skill, speed, decision-making, and possibly luck of the opposing party and the missed clues on one's own part. There is no reason to assume that an individual at risk of a joint-lock when not accepting the inefficient means of the game could not, or would not resort to eye strikes, throat gouges, and groin strikes. In addition, of course, a damaged joint, although cruelly slow to heal, is rarely fatal.

A submission is a signal that, like a strike, separates form from meaning: I have hemmed you into a corner not I am trying to destroy your will. Likewise, tapping out is a signal replete with meaning: I recognize that you've won, at

FIGURE 5.2 Tapping out signals trust in the parameters of the game.
Photograph courtesy of Patrick Becker.

least this time around, but I also recognize that you are not trying to hurt me and, implicitly, I promise that I won't hurt you when I gain the upper hand. Rather than seeing tapping out as a symbolic death, we could just as easily see it as equivalent to BDSM's explicit boundary setting: a parameter around a potentially dangerous activity that allows participants to exercise their agency even in a situation where they are physically compromised. "Tap" is an effective safe word.

Anthropologists have tended to look at trust in an evolutionary context, suggesting that trust includes putting self-interest aside in order to gain the long-term benefits of cooperation.[32] I am reluctant to suggest that trust always serves the same function or produces the same social effects in all contexts; however, there is something to the anthropologists' assertion that actions that signal goodwill produce mutual pleasure and that actions that walk the line of risk and danger but ultimately refuse harm generate a particularly intense enjoyment. It is enjoyable to act in generosity and to receive that generosity.[33] It is also pleasurable to exercise an ethics of care in a situation of danger,[34] even when that danger is self-created. The reminder that participants not only eschew violence but also come to each other's aid reinforces mutual support and respect.[35] Such reminders, in turn, enhance a sense of community.

Getting submitted is disappointing because of its reminder of failure, but it is reassuring in its direct and immediate reminder that what's happening is not violence. The symbolic violence of martial arts can, when handled with respect and consideration, operates as an emblem of trust that reinforces social relationships. Such an insight can extend from martial arts to the world beyond the mat.

Sports and Risk Aversion

Modern, commercial sport takes a paradoxical position on risk. Sports teams, especially professional and high-level amateur ones, routinely risk the physical well-being of players, as evidenced by the devastating, sometimes permanent injuries incurred by American football players, amateur and professional alike.[36] Professional sport fighters, like team athletes, are objectified by the system in which they participate. In both cases, viewers insist that players provide the spectacle the crowd craves, regardless of its effect on their physical and mental well-being.[37]

And yet modern sports remain risk-averse when it comes to the outcome of competition. For example, the Pacquiao–Mayweather match of May 2105 was billed as the fight of the century because, although the two welterweight champions had ample opportunity to compete against each other, they had not done so over their long careers. It seems neither side would take the risk of losing. The match finally took place and all that was evident was the professionalism of both fighters. Mayweather won by points; it was by most accounts a close match, but hardly one filled with suspense.

The real drama came later as lawsuits followed the match. One was a class-action suit against Pacquiao because he neglected to declare a shoulder injury, thereby, complainants argue, depriving fans of their money's worth and adversely affecting gamblers' odds. Such a case corroborates the claim made by Alex Channon and Christopher Matthews: that the demand in commercial sport fighting for spectacle supersedes a fighter's well-being and individual agency.[38] Pacquiao launched another lawsuit because the boxing commission allowed Mayweather a vitamin and mineral injection and denied Pacquiao an injection of a local anesthetic to manage his ligament damage. Rumors of a mole within Pacquiao's training camp followed: an informer ostensibly brought Mayweather's team details on Pacquiao's injury so the former could use the clinch to injure his competitor. Whether this is true or not, it suggests that a profound unwillingness to lose is common at the highest levels of the sport; it suggests that contenders are expected to work against the inherent risk of the encounter and to avoid its unpredictability not only by skill but also by a meticulous management of outside circumstances.

Spectators' rollercoaster ride around the career of UFC fighter Ronda Rousey constitutes another example of risk aversion in commercial sport. The last several years saw speculation as to who the previously undefeated UFC champion would fight. At first, she was reputed to be too skilled for the sport: her brisk defeat of Cat Zingano was rumored to spell the doom of women's MMA. Her stated goal, and that of UFC head Dana White, was to retire undefeated. As in the case of other competition fighters, her opponents were therefore carefully curated. Rousey's match with Holly Holm was supposed to be another easy victory; the surprise defeat produced a flurry of speculation that turned into outright disparagement when Rousey lost a subsequent match to Amanda Nunes. The ridicule fans and commentators leveled at Rousey equaled only the adulation she received as an undefeated champion.

The extreme care that goes into the selection of opponents,[39] as well as the highly focused and specialized preparation of sport fighters toward individual matches, works against the unpredictability of the game. Even more extreme is the role of journeymen in professional boxing—fighters who are hired to lose or with the expectation that they will lose to boost the record of rising champions.[40] When institutions need stars to continue to sell live tickets and pay-per-views, they rapidly move into a situation where the institution can't afford to let the athlete be defeated. A sport that seems to be all about risk can swiftly become risk-averse, at least in terms of outcome, even as the sport takes extreme risks with players' bodies and overall well-being.

As workers, sport fighters are, of course, entitled to rules that protect their safety and to opportunities for success and career longevity. I am not, therefore, suggesting that we should require sport fighters to take undue risk of injury or even to alter their desired career path. Indeed, I am arguing the opposite: that we allow athletes to make their own decisions about the acceptability of risk, regardless of its impact on the fans' experience. I am also proposing that a better public attitude toward wins and losses would go some way toward modeling generosity and an acceptance of unpredictability. Indeed, shifts in public attitude toward losing and winning could result in reduced dangers faced by athletes, given that competition, not training, represents the site of most frequent injuries.[41]

The most fascinating fighters in martial arts history are those willing to engage with the differences offered by other people competing against them. The most interesting moments, to my mind, are those when interpersonal exploration comes to the fore. When I watch the modern UFC, for instance, I can't help but think back to the early days of this competition, where there were no weight classes and competitors practiced entirely different martial arts, some of which were unknown to one another. Rorion Gracie, of the Brazilian jiu jitsu dynasty, launched these early events in order to promote their system because it was so unfamiliar and effective at addressing the weaknesses of other fight systems.[42] In this sense, organizer Rorion Gracie was confident of the outcome: universal victory and the explosion in popularity of their sport.

However, as a spectator, watching that first UFC match in 1993, the outcome seemed anything but guaranteed. The results mattered less than the process, at least for viewers such as myself who had no vested interest in one contender or another. The explorative element of those early matches was fascinating: grapplers had to contend, for the first time, with being hit. Kickboxers had to deal with takedowns. Small fighters got to see if their agility was sufficient against not only a larger fighter but also one with a different skill set. Larger fighters wound up in completely unfamiliar positions as a slimmer fighter (usually Royce Gracie) wrapped himself around their backs or attacked their limbs. A far cry from the reality-TV inflected, ad-packed broadcast of highly systemized matches now featured by the UFC, these matches formed an exploration of difference, in training background, fight style, and physique. It bought contenders into an encounter with the unexpected. An aversion to economic risk and an overemphasis on outcome in contemporary commercial sport lessens the possibilities for this kind of exploration.

The Politics of Risk and the Culture of Fear

The pleasures of risk don't only contrast with a simultaneous embrace of danger and risk aversion in professional sport. They also sit in opposition to a hyper-awareness of danger in the modern world, especially in American society, which gives a disproportionate weight to unusual dangers (terrorism, serial killers, flesh-eating bacteria), while being strangely oblivious to far more likely banal threats such as accidents, disease, and violence from friends, lovers, and family members. Sociologist Barry Glassner labels this phenomenon the culture of fear.[43]

Glassner argues that Americans, in particular, fear spectacular, dramatic threats, ranging from violent crime to plane wrecks to rare diseases, ignoring the many ways in which the world has become safer as well as downplaying commonplace dangers such as traffic accidents. The hysteria around fear, Glassner argues, leads to social violence as when, for instance, our society sees black men as criminals when they are more typically crime victims, and teens as threats to adults when they are more likely to be abused by adults than to harm them.[44] Journalist Daniel Gardner delves into the investigation of fear trends, suggesting that our understanding of risk is colored not by magnitude or likelihood but by specific factors such as personal control, familiarity, and origin of the risk.[45]

Misperceptions of threat have led us to seriously restrict our use of public space with, for instance, the rise of gated communities and the demand that minors of all ages be under direct adult supervision at all times. It has led to more dangerous behavior, such as when we fear flying because it is out of control and drive instead, which is far more dangerous.[46] We structure children's leisure time because we fear stranger-abductors and juvenile delinquents alike, but we urge them into increasingly competitive sports that expose them to concussions and other injuries with long-term consequences. It leads us to downplay serious threats such as climate change, because they appear to come "from nature." A culture of fear adversely affects our ability to handle risk and appraise danger effectively.

Reflecting on Shilpa Phadke's argument that creating opportunities for managed risk-taking is an obligation of society, I am interested in considering how a hypothetical, society-wide exploration of risk contrasts with a culture of fear. The North American context in which I write differs in crucial ways from the South Asian one that Phadke et al. consider, notably in that public space is not as obviously dominated by men in North America. Some of the issues they address carry over across any number of patriarchal societies, such as the ways in which women are blamed for their own victimization and that men are seen as invulnerable even when men are statistically more likely than women to encounter violence in public. However, I want to extend their argument beyond a gender analysis to consider the status of risk in Western capitalist countries and in the United States in particular. Central to Phadke et al.'s analysis are two points: first, that risk is directly tied to agency, access, and citizenship and second, that societies owe their citizens opportunities to manage their own encounters with risk rather than being shielded from risk or unduly exposed to it.

Following Phadke's suggestions, I question what happens to risk assessment in a society that exhibits a dread of risk, whittling away at opportunities to manage danger through decision-making while also blaming those who come to harm for taking risks. In the absence of opportunities to assess danger, what becomes of the sense of personal mastery and accomplishment that accompanies risk-based play? I question what happens to the sense of community that develops through rituals of trust where we willingly expose ourselves to danger and allow others to demonstrate their goodwill. What are the implications for a society that cultivates fear and preaches risk reduction while erasing much of the safety net that allows its citizens the ability to decide when and where to take risks?

I don't want to overstate the pleasures of risk, nor do I want to ignore the nuances of risk-taking. Risk, like vulnerability and failure, can work to reinforce the status quo and to reiterate difference and hierarchy as easily as it can unsettle them. In addition, as sociologist Mark Stranger argues, the pursuit of risk in the interest of thrills can distort risk assessment instead of bolstering it.[47] Pursuing risk can mean chasing ever-higher thrills; even if this happens unintentionally, it can muddy the risk assessment that counterposes exposure to danger. Moreover, risk-based play can produce, in Stranger's terms, the "feeling that participation in the activity is good in itself."[48] This sense of a good in itself can foreclose the possibilities for introspection and the sense of community that physical play can produce. Like more organized sports, then, alternative sports and other forms of play can become hermetically sealed worlds where ethical and political critiques are evacuated.

In addition, it's important to note that the pleasures of risk only emerge when risk is taken on willingly. Without such a distinction, the effort to separate risk from danger becomes an abstract undertaking. The homeless are both at risk and exposed to danger by virtue of their condition. Low-income people exposed to environmental toxins risk their health in order to maintain the safety provided by a roof over their heads. Women and nonbinaries risk violence from cisgender men in order to move through public space. Communities of color risk injury and death both when police neglect their neighborhoods and when they patrol them. A risk not chosen is a danger, whether it results in damage or not. A subjective danger that is imposed is a threat, regardless of whether it could theoretically be managed in other circumstances.

Exposure to risk is not "a good in itself." Risk is related to consequence, and, like vulnerability, has ethical and political implications.[49] However, it requires consideration, management, and reflection to produce the sense of mastery and community that I have suggested it has the potential to do. In order to better understand both consequence and the importance of introspection, we need to consider the stakes of action and interaction. We need to consider failure.

6

Fail Better

THE PARADOX OF DEFEAT IN MARTIAL ARTS TRAINING

DURING THE SUMMER of 2017, I attended an empowerment self-defense instructor training program at a YMCA Camp in rural New York State. Run by Yudit Sidikman, founder of the women's self-defense organization El HaLev, the program offered templates for teaching self-defense through games and tasks rather than only through drills. Designing ways of signaling accomplishment at the end of sessions and programs is part of the El HaLev method of promoting enjoyment within self-defense training.

Toward the end of the instructor training, Yudit brought us together to break boards, in conventional martial arts fashion, where an instructor holds a plywood board and a participant smashes through it with a palm strike. Yudit introduced an innovation designed to link to the work we had spent the last several days doing: we wrote, in Sharpie marker, on the board, a perceived restriction we intended to smash through. After the palm strike, our burden was destroyed.

As with the other tasks we engaged in, our opportunity was both experiential and meta-instructive. We broke boards and we learned how to teach people to break boards. Yudit drew our attention to how difficult it seems to be, in contrast to how easy it is when done with correct technique. I hadn't broken a board in decades and so I felt some of the anxiety she attributed to newcomers. Plus, I was fascinated by her description of teaching board breaking.

When breaking a board, she said, a novice woman usually thinks, "I can't." Whereas a novice man typically thinks—"I can," someone interrupted. "What if I can't?" Yudit said.

This distinction between these contrasting forms that self-doubt takes when expressed by men and women sheds light on the cultural weight assigned to failure and its negative associations. Failure, as it operates here, signals inadequacy. Failure, in both the stereotypically feminine and masculine responses, invokes incompetence rather than representing an opportunity for learning, restrategizing, or responding creatively to a problem. Yudit's reflections also reveal how failure expresses itself along the lines of social identity.

If, as the phenomenologists tell us, we experience our status as human subjects through our mastery over physical tasks, then there is something inherently unsettling about failing to complete a physical undertaking. And yet as Greg Downey points out, failure, or at least incomplete mastery, undergirds the learning process of any physical skill.[1] Such an association of mastery with personal identity is complicated by gender. As Iris Marion Young argues,[2] mastery allows us to experience ourselves as subjects and not objects at the same time that mastery is seen as a masculine attribute. In this context, as in others, masculinity generalizes as human at the same time that it restricts its proper domain to that of cisgender men.

Young discusses the association of masculinity with competence and femininity with ineptitude as it pertains to women's experience of incomplete subjecthood. The flip side of this equation is that men don't simply exist as men; they must prove themselves worthy of being a man. This is evident in phrases such as "be a man about it" and "man up." The use of the word "man" as a verb is particularly telling: masculinity is a doing, not a being. It reveals the threat of, in Judith Halberstam's terms, "the failure of ideal masculinity."[3] The social demand that men prove their masculinity expresses itself through the requirement to perform mastery at all times. That men are expected to continually perform competence leads to a toxic masculinity that precludes admitting failure or weakness of any kind. Men are therefore denied the right to fail.

A woman who fails, by contrast, confirms an already inferior status. For women, especially when performing physical tasks, failure is often expected. Failure is also attributed to her womanhood as a conditional state. When a woman fails, she doesn't fail *to be* a woman; instead, she fails *because* she's a woman. For some women, especially those who are middle-class and cisgender, "I can't" becomes the fallback position, the identification of themselves as the incomplete subject that Young described nearly forty years ago.

The acceptance of the incomplete subject position operates as the baseline only for women who have internalized messages of feminine weakness and incompetence. Women who strive for competence and success, paradoxically, end up in an analogous situation to men, less assuming failure than fearing failure's implications. However, while a man who fails fails to be a man, a woman who fails fails all women. A difficult task is not a test of whether this particular woman can measure up; it is a test of whether *a* woman can.[4]

In contrast to the requirement that men prove themselves as men via accomplishment, a woman only has to confirm her status as a woman when she's in danger of succeeding too much. So, for example, sexualization and hyper-feminization of female athletes accompanies their otherwise patriarchy-challenging success on the court, on the field, or in the cage.[5] A failure can make a successful woman more appealing, as seems to have happened in the wake of Hilary Clinton's loss of the presidential bid, or it can turn a women from glorified to disdained, as did Rhonda Rousey's losses. A woman's competence can be threatening for the same reason that a man's competence appears necessary: if success is necessary to confirm masculinity, a woman's success takes away something that a man "needs" for something she, apparently, merely "wants."[6] Such a perspective, usually held unconsciously, suggests that success is a zero-sum game, a problematic assumption in itself.[7]

Failure is not just gendered; it is also racialized and class-marked. The consequences of poverty and racism, ranging from poor performance in school to addiction and imprisonment, are treated, in American public discourse, as individual failures rather than as the product of an unjust system that disproportionately attributes resources to some communities at the expense others. The labeling of poor youth of color as "at risk" rather than as "underserved" is a linguistic example of the mapping of failure onto individuals rather than systems. Consequences for failure, likewise, divide along the lines of race and class (as well as sexual orientation and gender conformity) with, for example, zero-tolerance policies in schools, three-strikes laws, and the war on drugs producing a school-to-prison pipeline.[8] This is a process that begins in school, as ordinary adolescent behavior is increasingly criminalized and minor infractions are met with stiff penalties,[9] a bias toward punishment referred to as a carceral logic.[10]

As Michelle Alexander indicates, although it's no longer acceptable to overtly discriminate on the basis of race, it is acceptable to discriminate in exactly the same ways (housing, employment, legal rights) against former felons.[11] Alexander points to racial profiling, police brutality, and harsh drug laws as the ground for a shocking surge in the institutionalization of US populations, with the prison population quadrupling over the last forty years and black men suffering the worst effects of this increase in incarceration.[12] Racial profiling and "broken windows" policing means that the consequences for minor infractions, such as traffic violations and recreational drug possession, among the poor and among people of color, are far graver than for the white middle class.[13] Ordinary failures, such as struggling in school or neglecting a broken taillight, become etched onto an individual through a legal and economic record that follows them through life. What Alexander calls the new Jim Crow logic condemns a large segment of the population to permanent social and economic failure, making it difficult for them to enter higher education, get a steady job, or acquire stable housing.

The consolidation of wealth in corporations and the ultra elite and the erosion of the public sphere normalizes certain kinds of failure: neighborhoods and cities now fail, falling into long-term decline. Although banks are too big to fail, cities and towns, apparently, are not. In this instance, states of economic failure cut across communities divided by race and geography. Once-thriving communities that lose their industrial base of production now enter into a permanent state of decline rather than experiencing regeneration, creating the so-called Rust Belt. Formerly middle-class, urban African American neighborhoods in cities such as Philadelphia and Detroit that have suffered from the shrinking of the public sphere experience a tragic parallel to their rural counterparts: the decline in the vitality of the public sphere has lead to a disenfranchisement of the black middle class, and formerly middle-class neighborhoods and even cities have sunk into a state of seemingly permanent failure.[14]

Failure is therefore not something that can be simply re-evaluated to reduce its sting. It is not an abstraction that merely needs to be rethought. Even among the more privileged segments of society the American dream now seems unattainable, as a younger generation contends with large post-college debt and sees themselves permanently priced out of homeownership. Our politicians debate whether to return to a situation where some are permanently denied health care. Homelessness occupies the extreme end of failure, and yet it appears as the fate of individuals and families who have simply made one or two mistakes or have experienced one or two grave losses. Many of us experience greater economic precarity than ever before, exposed to fundamental kinds of failure. The dismantling of social safety nets, in the United States and elsewhere, means that we have created an economy that disallows failure.

Failure, like vulnerability, gets mapped onto certain populations. Failure, unlike vulnerability, results not in paternalistic protection but in exclusion. Although failure is positioned differently for men and women and across racial and economic groups, in all instances, failure is treated as and poses a threat. In sharp contrast to the idea of failure as threat is a counterposing one, expressed in contemporary educational and aesthetic theories (and practices): that failure offers opportunities for experimentation, growth, and reflection.

Our most successful segments of society, especially the young, are characterized as "failure deprived."[15] Think pieces suggest, with a fair amount of evidence to back up their claims, that a lack of exposure to consequences clouds the judgment of children while an insufficient experience of failure leaves young adults lacking in resilience and adaptability.[16] We live in a society where every child on a sports team gets a medal and every student expects an A. As a result, colleges have introduced programs to teach students how to fail.[17] While the experience of the inner city child whose every actions are under surveillance could not be more different from that of the middle-class youth who has only ever experienced success, the cultural message is similar:[18] errors are intolerable.

Failure-into-success stories are, meanwhile, the new rags-to-riches narratives. The idea of "failing up" is celebrated.[19] This is especially true in the dot.com sphere, where certain kinds of unconventionality are lauded. You can't have success without failure, this narrative goes. Implicit in it, however, is the related idea that failure is only acceptable when it results in success.

Failure is, by its nature, paradoxical. Learning cannot happen without failure. Nor can creativity. It is not possible to acquire mastery without a lot of failure along the way. Failure, like vulnerability, inheres in all action; whenever we do anything, we create conditions in which failure can happen.[20] And yet psychologists remind us that losing is inherently painful; failure produces psychological stress across a range of circumstances.[21] Social psychology studies, such as those initiated by Daniel Kahnemann, suggest that loss aversion typically outweighs the incentive provided by winning.[22] Losing generates anxiety and reluctance to re-enter the stressful situation.[23] Conversely, winning encourages the desire to re-enter the competitive context.[24] The resilience and adaptability that failure is supposed to (and often does) generate is not easily acquired.

However, as we've seen, failure inhabits a *particularly* paradoxical situation in contemporary American society. My aim is therefore not to write another piece that celebrates failure and castigates a younger generation for refusing to embrace its potential.[25] In order to truly comprehend failure and, paradoxically, in order to experience its benefits, we need to acknowledge that failure does not always lead to success. Sometimes a failure is just a failure.

My interest, then, is in unraveling the complexity of failure and recognizing its inherently incongruous nature. I suggest that the complexity of failure, combined with its inevitability, can allow us to reconcile its contradictions. Instead of mapping this failure deficit onto individuals, I am suggesting that we rework our societal understanding of failure as well as our provision for it. Much like Phadke et al.'s argument regarding risk, that it is the obligation of society to provide opportunities for managed risk-taking, it is the obligation of a fair and just society to make provisions for failure. An enhanced awareness of the pain of losing and the disappointment of failure can facilitate a more accurate understanding of the potential benefits of failure. Integrating failure into a narrative of eventual success masks the dismay associated with failure. In line with Judith Halberstam, I'm suggesting that failure can generate different kinds of knowing than those proposed by a mainstream success narrative,[26] opening up "more creative, more cooperative, more surprising ways of being in the world."[27] Kinetic play provides a useful opportunity for thinking about both the consequences and the inevitability of failure.

Martial arts, in particular, represent a useful arena for investigating failure. Failure is inevitable in martial arts: when it comes to any kind of live practice, every practitioner, no matter how skilled, gets hit, kicked, or taken down. Even drills can be predicated upon the idea of training to failure, increasing in complexity until the exercise exceeds the ability of the practitioner to handle it. Small, ongoing failures become the basis for problem-solving and strategy-building. Large failures produce opportunities for re-evaluating a game plan.

Martial arts provide a double encounter with failure. Not only do sport fighters frequently get hit, they also fail to land their strikes. They find their tactics rebuffed and their strategies interrogated. The chess game aspect of martial arts that I discussed in chapter 3 relies not on continual success, but on an exposure to failure that generates new approaches and that requires the reworking of a game plan on the fly.

And yet failure in martial arts produces pain, directly through the sensation of the opponent's hit and indirectly through the emotional encounter with error that reveals flaws in approach or technique. The ability to withstand the emotional consequences of failure and to adapt to the changed circumstances it reveals forms the basis of the humility that martial arts training ideally cultivates. Understanding failure as both painful and revealing contrasts with the celebration of "soft landings" and "failing up" in the American business sector.

It also sits in opposition to the much-vaunted status of winning in American cultural life and, as such, reveals the investments of a success-obsessed society. Attending to the role of failure in learning and playing can highlight the status and meaning of failure in a society focused on competitive outcomes. Such an approach considers whether we can re-evaluate the meaning of failure while acknowledging its material and emotional consequences. Given how central sports have been to cultural attitudes toward success and failure, it's worth considering whether an effort to revalue failure while acknowledging the pain it causes can encourage a shift in societal investments in winning at all costs.

Live Losing: Martial Arts, Performance, and Failure

It's Sunday morning and I'm sparring with Anna. We're training in her garage, as we often do. No one else showed up today so I've gotten a private class. That seemed like great luck until we near the conclusion of our session. Because now it's time to spar and I'm the only one for Anna to fight.

Anna is small, slight, and quick. Her footwork is stellar and her training in panantukan, Filipino boxing, gives her the ability to angle off nearly any attack. Her panantukan training has also given her a wild jab, one that swoops in from directions I can't track: unexpected diagonals, surprise backfists and even the occasional overhand. She likes to spar with untimed rounds, so I can't count on my usual reassurance: I only have to live through the next three minutes.

Next to her I feel heavy, slow, and numb, launching obvious attacks and fending off her strikes with awkward, twitchy deflections that come too late.

"Kicks only," she declares, and off we go. Her heavy Thai kicks land on my thighs, but I manage to evade any hard shots to the ribs. I land one or two kicks on her and I think I'm doing all right. I'm moving, light on my feet at least, and circling. When kicks are allowed, I can, at the minimum, keep my opponent away from me. Besides, using the longer weapon of my legs, more of her body is available. It's easier to create a disincentive to her attack than when we're restricted to punches.

"Jab only," Anna says and we move in closer. I'm confronting that unpredictable front hand without the comfort of distance.

"All punches." Her brisk footwork and rapid strikes truly begin to confuse me. She gets me focused on deflecting punches to my face and lands a body strike, a kidney shot that crumples me. It's just a split second but it's long enough. Her right cross lands square to my nose.

I taste metal and feel warmth in my throat. No cracking sound, so I keep going. I sniffle and focus on getting my feet moving.

"Clinch allowed," she says, and now I'm deflecting her hands off the back of my neck. We battle for the inside space, gloved hands slipping in between arms, latching on and landing knee strikes to the body. I can muscle my way through this, at least enough to evade her knees. The knee strikes that do get through bring the comfort of not being punches to the face.

"Back to punches." Out in striking range and I'm feeling particularly vulnerable as a trickle of blood runs from my nose and onto my lips. It's all I can do to play defense.

I call time before we return to kicks, exhausted and wondering if a second strike to my nose would break it. I don't know if getting hit in the nose is cumulative. It's probably not, but the idea distracts me and distraction is the last thing I want when up against Anna.

We hug and I grab a tissue to staunch the blood from my nose, filled with that weird euphoria that follows a challenging round. There's the awareness of being nowhere near good enough but right next to that, the sense of accomplishment: I got through it. I didn't even complete the designated round, not making it through the return to kicks-only fighting. I confronted one failure after the next, managing only a few successes. But I endured.

Rounds like these, when I go up against someone much more skilled than I, illustrate the paradox of martial arts training: failure can be a kind of success. There are people who are so much more capable than I that getting through the round with them is an accomplishment in its own right. Finding accomplishment in responsiveness to a challenging situation—weathering the storm even when failing to inhabit the eye of the storm—is not unique to me or even to the more inconsistent of fighters. Accomplished fighters speak of rounds with those more skilled than they as "mere survival."

Live training, in martial arts, thus consists of finding success in failure. An exposure to failure is, perhaps, the single most important element that distinguishes martial arts that rely on live practice—sparring and grappling—from those that do not. Indeed, those who shy away from sparring cite its high rate of failure as one reason for their discomfort. For others, myself among them, feeling unsettled in order to feel capable is precisely the point.

Martial arts training allows us to find success in failure partly because failure undergirds learning, and martial arts training makes the role of failure in learning obvious. The direct engagement with failure as the basis for understanding constitutes an experimental approach, which parallels that of the scientific method.[28] It also runs parallel to an approach engaged in the avant-garde arts. A trial-and-error process is central, particularly, to the live practices of sparring and grappling. Live practice is the ground on which this experimentation, this consideration of "what works,"[29] happens. As such, it's worth considering the meaning of the term live in martial arts parlance as well as in performance and team sports as a way of exploring its relationship to experimentation and to failure.

The term "live," in martial arts, carries several meanings, some of which connect directly to connotations of "live" in performance and some of which diverge. The parallels and differences in meanings of the concept of the live reveal understandings of the risk of failure that likewise both align and differ. In martial arts parlance, a live encounter is one that is not set or choreographed; it is one in which participants attempt to strike or subdue one another while evading or deflecting their counterpart's attempts at the same. Partners, in a live interaction, do not take turns kicking, striking, or submitting; instead, they attack and defend as need be. When training goes live, partners become opponents.

Martial artists also use the term "live" to refer to weapons that are capable of inflicting their full potential harm: a soft stick is juxtaposed with a live rattan stick, and a trainer blade is juxtaposed with a sharp metal knife. This aligns with the definition of live ammunition as containing explosives and live coals as retaining sparks.[30] It is not the possibility of harm per se that renders a weapon live, as a poke in the eye with a wooden knife would still injure and blank ammunition still kills. Rather, a live weapon is one that does the specific harm for which it is designed.

FIGURE 6.1 The same drill uses a trainer blade and a live stick because of the nature of the weapons.
Photograph courtesy of Tim Becherer.

The term "live," when used in relation to performance, can refer to events that are choreographed in terms of their movement being set, their notes preestablished, or their lines committed to memory. The dictionary definition of a live performance defines it in terms of its opposite: a live performance is one that is not recorded.[31] The seeming paradox of a live recording is one that represents an accurate, continuous take of a performed event without the editing that would make it appear more seamless than it was. In team sports, a live ball is one that is in play. This runs parallel, in a sense, to a live weapon in that it is an object that fulfills its designated function.

An exposure to failure links these disparate meanings of the term. "Live" connotes a vulnerability to the consequences of failure via the terms of the engagement of the encounter. A live event in both martial arts and performance is one where error becomes a distinct possibility. Recorded events can be repeated in sections until they pass muster, or they can be edited in order to render errors invisible or inaudible. A martial arts drill can allow participants to repeat an evasion, deflection, or strike until it is executed accurately. Even rapid-fire, counter-for-counter drills such as Filipino martial arts' sumbrada allow a participant to back up and restage a strike in order to correct her response. In martial arts, as in performance, actions in live events cannot be corrected.

Habits can be altered and tactics changed in the wake of live training, but these adjustments happen via retrospection. Even when the best of fighters reveal an eerie ability to modify their tactics and their style in the course of a round or match, this shift happen on the heels of feedback while anticipating what will happen next. In live performance and live training, both martial artists and performers contend with what is there, not with what they wish were there. Participants face the circumstances before them, adjust to what they find, and adapt to another person's adaptation. Thus, the chess game I explore in chapter 3 is constituted not just by interpersonal exchange but also by incorporation of error in real time.

The meanings of live interaction differ because the terms of engagement that constitute that interaction vary. The phrases "live blade," "live ball," and "live performance" all convey immediacy and a sense of risk, but they refer to different circumstances in which such risks play themselves out. Guro Dan Inosanto, senior student of Bruce Lee and head instructor of the Inosanto Academy of Martial Arts, relays a story about using a live blade in a demo that indicates how the different meanings of the term suggest contrasting threats of failure. In his early days of demoing, Guro Inosanto says, he used a live blade. At one point, as his training partner moved through a rapid-paced drill, the knife struck Guro Inosanto in his thigh. He felt the sting of the blade but

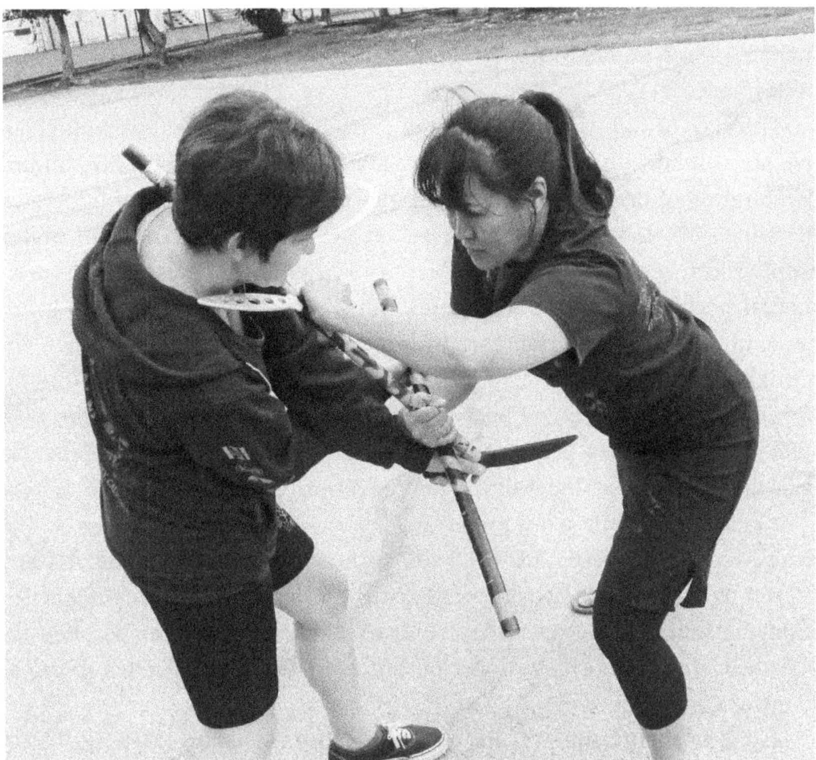

FIGURE 6.2 A trainer blade allows actions that with a live blade would be perilous. Photograph courtesy of Tim Becherer.

kept going to complete the demo. Then, he demonstrates, he hobbled offstage to check the wound and stem its blood flow. The lesson there, he said, was not to use live blades for demonstrations.

This mishap reveals the different connotations of live as they relate to failure. In relation to the blade, Guro Inosanto was on the receiving end of his partner's failure to fully account for the risks associated with the live weapon. Although he suffered the effects of the live blade, Guro Inosanto masked it to maintain the integrity of the performance, avoiding its failure, a crumpling of demo into daily life. He maintained the frame of the live performance even as his partner failed to accommodate the live blade.

While the consequences of failure differ between live sport and live performance, they also converge. Failure, in martial arts practice, brings with it the immediate threat of pain and the more serious threat of injury. In performance, especially in dance, pain can arise from success as well as from failure, but injury usually results from error.[32] Moreover, the consequences of failure are not only physical; they are emotional. The risk of embarrassment at having others witness a failure is common both to live sport and live performance.[33]

The risk of failure and its related consequences is central enough to live performance that theater scholar Sara Jane Bailes puts forward an understanding of performance that is rooted in failure. Bailes highlights, for instance, the "innate precariousness" of performance.[34] Although Bailes emphasizes representational failure and therefore focuses on experimental performance, her arguments can be applied to live events more generally. Their application can prompt insights as to the productive potential of failure.

Citing dramatist Samuel Beckett's admonition to "fail better," Bailes asks "where else but in live performance are we given the opportunity to rehearse the experience of that directive without the catastrophe of its events?"[35] An answer to Bailes's question lies in the arena of physical play. Kinetic games, like live performance, present us with an opportunity to rehearse failure, to learn from it in the absence (usually) of devastating consequences, and to practice resilience without the true suffering that real-world failure can so often induce. Creating sport events where no one ever fails evacuates this potential for exploring failing.

Avoiding opportunities to practice failure doesn't shield us from the threat of failure, it merely denies us the opportunity to practice our responses. More than that, avoiding failure means losing the opportunity to understand the consequences to action. Journalist Hanna Rosin points out, for instance, that, as children's playgrounds became standardized, they reduced opportunities for threat appraisal while not reducing the most serious of injuries. Less serious injuries, in particular long-bone fractures, have increased, possibly arising from a phenomenon known as "risk compensation": if there's less to be concerned about, we act with less concern for our actions.[36] Failure, like risk, enables us to discover the consequences that follow from our actions and to build upon this knowledge, changing approach according to failures and successes alike. Consequences don't go away just because we stop practicing to face them.

We need an understanding of failure that accommodates both the pain of error *and* the necessity of failure to learning. The live event, as rooted in potential error, typifies the paradox of failure: that it is necessary to learning and creativity at the same time that it carries distressing and potentially dangerous consequences. Understanding the live as the negotiation of failure suggests that a move away from failure aversion need not disavow the pain of failure or the consequences of serious error.[37]

Sweet Science(s): Improvisation, Losing, and Experimentation

Embrace the Suck. That's where the learning is.

—GURO CONRAD CAYMAN, *quoting his music instructor*

When I first started grappling, there were days when I felt invincible. I would show up to class, learn a few techniques, and when it came time to roll, I was dead on. I would pin other white belts and work my way out of their grasp. I occasionally found a joint-lock and got more than a few chokes on. With the more experienced grapplers I got choked and submitted, but not without foreseeing at least their first few moves.

Other days, I was useless. In the same class with most of the same students, I was taken down by the very people I had run circles around only a day or a week before. I missed the most obvious clues as to their intentions, and found myself lured into the most foolish of predicaments: my gi pulled over the back of my head, my hands tangled up in a foiled attempt at defending a choke. I thought, for a while, was that this was how it was: grappling, like sparring, was a rollercoaster of success and defeat. It took several years before it leveled out, less an amusement park ride than a marathon course through city streets.

This one day on, one day off pattern was predictable in its variation but uncontrollable. If I had sparred or grappled well last time, I prepared myself for disappointment. It reminded me, in a peculiar way, of my daughter's sleep patterns when she was an infant and a toddler: one good night, one bad one. A nonsensical comparison, it seemed to pop into my head randomly without explaining anything, but Daniel Kahnemann's writing on the function of intuitive thinking helps to explain this phenomenon: chance produces variation that skill can, at least in part, correct for.[38]

As we've seen, skill develops in a context where a practitioner of an art, science, sport, or other undertaking receives regular feedback and where the environment is consistent enough that the feedback can be trusted.[39] Feedback often comes through failure. Failure creates opportunities to practice adaptation, a continual adjustment to circumstances. As Sarah Lewis points out, "errorless learning does not lead to certain wins."[40] In fact, errorless learning can produce long-term failure, as it disallows the possibility of feedback. Failure, then, is the ground on which learning occurs.[41] Mastery can only come about throughout repeated effort and repeated collision with error and its consequences. Learning requires that we accept uncertainty. As the adage goes, a master has failed more times than a beginner has even tried.

Errorless performance is also not necessarily the most engaging or enriching; it doesn't provide the most opportunities for creativity, exploration, and problem-solving. Discussions of visual art abound with considerations of failure, ranging from speculation as to whether religious artists deliberated insert flaws into their work to acknowledge human imperfection to reflecting on the beauty of intentional error in photography.[42] In most concert dance, performers obscure failure just as they minimize the display of effort. Even in modern and postmodern dance, where dancers and choreographers foreground effort and its engendering relation to gravity, rough edges have smoothed out over time so dancers fall to recover, and drop to rise.[43] Experimental dance, like experimental theater, calls attention to ruptures, interruptions, and other kinds of failure in order to provide a meta-commentary on performance.

Given that sports center on one player or one team besting the other, failure is front and center. Players strive to trip each other up; they project one action only to take another. Failure undergirds the excitement of the sporting event.[44] It is also what makes a game interesting: the fumbled play, the ball that barely clears the net and forces the opponent to run forward. In martial arts, failure is even more prominent: the kick that is evaded and countered; the punch that starts strong but leaves the fighter open to a return shot; the takedown that is reversed.

Sports bear a complex relationship to effort: we see athletes' sweat and the evidence of their accelerated breathing; we often see the dirt that echoes the fall or the tackle; in martial arts we see the blood of competitors, failure in the form of blows received. And yet competitive sports hinge on our being able to witness nearly superhuman accomplishment. The fascination that live (and on-screen) sports injuries produces arises in part from the contrast between the excellence of physical accomplishment and the frailty of the human body.

The scientific method, like experimental art, bases itself around the possibility of failure. The idea that an experiment must be repeated and repeatable to be valid hinges on success. However, it also acknowledges up-front that failure necessarily occurs. Such an approach shares much with sparring-based martial arts training. As we've seen, Bruce Lee, who encouraged traditional martial arts to move beyond light-touch sparring and into full or near full contact, called his approach "scientific street fighting." Lee's approach centered on the question: "Does it work?" Particularly when applied to martial arts training, where the consequences to this inquiry are direct, immediate, and painful, asking if it works automatically comes with the question of whether it doesn't work.

"Find it in sparring" is a frequent refrain when attempting to integrate drills with live training. The relationship between risk, failure, and experimentation explains one of the terms of affection boxers bestow on their craft: the sweet science of bruising. This understanding of confrontational play as rooted in risk and failure signals how martial arts align with both art and science, through their potentially experimental nature. The idea that failure can contribute to an experimental mindset extends beyond martial arts training to physical play of all kinds.

A Society of Winners? Failure beyond Success Narratives

Sociologist Francisco Duina holds a dimmer view of failure than those who emphasize its centrality for learning and creativity.[45] Duina suggests that failure is threatening enough that the joy of winning is largely relief at avoiding failure. He argues that we are excited by risk because we fear its detrimental consequences. His perception of winning and losing is negatively defined: when we win, we are happy because we didn't lose. When the risks are (or seem to be) substantial and the competition is close, the relief that accompanies winning (or not losing) is intense enough that it produces pleasure.

I disagree with Duina, seeing in his analysis little space for competitive pleasure or for the experience of mastery through physical action that may or may not result in a win. However, his argument can be read against its grain to explain why losing after finishing a game isn't always a failure. Emerging from a round of sparring with a bloodied nose, gasping for breath, and having been stymied at all turns can still constitute a kind of success. Giving a good opponent a run for her money brings intense satisfaction, even when that opponent is the superior fighter. Especially when that opponent is the superior fighter.

Completing a match, round, race, or route in the face of difficulty produces its own joys even when that completion doesn't result in a win. This is especially the case in individual, highly taxing, and high-stakes sports such as marathon running, rock-climbing, and sport fighting—satisfaction can accompany a "good" failure just as it does a win. If you don't place but you still run 26.2 miles, if you complete a route no matter how many times you fall, if you get through the round or through the fight, you have accomplished something. Seeing the game through to its conclusion is a kind of success, a success that can endure even in failure. The avoidance of a worse outcome can produce not just relief but intense satisfaction in itself.

A matter-of-fact attitude toward error, an ability to see success in a productive failure, constitutes the resilience that is the much-discussed benefit of failure. Resilience, we hear, is something that today's young people don't have enough of. However, if surviving failure were all it took to develop resilience, our inner cities and our rural poverty zones would produce more success stories and fewer tragedies.

Failure is a solid, tangible marker of something going wrong, one that is felt more acutely depending on where we're placed and what kind of safety net we have access to. Failure can arise from luck or circumstances as well as from flawed decisions. Failure is not, then, merely a hurdle to be overcome. The famed resilience and persistence that failure produces carry their own consequences. Optimism has its own perils.

Increasingly, in American society and much of the English-speaking world, success and failure are seen as the responsibility of the individual. Neoliberal economies provide little space for failure and offer little in the way of protection against its consequences. As we've seen, failure is celebrated when it feeds into narratives of success and triumph over adversity. We omit the privilege at the center of "failing up" narratives and castigate young adults, in particular, for, in Emilyn Claid's terms, "failing to fail."[46] At the same time, in contemporary English-speaking societies, as commentators from journalists to philosophers have noted,[47] we encounter a cultural imperative to be happy at all costs.

In studying optimism, social psychologists and philosophers have remarked upon its recurrence as well as its hazards. Optimism is usually defined as a confidence largely focused on positive future outcomes.[48] Optimism represents a willingness to expose oneself to risk despite the likelihood of failure, also consisting of an ability to move forward in spite of setbacks. It's often remarked that insanity is doing the same thing and expecting different results, but optimism follows a similar pattern. Psychologists have argued that those with the most accurate view of reality are those who are mildly depressed.[49] Those with a "normal" mindset tend toward optimism, but also slightly misperceive the likelihood of success.[50] Optimism, then, is useful, perilous, and reassuring all at once.

Despite optimism's complexities, American culture—and, increasingly, international ones—encourages us to be continually upbeat and always look on the bright side of whatever situation we end up in, no matter how grave.[51] Those who position themselves outside this imperative toward happiness are, as philosopher Sara Ahmed points out, maligned as disgruntled killjoys.[52]

Optimism is valued, at least in part, because it drives capitalism. As Daniel Kahneman reminds us, the optimistic predictions of entrepreneurs, for instance, fuel the economic engine of capitalism.[53] In the United States and in much of the English-speaking world, we are taught to ignore failure, to keep our chins up, and to carry on in spite of the odds against us. Simultaneously, the cultural imperative to be happy runs parallel with a neoliberal system that has eroded the social safety net.[54] Particularly in the United States, where we map the responsibility for success onto the individual, we are reluctant to account for the effects of circumstances and luck, and so we disparage the underserved for succumbing to failure and we disparage middle-class youth for their lack of resilience. Optimism can set up expectations that go permanently unrealized, particularly as we live in conditions of economic precarity that increasingly obliterate the middle-class and preclude access to its comforts, a condition that literary critic Lauren Berlant has labeled "cruel optimism."[55]

Like failure, optimism is a mixed bag. An optimistic mindset boosts resilience but at the same time, it produces a confidence that all will be well, even in situations where a positive outcome is unlikely. Optimism can produce an inability to know when to quit.[56] Such an outlook can cloud decision-making in situations where consequences are grave and rewards are few.

To insist that optimism is inherently bad would be not only curmudgeonly but also inaccurate. My intention, then, is not to discourage optimism but to counter both the disparagement and the celebration of failure through a consideration of its multiple effects, including the pain and disappointment it creates. Confronting the consequences of failure can work against narratives of success and a cultural imperative to be happy at all costs while valuing the resilience and the opportunities for learning that failure produces. In line with Judith Halberstam, I suggest that an engagement with failure can produce a new kind of optimism, one that challenges self-importance and that links overtly to efforts toward equality.[57]

Addressing the consequences of failure requires a sustained consideration of competition. By most accounts competition is a feature of modern life. A capitalist economic structure is predicated upon competition among both those who sell and those who buy, assuming an equal playing field on which this opposition can take place. Democracy rests upon competition among candidates, who vie for public approval and who oppose one another in order to reach policy compromises. Modern sports, as sport historians tell us, structure and quantify competition to standardize it, theoretically rendering it fairer.

Americans, in particular, tend to value competition.[58] We are the most likely to think competition is beneficial for individuals and for society, that the outcome of competition accurately reflects effort, and that competition is inherently fair.[59] American viewers disparage those who come in second place in athletic events, associating them with the act of losing rather than with the accomplishment that lead to their competition in the first place. For example, as sociologist Stanley Eitzen points out, the football team that is defeated in the Super Bowl are known as losers when they are the second-best team in the American football league.[60] The ridicule that followed Rhonda Rousey's second loss in the octagon after an unbroken winning streak turned losing into her defining characteristic rather than a necessary consequence of competition.[61]

Such attitudes toward competition are particularly pronounced in the United States but are not uniquely American; rather, they seem to be prevalent through much of the English-speaking world. For example, in Britain, until Paula Radcliffe's 2002 marathon win, it had become commonplace for sports journalists to describe the long-distance runner as "Loser Paula," after numerous instances in which she led a pack of runners only to miss a medal by several places.[62] This is particularly strange in the world of marathon running, where simply completing the race constitutes a success out of the grasp of most people. The disparagement of an athlete who is one of the world's best distance runners and the peculiar choice to identify being bested by a handful of superior athletes as "losing" indicates the failure aversion of sports-viewing publics.

Because modern sports culture disparages losing, we are now in a peculiar, paradoxical position where children's sport, which is supposed to foster resilience, enhancing character traits such as "courage, determination, fairness, and respect," won't even countenance the possibility of failure.[63] We have tournaments where everyone gets a medal and competitions where everyone who participates gets trophy.[64] At first glance, this appears to be the opposite of high-level amateur and professional sports where losers are shamed and disparaged. However, by teaching children that failure is so devastating that we can't even acknowledge it, we continue the celebration of winning and the disparagement of losing.

While competition may well inhere in sport, a disparagement of losers and a lionization of winners does not. The Scandinavian countries feature a proliferation of independently organized, local sports clubs. These clubs are run by volunteer effort and they function independently of both for-profit entities and of public institutions. They provide an opportunity for members of a community to come together, interact with their peers, and build a sense of commonality even as they compete. Who wins and who loses in these events is largely immaterial. Indeed, Scandinavians seem to value sport not for competition but for its opposite: unity.[65]

It is possible, then, to reconsider the relationship between play, competition, success, and failure. Losing is necessary to competition; it authorizes and enables play. Losing isn't even a regrettable necessity; it is fundamental. The participation of a losing team or losing contender occasions victory. Such a re-evaluation opens up further questions. Is it possible to revalue failure without working it into a narrative of success and without forcing it into a straightjacket of optimism? How can we rethink failure without disavowing the pain it causes? In other words, is it actually possible to fail better?

Francesco Duina maintains that the product of winning is confidence. The product of losing, he says, is doubt and introspection. The loser doubts his or her abilities and goes off to think about what she or he could do better. Presumably, this is a negative effect. However, doubt and introspection are not, in themselves, harmful. The absence of doubt isn't only confidence; it is also ruthlessness. The absence of introspection isn't only optimism; it is thoughtlessness. Introspection may be the key to resolving the paradox of failure, understanding that it is central to learning while also being inherently painful. Introspection can allow us to recognize and value failure while escaping the cultural imperative to always only look on the bright side.

Competition, as we've seen, can enrich experience.[66] And yet competition can also tilt attention away from the process of interacting and toward its outcome: success or failure. Competition is a frame within which the drama of success or failure plays itself out.[67] Yet as we've seen, competition can be pleasurable and even collaborative. Competition is more complex that it first appears.

7

Making Play Work

COMPETITION, SPECTACLE, AND PERFECTION IN SPORT

Not that you won or lost, but how you played the game.

—GRANTLAND RICE

Winning isn't everything, it's the only thing.

—HENRY RUSSELL SANDERS

IT'S AN UNSEASONABLY hot March morning in the flatlands of the San Fernando Valley. Ten of us are training in a small, matted space behind a yoga studio. A chainlink fence surrounds the mat; its large gate swings in the occasional breeze. My instructor, Coach Alain, rents the space for classes with a small group of students. Borrowing the parlance of UFC and other MMA competitions, I've taken to calling the space Alain's Cage.

We open the class with rounds of sparring. We start out light and slow, our contact barely more than a touch. I'm working with Roland, a more senior student. He's more skilled than me but gentle in nature, and when sparring light, I can use that as a way in. But Roland's got a good repertoire of moves; reading his actions and responding to them is hard work.

The round is long. My stamina drops, returns, and drops again.

"Dig deep," Alain says. "You guys are fighters."

In common speech, I am, indeed, a fighter: bold, aggressive, and unafraid of challenging situations, including verbal and physical confrontation. Within the martial arts world, however, I am not a fighter. In martial arts parlance a fighter is a competitor, an athlete who participates in public matches on a regular basis. What separates a fighter from a "fighter" is competition, the realized intention to take martial arts off the mat and into the ring or the cage. For a fighter, in this narrower sense, martial arts belong not only to the training space of the academy, dojo, or gym, but also to the performance setting of sport. For someone like me competition is an attitude, as in a competitive spirit; for a fighter, it is an action undertaken as part of an organized, possibly institutionalized event.

These differences open up to the multiple connotations of competition within the overlapping spheres of game and sport. Sport fighting, as its name implies, aligns with sports as much as with games and play through its emphasis on competition. Combat sport is based around not just competitive pleasure but formal, structured events where contenders go up against one another. Amateur and professionals alike face one another in public bouts where an audience watches and officials determine the outcome of the match.

Sports refine but also amplify and standardize games. If a game is about the tension between playing and winning, sport tilts the balance toward success. Sports retain the inefficient means of the games on which they are based, but competing athletes are less likely to cede an advantage in order to continue the game.

If games hinge on a primary tension between playing and winning, sports consist of multiple tensions. As sociologist D. Stanley Eitzen points out, these tensions include those between unity and division, inclusion and exclusion, health and injury, expression and control. Sport is also characterized by a friction between work and play. Although athletes and coaches speak of a personal best—overcoming one's own perceived limitations—the outcome of sport is central. It's not win or lose; it's how you play the game. Except that winning isn't everything; it's the only thing.

Keeping Score: Sports, Spectacle, and Quantification

Sports, like games, center on experience. To be played with any degree of skill, let alone enjoyment, sports require that athletes immerse themselves in the situation at hand. Athletes enter the state that Csikszentmihalyi describes as autotelic or flow, where the relationship to one's body, instrument, and tools is seamless. Learning to play a sport involves not only skill building but also learning how to get into the flow state within the parameters of a particular activity—how to move, in phenomenological terms, from immanence, where the focus is on the mechanics of the task, to transcendence, a seamless moving through the activity.

A person who is in an autotelic state, by definition, focuses on the immediate; a person who attends only to an outside goal is typically not in the flow state. For competitive athletes, however, the immersive experience is channeled toward winning: finishing the race ahead of other competitors, besting the opponent in the ring, accumulating the points required to succeed. The state defined as "the zone," then, is one of peak performance combined with full immersion.[1] Csikszentmihalyi describes how a honed sense of time becomes part of the skill-set of athletes, such as runners and competitive cyclists, whose accomplishment is measured temporally so that their state of immersion includes an attention to how their performance will be evaluated.

A clear, defined goal is only part of what constitutes a sport. The presence of viewers as well as their relationship to the event—ticket holders versus informal observers, for instance—also shifts an activity from a game into a sport. If no one is watching, it's just a game, even if the players compete against each other, even if their competition is fierce and they keep score, deciding on a winner at the end. Sports, then, are performances as much as they are games.

Sport centers not only on visual display but also on high and low points that determine the fate of the match. The possibility of failure that is so central to sport allows sport to operate as a performance. For this reason, journalist Malcolm Gladwell describes the liveness of sports as the "drama of athletic competition."[2] Sociologist Francesco Duina likewise compares sport to performance: "The more drama we witness, the more delighted we are."[3] This use of theatrical terms is not incidental; although physical games share with performance a management of risk, the navigation of failure, and clear structures of engagement, the presence of spectators turns a game into a show.

The more spectacular a sport, the less the interior experience of the athlete factors into the evaluation of the event. Because watching is so important in sports, the audience's pleasure in viewing takes precedence over the enjoyment of the athletes. While athletes clearly experience competitive pleasure (at least, most of them seem to), viewers care more about what we see than about what athletes feel. It is possible, for instance, for observers to enjoy an event even when athletes suffer. If the goal for an athlete is to move, in phenomenological terms, from immanence to transcendence, the goal for the audience is to see transcendence, seamless activity, at work. There's a paradox here: the point is for the activity to appear effortless, even as we see the signs of effort, the sweat, and, in martial arts, the blood of the competitors.

Former professional football player Nate Jackson describes the consequences of this desire for both effortlessness and dramatized effort.[4] Jackson, tracing his career as a low-level NFL player, speaks of the torment that football inscribed upon his body, through multiple injuries incurred in training and in competition. Jackson tells us that his injuries were particularly destructive because the machine of professional football refuses to allow time for recovery. Jackson's interior experience of suffering differed radically from the experience of viewers focused on the nearly superhuman performance of highly skilled athletes.

The masking of injury bears a similarity to author and choreographer Emilyn Claid's assertion about ballet: in hiding the dancer's interior sensations of effort, awkwardness, and pain, ballet creates an impression of otherworldly effortlessness and subsumes real experience into this illusion.[5] High-level sports likewise foreground the larger-than-life accomplishments of the players while denying their human fragility and fallibility. In professional sports, however, unlike in ballet, injury becomes part of the spectacle and devastating injury turns into a subject of fascination. Whether it's the lists of the most devastating NFL injuries of all time peppered around the Internet or the instant replays of Anderson Silva's shin shattering during UFC 168, these images invite attention because they reveal the vulnerability of the human frame underneath the apparently superhuman accomplishment.

Injuries form part of a larger structure of crushing lows and spectacular highs in elite sport. Viewers root for a dramatic win and disparage (but also crave) a devastating loss.[6] Suffering is engaging when it serves a positive purpose, when it leads to an outcome that makes it worthwhile. Indeed, the most pleasurable matches feature an unlikely outcome that the events of the match lead up to with a seemingly inevitable force. Sport, in this regard, is like narrative: filled with suspense, featuring twists at each turn, and often resulting in an arc of victory or failure.

Because sports are about spectacle as much as, if not more than, experience, most American adults interact with athletic games primarily by watching, not playing, sports. Few American adults incorporate physical play into their daily lives. For example, a 2015 Robert Wood Johnson Foundation study indicates that only 25 percent of American adults play sports, although 75 percent participated in sports when they were younger,[7] with nonparticipation being more common for women, older adults, and those with lower incomes than for men, younger adults, and the wealthy.[8] Nor is this gap filled by adult nonsport activities, such as practicing yoga or dancing: a CDC report indicates that 80 percent of American adults get insufficient muscle-strengthening exercise, suggesting an overall lack of participation in physical recreation.[9]

Meanwhile, the Super Bowl and other televised sporting events attract national attention; many Americans plan for game day with genuine excitement and experience true enjoyment when watching sports. On a local level, adults retain an interest in sport but through youth involvement. Teen and young adult athletes grow up to become Little League and AYSO coaches, rather than remaining athletes themselves in adulthood.[10] Jokes about weekend warriors—middle-aged men lying on the couch with an ice pack after shooting hoops—reflect the idea that physical games are something to be outgrown. Viewing rather doing supports a sedentary existence among the majority of the population even as a minority achieves ever-greater accomplishments. Spectator sports outsource physical mastery and competitive pleasure to experts and relegate them to a phase of life that is swiftly outgrown.[11]

The focus of sports on viewing rather than experiencing moves sports toward quantification and categorization. Times, scores, ranks, and other statistics occupy a privileged space in modern sports. So strong is this link between viewing and cataloguing that some sports sociologists and sports historians suggest that quantifying games is what makes them sports. For sociologist Henning Eichberg, for example, sport is a product of the modern era, arising in the eighteenth and nineteenth centuries, in conjunction with the modern West's fascination with standardization and routine and in response to technologies of time keeping.[12]

Because of this emphasis on outcome, Eichberg argues that "sport is placed in a complex way between work and play."[13] Sports sociologist Eitzen agrees that the commercialization of sport, in particular, turns play into a kind of work, in which "the outcome supersedes the process."[14] Indeed, Eitzen argues, the highly structured and organized nature of contemporary sports diminishes its playful elements, such as enjoyment, self-expression, and creativity, which decrease as sport becomes more institutionalized, more specialized and hierarchical, and oriented toward extrasport concerns such as making money and generating publicity.[15] The commercialization of sports means that when two athletes—or two teams—compete, they do so not only as individuals but also as representatives of institutions. Institutions complicate the relationship between play, competition, failure, and risk as institutions do not experience pleasure, they have no interior experience, and they cannot engage in exploration; they have no subjectivity, so there is nothing intersubjective between them. That we do in fact *play* sports, rather than working them, signals that the line between sport and game, between work and play is a blurry one.

When games turn into work and sports become institutionalized, it is not surprising that they become specialized and outsourced to experts. If sport requires perfection over and above immersive experience, why would ordinary people participate? Why shouldn't we outsource play to experts if play requires excellence, demands constant training, and is focused on generating revenue and publicity? Why risk self-doubt, exertion, and possible injury to participate in something clearly beyond our grasp? While watching sports can be its own form of play,[16] sport watching is also serious: spectators calculate and track stats and results, viewers stake money on events, and, in the most extreme situations, fans riot when they don't like the outcome of the game. This seriousness excludes the nonelite adult athlete and diminishes the importance of participation. Instead of play, adults, especially in the United States and Britain, are offered exercise.

Exercise, Uniformity, and Obligation

For most adults in the developed world, except laborers who are increasingly marginalized and underreimbursed for their efforts, physicality no longer dominates the realm of work. Paid work, for much of the population, is sedentary. Domestic work, too, is partially mechanized. While mechanization and digitization have brought about improvements in worker safety and, theoretically, a freeing up of time, they also urge more of us toward inactivity.

Indeed, public health studies illustrate the association of physical activity with leisure and not with work: low-income Americans exercise less than wealthier ones, with the amount of exercise undertaken steadily increasing as income does.[17] Studies of leisure time also indicate a fragmentation of the nonwork time that could facilitate physical activity: although Americans now have more leisure time than in previous decades, the quality of this time is diminished. Increasingly fragmented, leisure time is placed between other obligations as many jobs require a near-constant availability.[18] Digitization of labor frees us from work sites but also allows our paid labor to spill over into all spheres of our lives.

Transportation, especially in the United States, is also increasingly sedentary. For many Americans, the privately owned car is the transportation mode of choice. In some places, it's a near necessity. While some American cities have created networks of bike lanes and have pedestrianized their downtowns, the majority of US cities and towns center on the car. Except in the most major of US cities, public transportation is an afterthought. Public transportation, although mechanized, at least requires the minimal activity of walking between bus, train, and metro lines as well as walking from stations or stops to destinations. This kind of physical activity, although limited, is ongoing and near continuous in cities and towns that depend on public transportation and absent in those cities that do not.

Movement, then, is increasingly distant from the functional aspects of our lives. Because physical activity aligns with leisure instead of with work, it has become a privilege. Tangible inequities express themselves in the distribution of leisure time and resources for physical activity, and an exercise deficit affects those marginalized by our society: people of color, those with low income, women, and the elderly.[19] Under these circumstances, physical activity becomes something that needs to be sought out.

Educational, medical, and governmental organizations put forward exercise as a solution to America's inactivity problem. We're reminded that a lack of exercise contributes to public health crises around obesity and degenerative disease. As we've seen, contemporary neoliberal societies place the burden for changing societal problems on individuals. This is as true of exercise deficits as of economics.[20]

The contrast between individual will and social support may be particularly pronounced for physical play. As we've seen, kinetic recreation requires spaces where it can happen, where a sense of community is created and maintained. It requires opportunity. Although people can organize in small groups to create these sites and to generate their accompanying possibilities, the greater the support for such opportunities, the more they are taken up. This is the case in Scandinavian countries, where a network of voluntary organizations provides opportunities for amateur sport practice and, not surprisingly, the majority of adults participate in sports.[21]

Moreover, when physical activity is framed in terms of exercise, the emphasis remains on outcome and not process. In this regard, exercise is the inverse of professional athletics, both focused on goals albeit of different sorts: in competitive sports, wins and loses are quantified whereas for exercise, personal goals are quantified. The benefits of exercise are often negatively defined: weight lost and disease averted. Even when those benefits are identified positively—better muscle tone, greater flexibility, increased stamina—they remain delineated by goals, not by the experience of reaching them.

Exercise regimens reinforce this emphasis on outcomes. Conditioning classes, circuit training, and personal training sessions feature instructions to raise heart rates via vigorous movement, to allow a specified amount of time for rest, to strength train particular muscles, often in isolation, and then to stretch. Calisthenics isolates body parts from one another, like the parts of a functional machine: "let's work on our hamstrings now," "let's move on to cardio," "work those deltoids."

On the one hand, this attention to muscular efficiency celebrates the wonders of human biomechanics. On the other, it resonates with Michel Foucault's idea of docile bodies, those that internalize a system of discipline and present themselves for observation and documentation.[22] Structured movement often gets us all moving the same way. Although we move in unison or in sequence, we interact more rarely. Circuit training occasionally allows for problem-solving in small teams (usually of two); the interaction is usually focused on an external task—Can you bench press ten pounds more? Do you need a spot?—rather than on understanding another person's intentions, strengths, and vulnerabilities. More often working out at the gym is a solo activity, done on our own at stations of machines with headphones on or while watching TV. Instead of our bodies bearing the traces of the activity, conditioning regimes perform activity to shape the body.

Diane Ackerman describes this as a situation in which we work at play.[23] She suggests that most participants seek out physical activities to achieve an end goal: a slimmer physique, improved cardiovascular fitness, greater endurance. As in the case of sports, this emphasis on outcome brings with it an obsession with statistics. Fitbits track how much distance we cover, the calories we burn, our changes in elevation, and even how well we sleep. Pedometers on our phones track our activity level to see if it measures up to plan. This may offer physical benefits but the psychic benefits of play diminish. It's called *working* out, after all.

Because sport and exercise affiliate with work, unlike play, they can be conscripted. Play ceases to be play when involvement is forced. It's possible to be drawn into a game that is not of our choosing, but as we've seen in chapter 2, when we are dupes to someone else's edge play, it's questionable whether we are actually playing. A sport remains a sport, however, and exercise remains exercise if we are required to practice them. If participation is demanded, the activity is not changed by a participant's reluctance. The gym-class dodge ball game that goes on despite the anxiety of a kid drafted into it indicates that we don't to have to consent to sport or to exercise for it to be what it is. If play is predicated upon freedom, sport and exercise can arise from obligation.

This sense of obligation extends from the individual to an institution. So just as children are required to exercise and participate in team sports by their schools, individuals can be coerced into mass exercise by totalitarian states. For instance, state socialist societies frequently deployed mass calisthenics as a way of demonstrating what anthropologist Susan Brownell describes as "the synchronization of the rhythms of the social body."[24] Fascist societies adopt similar tactics of illustrating unity through large-scale, synchronized movement. Used in the interest of creating a national spirit, sport can be practiced in large groups, moving simultaneously in an activity that marks out a group as both uniform, in relationship to each other, and distinct, in relationship to other groups.[25]

With its emphasis on exploration and experience, play has no quantifiable outcome that can be celebrated as an emblem of an institution. Play encourages us to celebrate our differences and find our points of commonality, but it doesn't render us all the same. Because it is intrinsically valuable rather than extrinsically functional, play cannot easily be used at the service of anything other than itself. Institutions that seek control over their members have little use for play.

In contrast to the suggestion that we "find time to exercise," psychologist Stuart Brown urges us not to make time for recreation but to assure that play—social, object, body, and fantasy play—runs throughout our lives. Just as it is important to create opportunities for social, object, and fantasy play, so too do we need the interpersonal exploration that makes up physical games of all sorts. The exercise–participation gap I've described suggests a play gap. We may get physical benefits from obligatory exercise but we lose the opportunities for personal transformation, creativity, and community-building that come out of generous and sometimes competitive kinetic play.

Work and the Making of the World

During the summer of 2013, I trained regularly at UCLA. Classes ran for only a few weeks, ending and beginning anew to fit into the brisk pace of an academic summer session. It was the start of a new session of classes and the wing chun instructor, Jim, was unable to make it to class. He sent Sifu Alain to teach in his place.[26] When I offered to make myself useful, Alain took me up on it, more enthusiastically than I expected. Class began with me, on the spot, teaching wing chun's first form, silumtao. Flustered and rusty, I was only able to recall about half of it. I stopped part way through but covered for the gaps in my recall by suggesting that learning half the form sufficed for the first day.

Alain resumed direction of the class and we fell into the expected groove: he, the instructor, leading and I, the senior student, demonstrating. Usually I get nervous when asked to demonstrate. But this was wing chun, familiar ground. More importantly, during the class before Alain and I had trained in dumog, Filipino martial arts' grappling practice. We hit pressure points on one another's arms. We worked chokeholds with sticks, which required attending to our own physical states—at what point, exactly, is that pressure too much?—and a rapid response when a partner tapped.

In the wing chun class that followed I found I could lock down on his intentions, read what he was doing, and fire back without pausing for an explanation. Because we had spent an hour reading one another's cues, that responsiveness felt natural.

Alain introduced a "bridging the distance" exercise, a way of working the pac sao, the basic wing chun block, into a conflict situation. He said, "a real fight doesn't usually look like this," taking a wing chun stance and throwing a series of vertical centerline punches that I deflected with wing chun hands like tan sao and pac sao. "A real fight," he said, referencing the conflict that self-defense instructors describe as a challenge fight, "looks more like this." He brought his fists up to his face, boxing style, and brought his stance into a lightly bent, springy, diagonal boxer's stance. I echoed his movements, threw a couple of light jabs at him, and we began to circle each other, light on our feet and tracking one another's movement. As we moved, one of the new students gasped.

How strange, I thought, all we're doing is circling. I'm not even throwing real punches. But then, for a second, I saw it as she did: Alain raised his hands and change his stance, which cued me to move into boxing mode. As soon as I did so, he started to circle. We tracked one another's footwork, stepping back when the other stepped forward, forward when the other stepped back. That movement, the simulation, of a sparring match brought the energy up almost automatically.

This kind of connectivity between teacher and demonstrator, teacher and assistant, and teacher and student is so common in martial arts classes that it usually goes without comment. It's only remarked upon when it fails: when the demonstrator forgets what to do or the teacher and assistant can't manage to match each other's speed, pace, or energy. Underneath the banality of the effective teaching exchange lies a myriad of possibilities for interaction, exchange, and improvisation. These possibilities suggest a sense of play within the work that is teaching and demonstrating.

Teaching is clearly a form of work. It's undertaken to produce a result: an addition to a student's knowledge base or a change in how students understand an issue, problem, or theme. While teaching can be, and frequently is, done as a volunteer effort, it's more likely to be remunerated than playing a sport or practicing an art. In martial arts, as in other sports and artistic undertakings, we are more likely to pay to do the practice and to be paid to teach it.

And yet teaching, when it goes well, can be remarkably like play. Teaching can put us in an autotelic state; indeed, it usually requires being in the flow state. Teaching can be responsive and improvisatory. It can allow us to develop imaginative problem-solving and creates opportunities for both developing mastery and exploring interpersonal exchange. Teaching, then, suggests that work and play are not simply opposites.

Psychologist and play researcher Stuart Brown says that "the opposite of play isn't work; it's depression." In refusing to contrast work and play, Brown provides an important insight: work, in itself, is not the absence of transcendence or flow. Csikszentmihalyi likewise maintains that the flow state emerges from any engaging task which challenges us and to which our skills are equal (but do not too easily exceed). Work, like play, can include states of complete immersion, of full focus. Diane Ackerman, in pondering the relationship of work to play, references the Bhagavad Gita and Krishna's famous statement about the virtues of karma yoga (literally yoking [of the mind] through action): "through action without attention to results one achieves enlightenment."[27]

Although valuing process over outcome characterizes play, it is not exclusive to play. As Csikszentmihalyi points out, we can work without attention to an end goal but simply out of fascination for the task at hand. While work focuses on outcome, the completion of the object need not be the sole point of attention. Indeed, when we are fortunate enough to have work we enjoy (and when it's going well), the outcome ceases to matter. The autotelic state can characterize work as much as play, especially when that work involves both risk and pleasure. A dancer onstage, a painter at the easel, a scientist in the lab, a runner heading toward the finish line, a fighter in the cage: all of them are working at the same time that they are in a flow state. Indeed, it is the paradox of sports and art alike that success usually relies on a state of immersion in which the outcome fades from view even as the goal retains importance.

Philosopher Elaine Scarry, in her work on the singularity of pain, takes this association of work with mindful immersion a step further, identifying work as the opposite of not of play, but of pain. Scarry comments on "the profound ambivalence" surrounding work in Western cultures; work, she suggests, appears as both "pain's twin and its opposite."[28] Pain, Scarry argues, is a state without an object; other states of being, such as desire and fear, orient outward from the body toward (or away from) something. We fear something; we long for someone. Seeing, hearing, and touch also connect us with entities outside ourselves. Pain, although it often comes from an agent outside the body, is a state that locks us within our bodies; we are in pain but we are never in pain for, of, or toward something.

For Scarry, work is the opposite of pain because work moves our consciousness outward from the self into the world. Work, and particularly the act of bringing an object or idea into being, rests upon imagination, a state as anomalous as pain. If pain is a state without object, imagination is object without a state.[29] Imagination, the necessary predecessor of creation, consists only of the "for," "of," or "to" that is lacking in the experience of pain.

Work, however, is only pain's opposite when it is consensual. Just as play cannot be conscripted and remain play, for Scarry, work becomes pain when it is forced (or required) and when the worker receives none of the benefits of labor. Slavery is an obvious example of work as pain with indentured servitude and serfdom close behind. On the less extreme end of that continuum appears work done solely for the purpose of earning a wage; the more perilous, uncomfortable, damaging to others, or mind-numbing the work the more it aligns with pain. A worker in a sweatshop, slaughterhouse, or export processing zone experiences more pain and less of the flow state of consensual, generative work. Drudgery carried out solely for a paycheck, while less brutal, can still appear on the pain side of the continuum. An office worker filing correspondence and a factory worker on the assembly line may find their work more painful than pleasurable as their focus is not the task they carry out, but the completion of it and a return home with payment to follow.

Work distances itself from pain when it brings something forth, when it has a result. Scarry argues that "the more [an action] transforms itself into its object, the closer it is to the imagination, to art, to culture; the more it is unable to bring forth an object, or bringing it forth, is then cut off from its object, the more it approaches the condition of pain."[30] In physical training pain serves the creation of an object, albeit an intangible one.

At first glance, then, Scarry's argument seems to undercut those who theorize immersion by attending solely to process. After all, she tells us that the ability to bring an object into being is what separates work from pain. However, for Scarry, as for theorists of play, process remains key. As games consist of a balance between playing and winning, work, for Scarry, features a balance between process and outcome. Attention to process is the point at which Scarry's ideas most clearly align with those who think about play.

The problem with obligatory exercise and conscripted sport practice is that such activity can undercut a feeling of mastery while simultaneously creating the physical capabilities that would otherwise produce a sense of accomplishment. At its worst, required sport can humiliate, creating a polarity between successful and unsuccessful participants, with the latter often shamed out of the same activities they are required to participate in. While the degree of suffering of a child mocked or bullied on the sports field does not compare to that of a worker in an export processing zone, there is nonetheless a tragedy in turning play into humiliation just as there is in turning work into pain.

On the flip side, athletes, dancers, martial artists, and others who love physical practices experience pain, an otherwise averse sensation, yet they typically develop methods for extending their practice beyond pain. This sensation, in the context of doing what we love and in the absence of injury, transmutes pain into work. Marathon runners, for instance, speak of a command issued from deep within the body to stop and the subsequent surge of pleasure at pushing past that point. Physical training systems give us the ability to turn pain into work because they operate as an act of imagination and creation. Pain is a common sensation in martial arts practice, whether that involves the sensation of a training partner's hand-trapping with a slap, the seemingly bone shattering sensation of an opponent's Thai kick, or the impact of a gloved fist striking the face or the body. Martial artists, dancers, and athletes learn to differentiate "good pain," a sensation that indicates fatigue, from "bad pain," which reveals injury.

This has its dangers, of course. Once pain is converted into work, it becomes easier to ignore its signals. Bad pain, that which signals injury, can be masked by the endorphins that course through our bodies when we're in the midst of an activity we love. Ballet dancers dance on broken toes. Athletes run until they collapse and sport fighters train despite damaged ligaments and tendons. These examples reveal a transformation in the meaning we give to sensation, however: when willingly undertaken and with access to and control over the outcome, pain can become work. Work provides opportunity for imagination. Work, like games, are world-creating. In the right circumstances, work can become play.

Competitive Pleasure and Amateurism

I picture games as a seesaw with winning and playing the game being the kids on each side. When players compete for fun, the kids on the seesaw are evenly matched in terms of weight and energy level. When one pushes off, the other drops, they ride up and down; sometimes they strike a balance. Sometimes winning is higher up and sometimes playing the game is. It doesn't matter who's up and who's down, because they won't be that way for long. The whole point of the activity is that these two elements constantly trade places. When games become standardized, structured, institutionalized, and commercialized, one side can become heavier and slower. The more spectacularized the sport the more institutionalized it is, and the more money behind it, the greater the discrepancy between these two elements.

If professional sports have moved too far toward outcome and away from process, will shifting a balance from watching sports to playing them rectify this? Can we support the process of playing as actively as we do the spectacle of sports? In other words, what is the place for amateurism in modern games and sports?

The term "amateur" carries pejorative connotations. Synonyms and near-synonyms for amateur include unskilled, bumbling, inexpert, dilettante, clumsy, awkward, and half-hearted. But the word amateur comes from "lover," and it implies someone who adores a particular activity or effort.[31] Reclaiming the idea of acting (practicing, performing) from love rather than from duty is promising. So, too, is renouncing the idea that deep engagement requires orientation toward a goal.

Sarah Lewis takes this idea one step farther, presenting amateurism as a strategy through which unexpected insights and discoveries can emerge. To make her point, Lewis sketches out the many accomplishments of physicist Andre Geim, who, in collaboration with Konstantin Novoselov, won a Nobel Prize for the first-ever isolation of graphene, the only two-dimensional object identified on earth.[32] Geim and his colleagues made this and other unlikely discoveries by "graz[ing] shallow" and querying what others "never bother to ask."[33] Lewis compares this approach to the Zen concept of the beginner's mind, an attempt to view circumstances anew with the fresh and open perspective of the neophyte. The intentional amateur, Lewis argues, taps into a "useful wonder" that urges the practitioner out of the expert's routine and, thus, opens up unforeseen discoveries.[34] Not surprisingly, Lewis links this sense of wonder, this ability to stay in the present, with play; like play, the intentional amateur's "constant now" is about process and not product.[35] The immersive state, accompanied by whimsy that circumvents the seriousness underneath exploration,[36] results in an ability to step out of the expert's routine and allows for the discovery of truly new terrain.

Reading about the genius of the intentional amateur, I find myself thinking about iconoclast Bruce Lee, who rejected training methods in martial arts that were based in secrecy, absolute devotion to a teacher, and adherence to a single system. Although Lee dismissed the traditional training protocol in which the teacher had absolute authority, he retained the importance of sustained, repeated practice. If we think about amateurs as dilettantes, then Lee, with his unwavering dedication to relentless training, was anything but an amateur. However, if we envision the intentional amateur as someone who makes unlikely discoveries because they are willing to "graze shallow," drawing from a range of approaches, as well as digging deep into particular systems, then Lee fits the bill.

Lee had the courage to do what we now blithely call cross-training when adherence to a martial arts style was not merely the norm but a requirement. He convinced wing chun master Ip Man to teach him although Lee's Eurasian ancestry excluded him from some traditional kung fu training systems. Lee observed Mohammed Ali's footwork and the way in which his outfighting gave him mastery over his opponents. Lee honed his own dexterity and mobility, shifting away from wing chun's grounded, inside attack while retaining its angularity and power. Lee studied a range of martial arts, seeking to extract what was most effective in each; he drew together fencing, Western boxing, wing chun, and kung fu snap kicks, as well as judo and Greco-Roman wrestling. He not only created a new martial art, jun fan kung fu; he also created a system, jeet kune do, through which practitioners "take what is useful, leave what is useless, and make it [their] own."[37]

At the Inosanto Academy of Martial Arts, I've had the privilege of training under Bruce Lee's close friend, student, and collaborator Guro Dan Inosanto. Watching Guro Inosanto teach, I am continually struck by the genius produced by the willingness to graze shallow as well as dig deep. In a Filipino martial arts class, Inosanto moves swiftly between training systems, as well between stick, blade, sword, and staff methods. And yet I have heard of him lingering over the nuances of the wing chun pac sao. Inosanto's classes are often an exercise in beginner's mind as he invokes traditional silat and modern muay Thai in back-to-back drills, all the while reminding us that our process is our own, urging us not just to practice but also to research, to "figure it out."

Such strategies of the simultaneous expert and intentional amateur open a practitioner to failure, acknowledging that error is necessary and, sometimes, informative. A celebration of whimsy and grazing shallow, as well as digging deep, can mitigate the disparagement of losing by highlighting the learning process and its insights. Francesco Duina, in writing about alternatives to our current model of competition, makes a similar point. He suggests that striving, in itself, matters: "the pursuit of something, regardless of outcomes, holds meaning in and of itself."[38] In line with Scarry's argument about work, Duina maintains that the pursuit of a goal is an act of imagination. He suggests that we could value competition not for its outcome, but because it gives an opportunity to envision possible futures and to pursue those possibilities.[39]

A while back, Lauren, a Brazilian jiu jitsu practitioner who I met at the National Women's Martial Arts Federation training, reflected on a competition in a Facebook post. Although Lauren took a bronze medal, she discussed the matches she lost as well as the ones she won, evaluating her performance and reflecting on how she'd improved and where she still needed work, with the concluding statement: "I didn't win against my opponent but I won against my former self." Lauren went on to win gold medals in both absolute grappling and in her division in a subsequent competition.

Lauren's comment indicates a balance between embracing competitive pleasure and sincerely engaging its demands, recognizing the importance of process as well as product. Her reflections reveal the value of individual accomplishment and striving for excellence. It evokes the possibility that the internal experience of the competitor matters as much as the external evaluation of judges and referees and that attending to process and outcome need not be at odds.

Lessons in the Physicality of Martial Arts: Competition that Embraces Failure

Recently, Professor Gary halted a jiu jitsu class partway through a round of grappling. We weren't just training hard, he pointed out; we were training combatively. Training hard is useful; fighting each other is counterproductive. If someone gets a submission, he said, don't get into a standoff. Accept it and move on. If you fight everything that your opponent does, you lose the opportunity to learn from it. Kru Maria made a similar comment in a kickboxing class: "Find your opponent's rhythm. Figure out their game and learn from it. If you fight their game, you miss the opportunity to understand it."

Martial artists use the phrase "no ego" when they discuss this kind of training, which acknowledges someone else's abilities and accomplishments even when they express themselves at the expense of our short-term success. This fighting without fighting ideal seems antithetical to the competitive, aggressive practice of martial arts, and yet paradoxically, it is crucial. Effective sport fighting requires attending to the "means rather than an end,"[40] even as the end, landing the strike or getting the submission, remains crucially important. The productive tension between playing and aiming to win requires a balance between a competitive and a generous spirit. The goal, in martial arts, as in other activities that center on competitive pleasure, is to find not just a meeting point, but also a balancing point.

As we've seen, an excess of competition runs the risk of evacuating the creativity from games. This raises the question of whether the pursuit of competitive pleasure can demand our best, while allowing for failure. Can we accept failure—celebrate it, even—alongside striving for mastery? Can we nurture the process of imagination that creates work out of pain? Can we accept that failure is part of accomplishment, that grazing shallow and holding onto playful and even fanciful preoccupations are necessary for creativity?

Bernard Suits suggests that egalitarian societies may privilege open games that provide opportunities for exploration, while more hierarchical societies prefer closed games that privilege a goal. Divided societies may not only crave closed games, but also demand a winner.[41] If this is true, our current fascination with winning and our vitriolic disparagement of losing may exemplify the polarization of American society. Success in extraeconomic arenas supports capitalist narratives of victory and continual expansion while losses suggest a failure of the individual.[42] The disparagement of a losing athlete or team evokes the market fundamentalist ideology that unfettered capitalism provides equal opportunities for economic success, and that therefore poverty arises from moral inadequacy rather than adverse circumstances.[43]

Play, games, and sport, depending on how they are structured, can create opportunities to explore dissent and contradiction without treating outcome as primary.[44] They can give us opportunities to practice disagreement with respect and to acknowledge difference, creating conditions for exploring oppositional civility. They can also attend to experience even when outcome remains important. Considering different formats for play can teach us about the balance between outcome and process. By creating opportunities for experiencing the flow state and the sense of mastery that goes with it, it is possible to turn work into play.

8

Making Work Play

RETHINKING COMPETITIVE PLEASURE THROUGH SELF-DEFENSE TRAINING

A GROUP OF us stands at the edge of the mat at a dojo in a Sherman Oaks strip mall. Lead instructor Jen faces us. Don approaches from behind and goes to grab her.

"What do I do?" she says.

"Base out." I refer to the need to ground her weight.

"Tuck your chin," offers another student, invoking the reminder we regularly receive about protecting our throats and shielding the knockout point below the jawline.

We're missing the central point, the most obvious defense, and, even as I speak, I'm aware of it, dimly, in the back of my mind.

"Turn and face him," Jen says, rotating with her hands up and chin down so that Don confronts her palms within range of his face.

"He's expecting this kind of fight," Jen says as they resume their earlier position and Don wraps his arms around hers, restraining her.

They break and he returns to a point several paces behind her. They repeat the scenario. This time as he comes up on her, she turns and faces him, hands raised, feet apart and staggered front to back, knees bent, and chin tucked.

"When he's facing my weapons," she says, referring to her hands, elbows, and knees, "it's a completely different fight."

In IMPACT self-defense classes, such as the one I describe here, the use of the term "fight" is strategic. Fighting, as we've seen, carries at least two connotations: a conflict that two people enter into with intention and a sport activity in which two individuals oppose one another in an effort to win the match. The term "fight," as well as the live, padded assailant trainings that are integral to IMPACT self-defense, invoke combat sport, reminding trainees of a subjectivity that is challenged by the violent scenario she prepares for. In calling a self-defense scenario a fight, a defender foregrounds her ability to make choices. She also claims gendered language typically reserved for men, challenging assumptions of female or feminine passivity. This terminology, as well as the physical training that accompanies it, restores the agency taken away by a sexist society with its mythologies of women's physical incompetence and men's invulnerabilities.[1]

Because fighting implies intention, it is something that we, and only we, can choose to do. An aggressor cannot force me to fight nor can he preclude my doing so. An assailant can provoke me by shouting but he cannot make me fight; he can try to intimidate me with abusive language but he cannot prevent my fighting. He can avoid my body's weapons (hands, elbows, knees, and feet) by sneaking up behind me; if we're on the ground, he can pin my arms. In all of these situations, I have options: I can deflect or confront his efforts at intimidation by turning to face him, naming his abusive language, or treating his efforts at insinuation at face value; I can break his grip, or feign compliance until he releases it in order to strike. An attacker may succeed in hurting me but he cannot preclude the possibility of my fighting, unless I am unconscious.

When someone is described as "getting into a fight," that someone is typically a man. Even when men are drawn into a violent conflict they didn't initiate, we still usually speak of the interaction as a fight. Women are described as getting into a fight only when confronted by another woman, and then, all too often, the violence is described as emulated male behavior instead of as a conflict in its own right. This is partially because of the nature of violence against men: men who assault other men typically provoke an altercation, based around an assumed slight. Men who target women, by contrast, create a relationship of indebtedness and control from which they execute violent action.[2] In accordance with this gendered script for violence, men who attack women do not see themselves as confronting an equal, nor do they expect to be violently resisted. This conventional gendering of violence emerges out of societal investments in men's aggression and women's passivity.[3]

Long before I encountered IMPACT Personal Safety and its padded assailant training, I referred to self-defense situations as fights and, invariably, would be met with puzzlement: "What do you mean you got into a fight?" When I described the scenarios in which I used violence in the interest of self-protection, the response was typically to emphasize the aggressor's actions and not mine: "Oh, you mean you were attacked." When I clarified the nature of my response, the confusion diminished only slightly: "You were attacked and fought back." When I encountered IMPACT training, I finally understood why this subtle change of words disturbed me: the addition of a single word shifts an understanding of agency and intention toward expectations that favor an aggressor.

It is typical to speak of self-defense as "fighting back" rather than as "fighting." This phrase has its merits. It is important legally and ethically, to distinguish between retaliating when faced with violence and provoking violence. The term "fighting back" acknowledges the gap between appraising and acting known as the OODA loop, a gap that puts a defender at a disadvantage. However, the term "fight back" implies that a response to an attack can only be a reaction; it cannot be an action in itself. It implies a position in which an aggressor drives the interaction and a defender struggles to keep up. It suggests that the aggressor has a script for violence and the defender does not.

"Fight back" is better, certainly, than "put up a fight," a phrase applied exclusively to women and almost always in reference to men's violence, specifically sexual assault. The phrase is particularly unfortunate as it implies that violence is inevitable if an aggressor intends it—and, worse, that a defender doesn't react but only appears to be reacting. "Putting up a fight" suggests a defender's actions don't actually harm an aggressor; they are a mere visual, and perhaps auditory, display. The phrase insinuates that whether or not violence occurs is solely up to how committed the assailant is and that the defender herself cannot alter the course of the interaction.

Seen in this light, using the term "fight" to describe a self-defense situation (as well as to refer to live training in self-defense scenarios) takes on particular urgency.[4] The term fight is equalizing: a fight happens between two individuals and not between predator and prey, assailant and target, or criminal and victim.[5] A defender who fights, rather than puts up a fight, forcefully insists on her equivalence to an aggressor.

This is not a matter of mere semantics: self-defense by necessity requires (and teaches) a defender to reflect on her own ability to make decisions and to enact them under pressure, thereby altering the course of a violent scenario. It is crucial, in a self-defense situation, for a defender to remember that she has options, that she can take action, and that she has agency even in a situation that she did not choose.[6] Self-defense, in this sense, hinges on turning an assault into a fight. The actions a defender takes render predatory assault a conflict between equals.[7] This shift starts with the language used to describe the encounter but it travels, by necessity, to the movement involved.

Fighting It: Improvised Self-Defense Scenarios and the Space between Work and Play

It's my turn to fight. Jen asks me where I am. I say coming out of a café not because I've been threatened outside a coffee shop but because the anxiety that sweeps over me before a fight overrides my creativity.

Don and Michael stand at the far end of the mat, clad in their padded suits. Michael steps toward me and I feel a surge of dread: Michael is more intense than Don. He's a jiu jitsu player and a member of a minimal-rules, live-stick fight club.[8] He's got a competitor's edge to him. Plus he's wearing the helmet he labels "Chad";[9] the smaller head protection allows him to move more easily. This is going to turn scrappy fast.

Chad makes a beeline toward me. I change my stance, placing my right foot behind the left. I clasp my hands in front of my sternum, an innocuous, almost prissy gesture. But it makes my hands available for a raised guard or a strike.

"What's going on?" I ask.

"I wanna to ask you a question," Chad says, approaching on an angle.

"Uh-huh," I say, rotating, moving my right foot then my left and turning my body at the same time so I've squared off to him again.

He tacks to the other side. I rotate again, deliberately moving one foot then the other as I turn my torso and my shoulders.

"What's this place like?" Chad asks. "The coffee any good?"

"I think it is," I say. "Go on in and see." It's an attempt at diversion.

Chad takes a step toward me. He's closer than our arms length combined, inside what in sport fighting we call the pocket. I feel that queasy frisson that comes when someone with opposing intent enters striking range.

I step into a ready stance. My hands come up, palms facing out, arms at a ninety-degree angle, a guard strategically modified for real-life conflict. The stance could look conciliatory—"I don't want any trouble"—but it could also become authoritative: "Take a step back now!" It could just as swiftly turn aggressive: my hands are well placed to strike the throat, to gouge the eyes, and to palm strike the nose.

"Can you take a step back please?" I say. Grammatically, it's a question but I speak it as a command.

"Hey, whoa," Chad says in performed dismay, his gestures broadening as he throws his hand into an exaggerated shrug. "I just wanted to talk to you."

"We've talked," I say. "Can you take a step back please?"

"Well, where're you going?"

"Oh, I'm leaving," I say, my hands still in front of my face.

"Where you going?"

"Home," I say without thinking. It's the wrong response.

"I'll come with you," he says, stepping toward me.

"No." My voice is more forceful now. "Take a step back."

"Come on, let's go."

"No!" I'm about to continue—"I don't know you, leave me alone"—when he grabs my wrist.

I land a palm strike to his face. He recoils then reaches toward me, grabbing my shoulders and shaking me, preparing to throw me to the ground. I knee him in the groin, shouting "No!" He hunches over but doesn't collapse.

"Knee him again," Jen shouts.

I strike his groin a second time. This time he sinks to his knees. I knee his face. Once, then another time. He drops to his back and signals to Jen: that was the knockout blow.

Jen blows the whistle.

"Look," I say, scanning from left to right, taking my gaze through the space and engaging my peripheral vision as I look over each shoulder. I intentionally break my tunnel vision to appraise other threats and note possibilities for assistance.

"Assess," I recite as I scan Chad's prone form, making sure he's unconscious.

I run to the line of students at the edge of the mat.

"Go for help!" We recite together as I high five the row of participants to join the end of the line.

This interaction is typical of IMPACT Self-Defense training: a scenario that begins with an improvised verbal encounter and moves to a physical confrontation. IMPACT, like other forms of empowerment self-defense (ESD), focuses on the indicators that precede physical violence. Aligned with the ESD movement, IMPACT trainings treat violence as a tool of social control and self-defense as an initiative through which men and women can counter gendered violence. In contrast to most other forms of empowerment self-defense, however, IMPACT Personal Safety hinges on padded assailant training and live fights. Mugger-instructors wear full protective gear, including helmets that protect the eyes, nose, throat, and chin as well as groin protection and padding on their collarbones, chests, arms, and shins. As such, defenders can hit full force and can aim at the most vulnerable target zones. These scenarios run through from start—the initial confrontation with an aggressor—to the end: getting out of the situation and getting to safety. Because these scenarios include a narrative frame and because they include a verbal interaction,

FIGURE 8.1 The padded assailant suit allows a defender to strike with full force. Photograph courtesy of Pink Dahlia Photography.

constructed around accounts of violence, they create a realism so intense that the brain responds with a stress hormone dump that is similar to that which is produced in a real assault situation.

Most IMPACT instructors see their practice as fundamentally different from martial arts and combat sport, because of its emphasis on training for likely assault scenarios. However, IMPACT trainings, like other practices that emphasize live training, take an experimental approach, based around testing actions to figure out what works. In IMPACT classes, as in combat sport, drills are taught, followed by an opportunity to apply them in live training, referred to in IMPACT as "fighting" the scenario. Also, like fight sports, IMPACT trainings include elements of both work and play. Such trainings provide an opportunity to reflect on the ability of self-defense training to reconcile play and work.

In contrast to combat sport, where a fight is a delineated, ritualized, physical contest between two people, IMPACT fights are intentionally ambiguous: they may or may not include multiple assailants and they incorporate the verbal prelude to violence as part of live training. These verbal exchanges are as live—as improvised, as unpredictable, and as contestatory—as the physical fights that follow. In addition, IMPACT trainings require that the defender decide when to start the physical fight and they teach her, through

FIGURE 8.2 IMPACT fights include forceful verbal boundary setting as well as physical confrontation.
Photograph courtesy of Pink Dahlia Photography.

a process of coaching, how to conclude the fight on her own. In this regard, IMPACT differs from most combat sport training in which live training comprises encounters between two, and only two, people who explicitly agree to fight and who are signaled as to when to begin and end their interaction.

The comparison I've just drawn between self-defense and combat sport is a contentious one. Martial arts and self-defense are both conflated and set up in opposition. Martial artists are often called upon, and frequently volunteer, to teach self-defense. Some martial artists maintain that the physical practice of sparring, especially in so-called no-rules sports such as shooto and MMA,[10] trains them for confronting real-world violence. A smaller subset of these martial artists insist that *only* their rigorous training methods, their grasp of a proliferation of techniques, and their vigorous conditioning regimens prepare them for what is problematically known, in martial arts parlance, as "the street." For some martial artists, then, self-defense is an attenuation of martial arts, a reduction to a few of its limited components.

Some self-defense advocates insist that the difference between the structure of real-world violence and fights in the ring means that martial arts are *not* training for confronting violence and that only designated self-defense training can prepare an individual for violence. They maintain that the structured and rational nature of the conflict in sport fighting, its rules, and its designation in time and place render it incomplete training for violence.[11] Both sides of this debate have examples to point to: some self-defense advocates point to the situations in which martial artists failed to successfully defend themselves while martial artists gesture to the many examples in which sport fighters used their striking, kickboxing, or grappling skills to neutralize a threat. Yehudit Zicklin-Sidikman, founder of El HaLev Empowerment Self-Defense, provides a useful metaphor for explaining the difference between martial arts and self-defense: training in martial arts is like pursuing a medical degree, whereas self-defense is like first aid. IMPACT training is like learning to be a paramedic.

In the pages that follow, my purpose is not to add another voice to this debate as to the relationship between martial arts and self-defense. I agree with Sidikman that martial arts and self-defense overlap but are not identical, that even doctors need some familiarity with basic first aid, and that the medical field sometimes offers solutions that first aiders and paramedics can put into practice. Instead, I want to examine the multifaceted relationship between martial arts and self-defense. Here I am interested in how self-defense training can balance work and play, saving discussions of how to handle personal violence for my self-defense teaching and learning. The complex relationship between work and play that self-defense embodies has relevance for daily lives beyond the realms of sport fighting and violence.

Harm to Degree: Self-Defense as Work

In several crucial ways, self-defense sits in opposition to play, games, and sports. As we've seen, play is intrinsically valuable and therefore unnecessary in any utilitarian way. For self-defense to be what it is, it must be necessary: a defender must face the threat of imminent bodily harm. While a fight is willingly entered, for it to be self-defense, it must arise from a situation that a defender did not intend.

While games use inefficient means, self-defense relies on efficient ones: neutralizing an attacker as quickly as possible in order to escape. A restriction of means in self-defense occurs in response to ultimate rules such as the moral obligation to do only as much harm as is needed to escape. Self-defense does not typically reply upon rules that only make sense in the context of the encounter. Indeed, much work of self-defense training lies in the need to undo an adherence to nonultimate rules, such as women's assumption that niceness is required at all times.[12]

If sport fighting disassociates sign and referent, self-defense retains that relationship. Aggressors maintain, and in fact, rely upon, a relationship between strikes and emotional damage. When an assailant grabs a woman with the intention of controlling and humiliating her or when an attacker shoves a man as the prelude to striking him, he unites sign and reference: this grab or hit means exactly what a grab or hit usually means. When a defender turns and lands a palm strike, she, too, retains that relationship between sign and signifier: the bloody nose is not the sign of respect that it is in sport fighting. It is a violent reprimand. The strike is a message enhancer.

In a threat situation, outcome matters more than process. In self-defense, the difference between success and failure can mean the difference between life and death. The process of self-defense, inflicting harm on another human being, is for most practitioners abhorrent, or at least regrettable. Such a distinction aligns self-defense quite clearly with work: an activity oriented toward an end goal.

Self-defense, like sport fighting, requires an acknowledgment of vulnerability in that it teaches practitioners to recognize the vulnerabilities shared by all humans. Self-defense training, however, is offered typically to those whose vulnerability has been exaggerated by societal narratives—that is, women and nonbinaries. In opposition to sport fighting, then, self-defense requires an undoing of perceived vulnerability rather than inquiry into vulnerability.

Such elements align self-defense with work, rather than with play. In addition, self-defense training, almost by definition, conjures the scenarios that most people fear and many dread thinking about. Indeed, because self-defense, when designated as such, sits outside the world of martial arts and sport fighting, it draws those who are uncomfortable reflecting on violence. Often, those who come to self-defense training are those who have experienced violence and are traumatized by its aftereffects.

Self-defense training can therefore be anxiety provoking. The atmosphere in the first session of a self-defense class is often tense and uneasy; students huddle near the wall, clutch their own arms, and avoid eye contact with each other and with their instructors.[13] In my experience, part of the effort of self-defense teaching lies in offsetting student anxiety and encouraging participation through drills that facilitate interaction and the successful completion of exercises.

The idea of self-defense as an obligation, rather than as a pleasurable undertaking,[14] plays into postfeminist criticisms of self-defense. The past few years have seen several instances in which women who define themselves as feminists have rejected the role of self-defense in the feminist movement and its efforts to end a culture of violence. Most recently, this took form as an outcry in social and conventional media in which commentators condemned women's self-defense as victim-blaming. Sparked by an article on *The Hairpin* and fueled by a suggestion from Miss Nevada winner Nia Sanchez that women learn self-defense,[15] the debate also happened to immediately precede the publication of a study by sociologist Charlene Senn,[16] which indicated a dramatic reduction in women's experience of sexual assault on college campuses following empowerment self-defense training. Feminist authors as visible as Jessica Valenti chimed in with complaints that self-defense muddied the issue rather than confronting the problem. Peculiarly, even Senn's study was taken to task for putting an undue burden on women. That the overwhelming majority of both empowerment self-defense advocates and researchers studying the effectiveness of women's self-defense are feminists fell out of the discussion.

The conflation of women's self-defense with victim-blaming is based in a logical error: an assumption that being prepared for an eventuality aligns with being responsible for it. However, this conflation acquired such emotional weight and impels otherwise progressive women toward a blanket dismissal of self-defense, despite the strong evidence in favor of its adoption, because of a perception of self-defense as conscripted rather than chosen. This perception of self-defense as work comes through in the content of criticisms of self-defense. "I shouldn't *have to* defend myself" is a common response leveled at women's self-defense advocates.[17] Some commentators insist that encouraging women to learn self-defense is inherently sexist. Women shouldn't learn to defend themselves; instead, men should cease their violence.[18]

In response, women's self-defense advocates point out that teaching women self-defense and teaching men to respect boundaries do not stand in opposition; indeed, they are compatible projects. Women's self-defense advocates also point out that women are systematically denied fight skills by a sexist society that dismisses women as passive, physically incompetent, and indecisive and that position men as invulnerable—characterizations that, far from dismantling rape culture, fuel it.[19] The self-defense is victim-blaming claim is so fraught with emotion, however, that such logical appeals have little effect. For those who oppose self-defense, it is self-evident; for those who support self-defense, the critique is incomprehensible.

Thinking about this response through Elaine Scarry's understanding of work versus pain can shed some light on the emotional intensity that accompanies the condemnation of women's self-defense. Self-defense, according to those who criticize it, is an obligation imposed upon women by a sexist society. Scarry, as we've seen, differentiates work from pain via four criteria: work is consensual, a worker has control over its outcome, its duration is fixed, and it has an object. As we've seen, effortful activity that lack these elements, such as slavery, child labor, and sweatshop work, become not work but pain.

According to those who would criticize it, recommendations that women learn self-defense operate as injunctions similar to restrictions on women's behavior such as policed hemlines and tabulations of drinks consumed. By aligning self-defense training with the many restrictions on women's behavior in sexist societies, critics of self-defense imply that women who practice self-defense do not consent to it but instead are conscripted into it. Despite the neglect of self-defense training as a primary intervention against sexual assault in CDC-funded initiatives and despite the resistance of university administrations to include (and pay for) women's self-defense training in student orientations, critics of self-defense maintain that empowerment training is imposed upon women by outside bodies and forces. This assumption enables critics of self-defense to make the paradoxical argument that self-defense is part of rape culture, despite the fact that women's self-defense offers women (and other people) the tools they need to alter conventional scripts for violence.

Similarly, when those who would criticize self-defense claim that self-defense doesn't work, they do not seriously investigate the existing evidence.[20] Instead, they insist that women participants do not have control over the outcome of self-defense training—their own safety—thereby questioning that the training truly has an object. When critics respond to statements on self-defense with the complaint that "not everyone wants to get a black belt," they emphasis the ongoing nature of martial arts training in contrast to the intentionally limited duration of purpose-designed empowerment self-defense. It is telling that much of the criticism of self-defense happens through the sound bites of electronic media; when brought into conversations and trainings with women self-defense advocates, it is hard for critics to maintain the idea of self-defense as imposed on women by individuals with greater power than they, as ineffective, and as a state of permanent training when personal choice, effectiveness, and fixed duration are built into the training.

Implicit in statements like "women shouldn't have to defend themselves" is the idea that someone else is responsible for women's safety.[21] Indeed, the flipside to the critique of women's self-defense is an assumption that men automatically or naturally know how to protect themselves and others. Such an assumption ignores the means through which boys and men are taught, encouraged, and even required to know how to fight. Parents, teachers, and coaches encourage boys toward roughhousing and team sports. Authority figures of all kinds condone playground tussles when they involve boys.[22] Although girls and women are now included in individual and team sports, combat sport, traditional martial arts, and everything in between remains dominated by boys and men. Boys and men who do not adapt to the rigors of incidental and formal fight training confront serious consequences: bullying, beatdowns, homophobic assaults, and transphobic violence.

The many ways in which (gender-conforming, nongeeky) men are taught to handle violence fall out of the "why should I have to?" equation. To many women, it appears that men "automatically" know how to protect themselves and others. It seems as if men were never required to learn these skills; they took to them so easily, it must be inherent. The ongoing process through which men acquire self-protection skills is overlooked not because it proceeds seamlessly from the existence of a Y chromosome, but because this training, for boys, happens through play. It doesn't appear to be an obligation because it occurs through games and sports. It only becomes an obligation for the boy who doesn't fit in.

By contrast, for most women, their first introduction to self-protection comes not through play, games, and sport but through a list of verbal admonitions: don't walk alone at night; don't open your door to a stranger; don't have more than a specified number of drinks. Mostly, these restrictions tend to prohibit behavior that is impossible to avoid and is inherent to being an adult in most Western, capitalist societies—such as being alone—and condemn actions, such as flirtation and partying, through which our most light-hearted forms of play are available.[23] They also place restrictions on banalities such as doing laundry and returning from the grocery store. Tellingly, these lists of "don'ts" almost never include suggestions as to how to fight an assailant. Instead, they often assume violence is inevitable if an aggressor intends it. Given the clear evidence that retaliating when attacked is, in fact, highly effective, such lists have softened admonitions not to fight when attacked and occasionally even recommend self-defense training. However, such suggestions appear at the end of a long list of warnings; they operate quite clearly as an afterthought.

A woman who pursues self-defense training, therefore, has much work to do to separate the wheat of empowerment training from the chaff of societal restrictions on women. Given the systematic process through which women's vulnerability is acquired through life in a sexist society, women's self-defense training is conscious and intentional in a way that self-protection for normative men appears intuitive and organic. The intentional nature of women's self-defense does not mean, however, that it needs to be devoid of enjoyment. Acquiring mastery, as we've seen, cultivates pleasure; as Martha McCaughey points out, the process of creating a new bodily self through self-defense can be a pleasurable one.[24] In response to the protestation of "why should I have to?" women's self-defense advocates can ask, "don't you want to?"

Participants in self-defense classes speak not only of self-defense as a healing modality but also as a source of enjoyment. Many are surprised at how fun it is. Empowerment self-defense trainings, in particular, are set up to generate enjoyment through their structure. Indeed, much of the effort of empowerment self-defense training, as opposed to more hierarchical forms of self-defense, hinges on the cultivation of pleasure through playful drills, exercises, and games.[25] In the process, they align self-defense with both the tenets of (satisfying) work and with play.

In response to the anxiety expressed by many self-defense trainees as well as in an effort to counter hierarchical self-defense methods, empowerment self-defense trainings cultivate pleasure and mastery through their structure. For example, ESD trainings don't just discuss consent; they practice consent through drills for stating and enforcing boundaries. They also encourage students to maintain their boundaries within class, with frequent reminders that it is acceptable to decline to participate or to alter a drill if it causes discomfort.[26] IMPACT courses emphasize duration by including a graduation at the end of a several-week long training, highlighting the deep, procedural memory that endures via stress-adrenaline training and eschewing the claim that coping with violence takes a lifetime of training, an assertion that is more common in martial arts. Trainings also include reminders as to the object of training by encouraging students to reflect on and verbalize self-defense success stories. Such elements mitigate student anxiety and bolster a sense of agency by aligning self-defense with both play and work. IMPACT trainings take this idea one step further, however, when they integrate elements of games and sport.

Reflections on Graduation: Self-Defense as Play

As we've seen, most IMPACT instructors contrast their practice with recreational and competitive sport fighting. However, like combat sport (and in contrast to the more aesthetic martial arts), IMPACT provides training fights in order to prepare a participant for an encounter with the oppositional intent of another human being. IMPACT sessions emphasize overtraining, demanding more of a student than she is likely to encounter in the "real" fight, running parallel to the idea that "you win your fight in the gym." The term "fight it" is used in IMPACT trainings to refer to the shift from drill to live training, much as sport fighters refer to their efforts to find the opening for a particular maneuver as pulling it off in sparring.

Instead of sparring other students in preparation for a fight in which contenders are (presumably) equally matched in terms of size, gender, professional versus amateur status, training style, and fight record,[27] IMPACT students fight instructors in padded gear based in attack scenarios structured around common, real-world styles of assault. The mugger-instructor, in the role as the sexual predator, tries to take hold of and knock the defender to the ground. The defender attacks with strikes, while shouting and grounding her weight; if she gets knocked to the ground or chooses to drop intentionally, she continues the fight from there. She may or may not fight multiple aggressors. The defender practices verbal scenarios for de-escalating the fight and uses her judgment to determine when the fight needs to turn physical. She practices how to respond once the opponent is in a (simulated) knockout: disengaging, looking around to break her tunnel vision, and assessing the status of the aggressor.

Fighters do not bracket the encounter with any gesture that would mark the fight as play rather than violence, because doing so would mitigate the ways in which stress hormones tricks the brain into perceiving the fight with the mugger-instructor as real conflict. Indeed, play markers are notably absent in IMPACT trainings. (Although a mugger-instructor once gave me a surreptitious thumbs-up at the end of a fight, mugger-instructors typically reserve their gestures of respect—compliments, handshakes, and hugs—for when they are out of their suits and have returned from their aggressor alter-ego state.)

Such conflict-based training scenarios contrast with the ritualized encounter of sport fighting which brings together two, and only two, opponents whose roles are similar and whose goals are identical. Each fighter attempts to dominate the interaction by landing more kicks and punches. Or they grapple and attempt to execute a joint-lock. Or they combine these efforts. Depending on the sport, a real, rather than simulated knockout may be the goal. In sport fighting the referee (or the coach in the gym) helps the fighter break her tunnel vision by calling time and, if need be, separating the fighters. The coach or corner man or woman has responsibility for assessing the circumstances of the fight and the fighter's well-being.

IMPACT is set up so that the defender will eventually "win" by delivering a knockout blow to the mugger. This results in some misunderstanding of the nature of IMPACT training with those who haven't experienced it insisting that "the guys are paid to fall down" and that the defenders are going full force while the mugger-instructors are not. Mugger-instructors adhere to a promise they call the mugger's code: to respond realistically to all strikes but to never fake a response to a strike. Their effort is apparent both in the scenarios and, especially, when they remove their helmets, wiping away their sweat. Their oppositional intent in the fights is as evident as the resolve of any sport fighter.

Similarly, the process through which this happens is as radically intersubjective as any sport fight: mugger-instructors push students to their limits, using the martial arts training they bring to their work with IMPACT. They gradually up the intensity of the interaction, fighting harder as students acquire competence. They contend with the actions taken by the student-defender, actions that are both verbal and physical. It may well be set up so the student eventually triumphs but in the moment of the fight, there is no remembering that the encounter will result in success.

The most marked contrast between combat sport and IMPACT training lies in IMPACT's ability to introduce live training to neophyte practitioners. In all but the most anarchic fight gyms, live fighting is a privilege earned through technical accomplishment and disciplined behavior, the ability to distinguish fighting from real violence; to keep the game going rather than attempting to win at all costs; and to create space for experimentation and exchange. The use of live fighting aligns IMPACT with combat sport while the method via which it is introduced, and the accompanying insistence that fighting is not only for experts, differentiates IMPACT from fight sports.

IMPACT trainings can introduce live practice right away because of the structure of the classes. The designated roles of attacker and defender allow participants to move swiftly to fighting without the stalking and studying common in sport fighting. Padded suits for the mugger-instructors allow even an inexperienced fighter to kick and strike with full force and to aim at target zones that inflict damage without concern for the difference between damage that is acceptable in sport fighting (a knock-out blow to the chin) and that which is not (an eye gouge). In addition, IMPACT students are unprotected (wearing not even mouth guards) and do not take hits. While this aspect of the training veers from real-world violence, it is included precisely so instructors can introduce live training early on and safely. The logic of IMPACT training is that the forceful grabbing, shaking, and throwing to the ground that the students experience prepare the student for real-world violence effectively enough that they are unfazed when, in a real violent encounter, they are struck. The success rate of trainings such as those offered by IMPACT indicates that this presumption holds true.

Despite the different end goal of IMPACT training and combat sport, IMPACT fights feel, in some ways, much like sport fights, albeit with a greater gravitas. For instance, the coach is on the mat with the trainees. She indicates the beginning of the fight with the same questions each time—"where are you?" and "any injuries?"—and signals to the mugger-instructor when the fight is about to start: "Jay's ready, no protected."[28] When the fight begins, the coach calls out suggestions: get your hands up, slow down, reposition before you strike, get in closer. As the fight's intensity increases, so, too, do the volume, intensity, and simplicity of the coach's instructions: my clearest recollection of an IMPACT class that I assisted was of Jen shouting, "Kick him in the head. Kick him hard in the head!" The coach is often physically proximate enough to the student that she can evaluate the student's distance from her target and can offer suggestions for more accurate positioning. In this sense, IMPACT proffers some of the same support as sport fighting, in the form of the coach,[29] but takes the role of the trainer to a heightened level, as the experimental and interpersonal process of fighting is nurtured through specific, immediate feedback and suggestions.

Classmates are encouraged to join in offering support. "Yell with her" is a frequent injunction. The participants who are not fighting stand in a line at the edge of the mat or the studio floor. Earlier on in a course, those who are not fighting stand silent and intimidated as their classmate fights. As the course progresses, however, enthusiasm and confidence grow so, by the end of the training, classmates are shouting "no!," "kick!," "eyes!" along with the defender. Much like the retinue of coaches, trainers, and sparring partners that follows a contender into the arena, the team of classmates stands alongside the fighter not just to offer her support but also to remind her, with their physical presence, of the rigors of her training.

FIGURE 8.3 IMPACT fights include coaching.
Photograph courtesy of Pink Dahlia photography.

When the student-defender achieves the knockout blow, the mugger-instructor signals that he's out. The coach blows her whistle to indicate the end of the physical fight. After the defender assesses the situation—"look," "assess"—she runs to the line as the instructor (or assistant instructor) calls out "all together" and the classmates shout "go for help" or an equivalent statement to reference getting to safety.[30] As the defender returns to the line, she high-fives her co-participants before taking her place at the end of the line.

Despite the apparently violent nature of the training, IMPACT's use of verbal training scenarios provide opportunities for cultivating oppositional civility. A defender is given practice with de-escalating and deflecting an assault, providing her with skills she can use to take control of a situation without the need to physically harm another human being. The mugger-instructors improvise ways of provoking conflict, and a defender learns to develop a

FIGURE 8.4 Returning to the line signals the completion of the fight. Photograph courtesy of Pink Dahlia Photography.

detachment even in the face of insults and accusations. She likewise learns to release her attachment to her own responses. This aplomb combined with improvisational skill teaches disagreement with respect at the same time that it provides the skills for the violent intervention needed for when respectful negotiation fails.

A defender also learns, in an intimate way, about the vulnerabilities of the human body, a necessary move in a society that purveys women's helplessness and men's invincibility through everything from academic theories to narrative film. Conversely, defenders learn to identify the weapons on their own bodies, an equally crucial maneuver in a context where women are taught to think of their bodies primarily as objects that can be hurt rather than as the extension of their will.[31] This understanding of comparable vulnerabilities and strengths is radically equalizing.

Just as games remind us that we are not alone in the world, these forms of self-defense remind us that we are not alone in our fight for our safety and our struggles to make the world a better place. For women who have experienced violence, the involvement of men in this process is a potent reminder that women are not solely responsible for ending gender oppression. Training fights remind us that our efforts of bringing into being a more just world are not isolated.[32] The physicality of these encounters renders this solidarity concrete; I find myself as grateful to the mugger-instructors for a tough fight as to any sparring partner.

Such conventions take the distress of a simulated assault scenario and turn it on its head. The fight becomes not just a means of surviving an attack but a method of triumph, of wresting its meaning from that which the assailant would give it. It turns threat into an opportunity to exercise mastery and accomplishment.[33] Evidence suggests that this strategy is effective in the world beyond the mat. For example, *The Safety Godmothers* consists of descriptions of self-defense success stories following IMPACT training. In one, a young woman who was attacked near a fraternity during a party describes her success with overtaking the assailant as motivated by her training, with this reflection: as I fought, she said, I heard my classmates cheering me on.[34] Such encouragement led her to both subdue her attacker and enlist the support of others in bringing him to justice.

In this regard, IMPACT mobilizes the paradoxical components of sport discussed in the previous chapter. The ability of sport to span work and play, uniting their competing elements, has a particular efficacy for self-defense training, an efficacy that is successfully mobilized in IMPACT training. While much hierarchical self-defense training is motivated by anxiety, IMPACT and other empowerment self-defense trainings build confidence and emphasize individual decision-making. Initially, most students dread fights, but most come to find satisfaction within them. In this regard, then, IMPACT trainings return attention to process from the outcome that is by necessity emphasized in self-defense training. Like other forms of play, games, and sport, it provides an opportunity to experience mastery through accomplishment and to mobilize that mastery in perilous situations. IMPACT trainings offer ways of managing risk, in stark contrast to hierarchical approaches to personal safety that emphasize risk avoidance. The live training scenarios offer defenders a way of working through failures to a satisfactory conclusion. The enhanced sense of subjectivity and the pleasure produced by this training come through an immediate, tangible, and radically intersubjective inquiry into shared vulnerabilities. It creates an autotelic state, a situation in which work becomes not an obligation but a satisfying undertaking. As such, IMPACT trainings take the work of self-defense and turn it back into play.

These scenarios allow us to reconsider the relationship between work and play, considering how their differences position them in an opposition that can be creatively interrogated and ultimately eroded. In sport and self-defense alike, elements of game structure and other features of play return a participant from a situation of (potential) obligation and toward one of immersion in process. Such realizations extend beyond the realm of sport and even of self-defense: attributes of play and of games can be extracted from the ludic context and extended into situations in which outcome is important so that work can take on features of play.

"I Know This One": The Autotelic State and the Satisfaction of Work

In the fall of 2015, martial artist, author, and self-defense advocate George (Susan) Schorn offered an empowerment self-defense training for UCLA students. Toward the end of the session, she took questions and I posed one that I had pondered for a while but struggled to formulate: what I have always found difficult about self-defense is not the biomechanics required to hit and injure an aggressor nor the assertiveness needed to issue a command and expect it to be followed. It is, instead, the difficulty of coming up with an appropriate response in a timely fashion when faced with an action that is not only threatening but also bizarre. Threat, by definition, breaks the social contract and is out of order, out of line, and often unexpected. The threats I responded to swiftly and with effective decision-making were ones I have been conditioned to expect: sexual harassment, attempted theft, and altercations to which

I was an intervening third party. When I have failed to respond adequately, it was because the threat lay so far outside of normal behavior I couldn't figure out how to respond to them: a mentally ill woman trying to gouge my eyes, a guy pickpocketing me while I turned to confront his friend who had harassed me, a man yelling at me on the bus because I woke him when I sat down.

"Practice," George said.

Review the scenario, she said, and go over your preferred responses until it becomes natural. At first, I thought this was just the standard martial arts recourse to doing the reps: put in the effort, do the repetition, and eventually it will become second nature. But she elaborated with an anecdote. She had a spent an afternoon at the dojo working on strategies for handling an erratic threat, someone whose behavior is unpredictable and hard to derail because it is not tied to an apparent goal. A few days later, she was walking down the street when a mentally ill homeless man came running up, apparently out of nowhere, and behind shouting at passersby. Her response wasn't "Oh, no what do I do?" or "Maybe someone else can handle this"; it was "I know this one!"

That response—"I know this one!"—sums up the ways in which self-defense training can create an enhanced sense of self through the experience of mastery.[35] This sense of mastery and the pleasure it induces creates a different way of being in the world from that of the incomplete subject that Iris Marion Young wrote about. The satisfaction that accompanies a task successfully completed can extend to situations that we didn't choose and even to ones we would rather avoid, such as those involving violent threat. The pleasure and self-satisfaction that accompanies such an accomplishment goes a long way toward explaining the paradox that Gavin de Becker identifies: how some people who fight when attacked go on to thrive after facing threat.[36] The gratification of a job well done extends into the realm of work, suggesting that work and play are not as distinct as they first appear.

Charlene Senn's sociological studies have indicated that women who take an empowerment self-defense class are 46 percent less likely to be raped than a control group; women who participate in an ESD training are 63 percent less likely to encounter an attempted assault. Not only do women learn how to fight attackers in an ESD training, they learn skills to prevent a situation from developing into a full-blown assault in the first place. Other studies show that women who are raped but who fight their attacker are less likely to blame themselves than women who do not fight.[37] In other words, women who fight end up less with psychological damage than women who don't even when they don't win the fight.

This is a striking revelation. Self-defense, which hinges inherently on outcome, is intimately tied to process. Acting in our own defense can enhance our sense of self even in the direst circumstances, where we are threatened and physically injured.

Self-defense indicates that work and play, although frequently set up in opposition, need not exist at odds. If self-defense, an undertaking that is inherently about product, hinges on process, so too might any number of other endeavors that we might consider work. The findings that women who train in self-defense are less likely to blame themselves after an assault suggests that intention and effort have their own value, even when they don't yield the desired result. Work can hinge on process, instead of only on product, and it can evoke our subjectivity and that of others. Work, like play, can remind us that we are not alone in the world and that we have choices, even in circumstances we don't choose.

Conclusion

A CRISIS OF PLAY?

IN 1995, SOCIOLOGIST Robert Putnam published an article titled "Bowling Alone: America's Declining Social Capital." He argued that American participation in voluntary public groups was on the decline, resulting in a diminishing of the "networks, norms, and social trust" that support a healthy democracy.[1] In 1996, journalist Nicholas Lemann wrote an essay in response titled "Kicking in Groups," in which he debunked Putnam's tenet that voluntary participation had diminished in the United States and its implication that America's mistrust of its public institutions could be blamed on a lack of participation in membership organizations. Lemann suggested instead that civic involvement had changed qualitatively—toward "open space and weekends"[2]—rather than diminishing quantitatively. Lemann further suggested that American societal ills were economic rather than social in their origins.

While I agree with Lemann that Putnam's ascription of causality is reductive, I find these authors' examples indicative of larger trends, separate from that which their articles address. Putnam titled his piece based on an example that he calls whimsical: from 1980 to 1993, 10 percent more Americans bowled on their own but 40 percent fewer bowled in leagues. Lemann mobilized an equally quirky example: participation in the American Youth Soccer Organization (AYSO) doubled, to the tune of one million participations, over the ten years from 1983 to 1993. These examples are not as fanciful as the authors would suggest: bowling and AYSO are paradigmatic of respective eras (roughly the 1950s to 1980s versus the 1990s to the present). As Lemann suggests, both involve participation and interaction among otherwise unrelated individuals, creating the "horizontal bonds" that Putnam sees as central to democracy.

However, bowling leagues and AYSO differ in central ways. Bowling leagues center on adult participation, while in AYSO, adults organize events for youth. Bowling leagues consist of continual, ongoing, sometimes casual competition across teams. AYSO and other kids' sports have become increasingly focused on training for designated competitive events—game days—similar in structure to elite sports. AYSO, then, operates as a spectator sport. Adults in AYSO organize, schedule, coach, and interact with one another. In the process, they create a community. They do not, however, play.

The shift from bowling to organizing AYSO reflects a larger trend in American life: as a society, we have moved away from kinetic, competitive play. We have shifted from doing to viewing, outsourcing physical play to experts and relegating it to particular phases of the lifespan. If, as I have suggested here, physical play provides opportunities for experiencing mastery and vulnerability, for accepting failure, and for confronting the radical difference of another's will, its neglect suggests negative consequences for individuals and larger society: higher levels of fear, increased preoccupation with success at all costs, and increasing rigidity of perspective and position. The neglect of physical play has implications for democracy and for economic stability, although perhaps not in the precisely the way that Putnam envisioned.

Sports and Play in American Life

Americans, by most accounts, are the most competitive people in the world.[3] We are the most likely to think competition is beneficial for individuals and society. We are also the most likely to believe that the outcome of competition accurately reflects effort and to think that competition is inherently fair. We celebrate competition in nearly all arenas of life, from business to sport to dance.

Given this love of competition, it follows that Americans would be the most inclined toward competitive play. At first glance, it seems that we are. Americans put more money and time into competitive sports than other nation.[4] Competitive, institutionalized sports are built into our education system, particularly at the high school and college levels. Coaches, teachers, and administrators track the success and failure of teams, with parents driving their children ever harder to win.[5] Structured kids' sports form a multibillion dollar industry not just as recreation, but also as training for a competition circuit.[6] College sports amplify this trend, with funding channeled into the most elite and competitive of sports to the exclusion of the less popular competitive sports,[7] as well as recreational sports.

The social and extracurricular life of high schools often revolves around sports, and, as sociologist James Coleman noted in 1961, the first thing we see when entering a high school is a case lined with sports trophies.[8] Even the schedule of the school day is determined by how many daylight hours are needed for sports practice. The intense fixation on and celebration of sport event outcomes as central to the identity of a school is, as Coleman points out, peculiar, creating the impression that these institutions are athletic rather than scholastic. At the tertiary level, colleges and universities in the United States literally center around sports: the football field often forms the focal point of the campus landscaping. Likewise, an entire college is defined by its sports teams' moniker: at UCLA, where I work, we are all Bruins regardless of what connection we have to sports. Similarly, the categorization of colleges and universities on a scholastic level often mimics its athletic categorization—as in the Ivy League and the Little Three.

This disproportionate attention given to competition sport leaves high-level college athletes in an ambiguous position as they generate money for their universities but, as amateur players, are not paid. They are instead rewarded with scholarships to fund their education but devote so much time to training that they struggle to fulfill academic responsibilities. Some of them go on to play professionally but most do not, raising questions about the consequences of the dedication of so much educational time to what is, after all, supposed to be a game. In the case of some sports, notably American football, unreimbursed, high-level play raises further ethical questions, given the severity of potential injuries associated with the game. The valorization of (some) athletes allows them to hover outside, or above, the structure of the educational institution. In the worst case, this creates a situation in which athletes operate outside the laws and regulations of their schools. In the best case they form a distinct elite—albeit in many cases, an overworked one.

Although I have puzzled at the near obsessive focus on team sports at institutions like UCLA, until recently I never questioned the institutionalization of sports within education. It seemed a given that competitive sport would be integrated into the operation of an institution that is fundamentally about research and teaching. While as a parent I am constantly seeking out opportunities where my young child can learn the skills of and experience the interactive and playful aspects of sports without its emphasis on competition, I also took for granted that sports competition would structure the childhood experience of many kids.

Only by thinking comparatively have I been able to grasp the peculiarities of American attitudes toward sports and competition. Organized sports have not always been central to educational curricula.[9] Similarly, sports do not occupy a central part in education in all societies. Kids in Asia, for instance, play pick-up games of soccer, cricket, and badminton during recess.[10] Or they play their sport of choice with their local club in town, not in school.[11] College campuses outside the United States center on plazas and quads, public spaces that people move through rather sites where they either play or spectate.

Although competitive sports create the horizontal bonds that Putnam praises, these bonds, as we've seen, often extend only as far as the team itself (and its alumni and coaches). For spectators, identifying as a sports fan likewise forges bonds, and according to psychologist Stuart Brown, even operates as a form of play. However, the playful elements of spectating happen without the immediate, interpersonal exchange and the experience of mastery and vulnerability so central to kinetic play. Notwithstanding the very real pleasure experienced by sports fans, the conflation of the individual with the group that occurs in team sports stands in opposition to the person-by-person negotiation of physical play. For the players, sport consists of moment-by-moment decisions that allow individuals to coordinate their efforts, on the one side, and to confront opposing intentions on the other. For nonplayers, these bonds operate horizontally but are structured from the top down; they are linked largely to outcome rather than to ongoing experimentation with vulnerability and mastery. They occasionally provide opportunities for oppositional civility but often produce its antithesis: constructed rivalry that turns real when violence flares up in the stands.

The centrality of team sports in schools, colleges, and universities not only puts sports, a form of recreation, where scholastics should be; it also foregrounds competition as paradigmatic for the educational experience. As we've seen, elite spectator sport emphasizes outcome rather than experience. Accordingly, as Stanley Eitzen points out, the more winning matters, the less creative we get to be. Sports have been criticized as a distraction from education in American high schools and colleges;[12] this is only one part of the equation.

The emphasis on elite competitive sports rather than recreational athletics also parallels a shift in education toward outcome and away from creativity.[13] While the rise of sports to prominence in schools anticipated the shift toward increased surveillance on schools via standardized testing, both factors have accelerated over recent decades. As numerous teachers and administrators point out, standardized, surveillance-based programs require that teachers abandon a personalized and context-sensitive approach to pedagogy. Play, including competitive physical play, can be personalized and context-sensitive; elite sport generally is not.[14]

The dismissal of creativity—and hence of the arts in education and in public policy—is a larger problem that reveals a utilitarian bent in American thinking. However, this neglect of creativity aligns with the importance of competitive spectator sport over and above other forms of play. Lest creativity be dismissed as inessential in a competitive global economy, it's worth remembering that creativity is a mode of thinking that is not only specific to the arts. Even when viewed in utilitarian terms, creativity drives innovation of all kinds, including the development of much-vaunted scientific knowledge. Elite sports, with their attention to outcome rather than process, are perhaps not the best model for educational institutions. If we are going to foreground sports, perhaps the incidental exchange, imagination, and context specificity of the pick-up game allows for a better example of the learning process. Since sports give us an ability to accept the vulnerability and failure that can drive innovative thinking when accompanied by introspection, perhaps their close relationship to scholastic efforts is less of a problem than their economic centrality and their exclusive focus on winning.

In 2012, Beverly Tatum, the president of Spelman College, created a particular—and striking—response to a disproportionate weight given to competitive sports in modern college life. She noted that the college spent one million dollars annually on athletic programs that served only four percent of students; meanwhile, nearly half the student population suffered from chronic health problems that could be alleviated by exercise.[15] Memorials to alumnae who died of degenerative disease marked ten-year college reunions.[16] Tatum undertook a radical initiative, closing the athletics department of her college and funneling the money it freed up into recreation athletics, including exercises classes, nonelite competitive sports such as 5K races, and intramural basketball, soccer, and volleyball.

Tatum intended this initiative to address the health concerns faced by students of her college, who as African American women confront some of the highest rates of degenerative diseases of any population, including hypertension and type 2 diabetes. Commentators have pointed out that African American women are also disproportionately affected by an exercise gap, with only 25 percent of black teenage girls engaging in physical leisure-time activity.[17] However, the phenomenon Tatum noticed points to a larger trend: American adults largely neglect physical play. Even youth are dropping out of sports at an alarming rate.

The majority of children play some kind of sport, but according to the Open Access *Journal of Sports Medicine*, by age fifteen most have quit.[18] And yet most Americans identify as sports fans. While options for physical play have proliferated, with yoga studios and rock-climbing gyms springing up all over urban areas and individuals and groups spending their weekends mountain biking, surfing, and canyoneering, the majority of Americans remains inactive. Kinetic play, for most Americans, becomes something to be outgrown or relegated to the select few.

Despite the money poured into competition-level sport, an assumption of limited resources seems to drive this tilting of the balance toward spectator sport and away from the experiential realm of recreation. Sport, in contemporary American life, is treated as a zero-sum game, in which seemingly ever-increasing accomplishment on the elite level seems to preclude participation on the nonelite level. This stands in marked contrast to the status of sport in other cultures, where professional accomplishment operates as a model for nonelite participation. For example, as we've seen, Scandinavians participate in a variety of forms of physical play, including competitive ones, throughout their lifespans. Two-thirds of Danish adults participate in athletic activities regularly, while nearly three-quarters of Swedish and Finnish adults play sports. Scandinavians are also, of course, known for their cooperative mentality and the social safety net it produces. This relationship may not be causal, or its causality may be reversed: it is not that people who play are content, but that content people play. Nonetheless, it raises some central questions: Why are the famously uncompetitive Scandinavians playing sports, competitive games, more than we are? And why are they so gratified as they do so? What does play offer their societies?[19]

It is possible that play, games, and sports are not incidental carriers of community and network. Adults who participate in physical play may activate cooperative skills and abilities through these activities. They develop the ability to work together and to disagree with respect through their participation in sports, which render them better able to access these capacities in other contexts.[20] Games provide an opportunity to practice interactions with other people; whether those opportunities are maximized is a different issue.[21]

Our American love of competition and fixation on winning may encourage us away from physical play. The need to win, or at least to excel, particularly for adults, puts us under a pressure that discourages the exploration of vulnerability and the encounter with failure that kinetic play can demand. Our obsession with outcomes not only convinces us that we have to be good at something to bother with it; it also encourages us to believe that everything in our lives, including our recreation, must serve a purpose. As we've seen, the obsession with fitness is one way in which play becomes focused on results. Play, by its very definition, serves no purpose. In an outcome-obsessed society, play can easily be abandoned because it doesn't do anything.

Spelman president Tatum is in line with most commentators in attending to the public health implications of this neglect of physical play. Public health studies investigate the physiological implications of a lack of physical play: insufficient exercise and its relationship to obesity, heart disease, diabetes, and other preventable diseases. Government initiatives urge us toward with exercise with exhortations such as "Let's Move." Play researchers emphasize the psychological costs of neglecting immersive, nonproductive experience.[22] Those focused on education, such as journalist Amanda Ripley, see sports as a distraction from academics, a diversion that adversely affects the American global standing in math and other scholastic subjects.

My purpose here has been to suggest an alternate, but complementary, view: the neglect of physical play has negative implications for sociality, creativity, for our ability to handle disagreement with respect, and to reach functional compromise. In line with my assertions in the introduction of this book, I am not suggesting that play directly serves a purpose. I am therefore not arguing that playing will automatically render us more peaceful, more communicative, or more willing to work through disagreement. There is some evidence to suggest that play teaches cooperation, but the beauty of play is that it is sufficient in itself. In addition, play seems best capable of enhancing our acceptance of vulnerability and failure, and our acknowledgment of the subjectivity of others, only when we are reflective about its outcome and its processes.

However, play's intrinsic qualities can operate as a model for how we want to live. Practices such as kinetic play allow us to mobilize our values and live them out. The United States is, by most accounts, facing a crisis of play. The country also suffers from an excess of fear, a distrust of public institutions, a plummeting civil discourse, and an increasing rigidity of position and perspective. It's worth considering the connections and the parallels between these two conditions.

Politics as Fair Play

In December 2016, political scientists Steven Levitsky and Daniel Ziblatt published an op-ed in the *New York Times* in which they analyzed Donald Trump's threat to US democracy. Comparing the businessman-turned-politician's proposed policies with those of the totalitarian leaders they observed in Europe and Latin America, Levitsky and Ziblatt argued that the checks and balances of a constitutional democracy do not fully guard against a concentration of excess power in any one individual. That's because democracies, despite their inbuilt suspicion of tyranny, take a lot for granted in terms of how politicians will behave once in power. Democracy, Levitsky and Ziblatt maintain, continues to function through shifts of personnel and party leadership because of informal norms: intentional self-restraint, a respect for opposition, and a dedication to unity in spite of differing opinions. This unspoken ethical code is as central to the maintenance of democracy as laws and regulations.

A democracy, Levitsky and Ziblatt argue, is much like a pick-up basketball game where players observe the conventions of the encounter in absence of a referee, where "unwritten rules . . . known and respected by all players, ensure a minimum of civility and cooperation."[23] A sense of fair play is necessary to democracy. A winner-takes-all attitude is a threat.

By all accounts, the United States recently witnessed one of the most divisive elections of its history. We have also experienced an election in which the suspension of fair play has been normalized. The interference of a foreign government in the election process has been received with little more than a shrug by leading political figures, simply because it put them and their party ahead. Voter suppression has become commonplace, and the legal but thoroughly undemocratic practice of gerrymandering rigs results to favor the politicians currently in power. In other circumstances, politicians change laws governing how much influence their position wields in order to curtail the power of the incumbent who follows them into office.[24] An incarceration system that selectively disadvantages African American men has permanently robbed a portion of the populace of their voting rights. Politicians suggest that we make it difficult for some people to get to the polls, and the public even considers rescinding citizens' rights to vote to favor a particular outcome. At one time we might have said "he/she/they won fair and square"; now we say "he won; we must move on" without addressing fairness or parity. A winner-takes-all approach has infiltrated US politics. While the erosion of democratic norms is particularly visible in the United States, the global rise of right-wing populism rests on a similar distrust of public institutions and a rejection of the conventional codes of fair play that would support trustworthy public institutions.

As in the case of Putnam and Lehmann, Levitsky and Ziblatt's reference to sports is not incidental, or fanciful. Rather it is revealing in indicating the kind of work that play does, individually and socially. Democracy, like play, relies on an acceptance of competing strategies, tactics, and worldviews. Democracy, especially pluralistic democracy, hinges upon the acknowledgment of the radical difference of subjectivity and experience and the effort and intentionality that constitutes unity. Just as the pick-up sports game can operate as a model for thinking about education and creativity, so too can kinetic play and the conditions of its support provide a paradigm for politics.

For instance, holding back on steamrolling an opponent is central to both politics and kinetic play because, as we say in martial arts, it's their turn next. This intentional self-restraint presents itself in a game as the paradox of the reluctant victor. In play, keeping the game going matters more than winning because play is pleasurable. In sport, keeping the game going is balanced against winning because the state of play is engaging. In politics, sustaining the state of "play" balances against winning because the state of play—interaction and exchange—creates the compromises necessary for functional governance. As recent occurrences in governmental politics indicate (such as the Senate's decision to rewrite the rules for a Supreme Court nomination), a focus on winning at all costs results in dysfunction and ideological intracability.

Democracy, like agonistic play, acknowledges that opposition is legitimate. Indeed, the acceptance of ideological disagreement and the enactment of that disagreement through competition for political office and debate over legislation form the basis of democracy. The assumption that competition can produce agreement undergirds democracy. An assumption that opposition is inherently illegitimate and operates as an existential threat is a watermark of totalitarianism.[25]

It would be far-fetched to assert that a lack of play has caused a decline in civil discourse, in democratic principles, and in economic equality. My intent is not to suggest that insufficient play has caused the multiple political, economic, and environmental crises we now face. Nor is it to claim that playing would restore civil discourse and democratic principles. Rather, I suggest that the decline in structured, competitive, but process-oriented play is symptomatic of larger societal crises. A society that neglects play is a society that devalues cooperation and respect for difference; it is a society that foregoes opportunities for interpersonal exchange and for acknowledging the subjectivity of others, opportunities for understanding that even as we disagree, we can acknowledge the advantages of our opponent's approach and maybe even learn from it. A society that neglects play is one that denies vulnerability and attempts to circumvent risk, thereby cultivating fear.

Play gives us as an opportunity to reflect on and reimagine how we interact with each other. I hope that this book has shown the many ways in which kinetic play can also teach us to value cooperation, respectful disagreement, and respect for the vulnerabilities and the skills of others both within and outside the game. Play gives us an opportunity to reflect on an ethics of experience. We can practice, for instance, agonistic or radical democracy via structured and unstructured interactions with others. By attending seriously—and whimsically—to play, we can embrace opportunities to practice oppositional civility in our daily lives.

Notes

PROLOGUE

1. O'Shea 2007.
2. I'm relying on David Harvey's (2007) and Lisa Duggan's (2003) definitions of neoliberalism. I'm also indebted to Linda Alvarez's overview of neoliberalism in her presentation at the 2017 People's Harvest Forum.

INTRODUCTION

1. I'm not the only one to encounter these questions. Susan Schorn (2009a) writes about facing a similar query after injury.
2. "Scientific street fighting" is a common descriptor for Lee's martial art style (Russo 2017; Bhumika 2016). The martial arts I discuss here are resolutely transnational, each with a history of global circulation. A full account of this transnational circulation is beyond the scope of this text.
3. Martha McCaughey comments on the assumption that "women must account for the very same activities for which men do not have to account" (1997: 224). Alex Channon, in a 2016 conference presentation, pointed out that it's common to assume that women practice martial arts for self-defense or for fitness, an assumption that falls into conventional association of women with potential victimhood or with sexual objectification.
4. Channon (2013) also comments on transformation as a recurrent theme in martial arts life narratives. Examples of martial art memoirs that highlight personal transformation include: Twigger (1997), Sheridan (2006), Polly (2011), Merz (2011), and Schorn (2013).
5. As Greg Downey points out, critics of UFC viewership suggest that fight spectacles' "primary appeal is prurient bloodlust" (2006: 109). Downey, by contrast,

argues that the UFC delivers "information about the body and fighting" (2006: 109), while also meeting audience demands for decisive outcomes provided through stylized, telegenic fighting (2014).

6. Mike Tyson, Floyd Mayweather, and MMA fighter War Machine are among the more famous examples of sport fighters who indulged in violence out of the ring or cage.
7. Jonathan Gottschalk's (2015) evolutionary psychology-influenced memoir is an example of this reductive view of sport fighting.
8. Loïc Wacquant (2004) reflects on the gentle nature of so many sport fighters, arguing that this sweet temperament is a compensation for the brutality demanded by their craft.
9. Studies that differentiate between sport fighting and violence are many. Some examples include Downey (2006, 2016), Gong (2015), and Matthews (2014). The similarities and differences between fighting and violence have received a great deal of attention in sociology, a full discussion of which is beyond the scope of this project.
10. The ability of martial arts to reduce (or foster) aggression has been the subject of quantitative study. Brad Binder (1999) reviewed a range of literature on the topic. A more recent, and more scientifically focused, literature review (Vertonghen and Theeboom 2010) suggested that although studies of martial arts and aggression are plentiful, the evidence they present is contradictory. Harwood et al. (2017) ran a study that suggested decreased aggression among youth who pursued martial arts training, although this is merely one study in contrast to the meta-reviews provided by Binder and Vertonghen and Theeboom.
11. The reference to Thoreau is intentional, although I recognize that my meaning is somewhat different than that suggested by "the squirrel shot in jest dies in earnest."
12. The relationship of risk management to a state of full focus is central to Mihaly Csikszentmihalyi's (1990) examination of the flow state.
13. The idea of play as intrinsically valuable is central to most, if not all, theories of play. For example, Johann Huizinga's oft-quoted definition of play includes the reminder that play does not serve a tangible function: "It is an activity connected with no material interest and no profit can be gained by it" (1962: 13). Roger Caillois, although departing from several of Huizinga's claims, nonetheless agrees that "the game has no other but an intrinsic meaning" (1962: 7). The intrinsic value of play carries over to Suits's (1990) theorization of games as well as to Diane Ackerman's (1999) reflections on play as well as to much of game theory, such as Rodriguez (2006).
14. In contrast to Johan Huizinga's (1962) argument that the play principle runs through all aspects of culture, I am assuming a difference between play and nonplay. However, to argue for a domain of nonplay does not necessarily

exclude the possibility of creativity, a play principle, or playfulness intersecting with nonplay arenas of life.

15. Richard Schechner also comments on the relationship between play and danger, maintaining that the fun of play is "playing with fire" (1988: 5), a metaphor I also take up later in this book. However, Schechner's argument and mine diverge around the issue of consent.
16. Oxford English Dictionary, s.v. "Play," http://www.oed.com/view/Entry/14575.
17. Play as voluntary and freely chosen is central to most of its definitions. For example, Ackerman (1999: 93) highlights the voluntary nature of play, as does Caillois (1962: 7, 9). Consent is also central to Stuart Brown's (2010) understanding of play.
18. Philosophers and game theorists agree that play is typically differentiated from quotidian life (Suits 1990; Ackerman 1999: 118; Rodriguez 2006). Huizinga identifies play as "consciously outside 'ordinary' life" (1962: 13). Similarly, for Caillois, play is "carefully isolated from the rest of life" with "precise limits of time and place" (1962: 6).
19. Caillois sums this up as a distinction between property being exchanged and goods being produced (1962: 5).
20. Brown 2008.
21. Scarry 1985.
22. Csikszentmihalyi 1990: 66.
23. Caillois (1962) uses the stakes of play, including material ones, to nuance Huizinga's theories of play.
24. Certainly some of the anger that erupts over the outcome of card games and sports matches arises from the financial stakes of betting. However, violence sometimes erupts even when no money is on the line.
25. Lewis 2014.
26. Lewis 2014: 155. Play does not, of course, have the same connotations in all languages. Tamil, for instance, differentiates between playing a game and playing an instrument. Others, such as English, French, and German do not make this distinction. Huizinga (1962) tracks contrasting word for play across languages, noting that some languages have multiple words for different kinds of play such as joking, teasing, imaginative play, contests, etc.
27. When Chinese speakers translate from Mandarin to English, they speak of playing Kung Fu. Just as some languages distinguish between playing music and playing a game, so too do some languages separate playing a sport from playing a game.
28. Richard Schechner (1988: 17) also signals this understanding of play as associated with looseness as in play in a rope as well as play with an idea.
29. Schechner 1988.
30. Brown 2010.

31. Consent is central to most definitions of play, including those proposed by Huizinga (1962), Caillois (1962), Suits (1990), and Ackerman (1999).
32. Channon and Matthews, n.d. My emphasis on consent in sport fighting puts me at odds with a body of evolutionary psychology literature, such as Gottschall (2015), which treats sport fighting as an extension of violence. However, as Martha McCaughey (2008) points out, evolutionary psychology blurs the distinction between ordinary behavior and violence because of its tendency to look at violence from the perspective of the aggressor rather than of the victim or defender.
33. Roger Caillois (1962) devotes a category of play, *agon*, to those that create structured, artificial conflict.
34. The undercurrent of danger to various forms of play has produced a literary interest in high-stakes and menacing games that blur the line between reality and play. Among these are the thriller film *The Game* (1997), Richard Connell's classic short story "The Most Dangerous Game" (1924), Shirley Jackson's short story "The Lottery" (1948), and the dystopia novel series *The Hunger Games*.
35. The blurred distinction created by the term "fight" is enough of an issue that at least some combat sport practitioners take issue with the term. For example, Loïc Wacquant (2004) points out that his trainer, Dee Dee, objected to his boxers referring to their matches as "fights."
36. Sociologists have investigated the idea of fighting as consensual in some detail. See Channon and Matthews (n.d.) for a detailed literature review on fighting versus violence.
37. Manning 2007: 12.
38. A number of blog posts on the Love Fighting Hate Violence website address such a conundrum where combat sport is predicated on consent while also blurring consent in its practice.
39. Cristina has since told me that her friend, Lev, is the source of this remark. However, I am attributing it to her in recognition of the conversation in which we discussed this idea.
40. Wacquant 2004.
41. Csikszentmihalyi 1990.
42. Joan Roughgarden (2004) makes a similar argument regarding violence in nature, suggesting that aggression is not its baseline state but is, instead, an aberration, a result of negotiations that have failed.
43. Kru means "teacher" in Thai and, as such, it is an honorific like sifu, sensei, guro, or coach.
44. I'm grateful to Inosanto Academy instructor Tim Becherer for summing up this paradox in such a concise way.
45. Caillois 1962.
46. Palmer 2005.

47. Manning 2006: 14; Connolly 1993.
48. Palumbo-Liu 2014.
49. Alongside the association of civility and politeness with the maintenance of the status quo is the association that Norbert Elias (1994 [1939]) illustrated: of "civilization" with hierarchy and encroaching control.
50. The precarity of our current age is, as Naomi Klein (2014) points out, a product of corporate excess and a dismantling of the public sphere, not of inherent scarcity.
51. Fairey 2016.
52. Fairey's position aligns with Elaine Scarry's (1985) understanding of civilization as generating not control but comfort. For Scarry, civilization is not the unique domain of Western, large-scale societies but is instead a component of all human societies. Scarry sees civilization as the extension of the imagination into acts of creation. While civility and civilization are not identical, I suggest that the work of the imagination is central to practices of oppositional civility.
53. Flock 2017.
54. Palmer 2005.
55. Mouffe 2014.
56. Mouffe 2014.
57. Halberstam (2011) credits Eve Sedgewick with this idea, but I have been unable to trace it to Sedgewick.
58. Schorn 2009b.
59. I'm indebted to Judith Halberstam's consideration of failure as revealing "different ways of being in the world and with each other" (2011: 2). Mihaly Csikszentmihalyi likewise describes play as including "the possibility of changing our goals and therefore the restructuring of what our culture states to be reality" (Csikszentmihalyi in Turner 1983: 233–234.)
60. Projects such Love Fighting, Hate Violence investigate what practices facilitate respect and empathy in sport fighting and how to promote such practices in gyms, dojos, and academies.
61. I understand practice theory primarily through the work of Pierre Bourdieu. In this sense, I align my project with others that make use of Bourdieu's (1977) idea of the habitus, a repertoire of actions from which we draw to live out our sense of self in the world. Unlike authors such as McCaughey (1997) and Wacquant (2004), my use of the habitus is implicit rather than explicit.

CHAPTER 1

1. The old French *estiquette* is also the root of the word ticket.
2. Of course, soccer players sometimes fake an injury so that the other side is penalized with a foul. Cheating by faking injury still signals the difference in the contract between players in a soccer match and a sport fight. Hockey represents

another important, and peculiar, consideration in this examination of sport fighting versus other sports. Hockey is not a sport fight. Its goals are not to land strikes on human bodies. Fighting, in hockey, is against the rules. And yet it is accepted as part of the fabric of the sport, so much so that hockey players train in martial arts not just to improve their defensive abilities but also to improve their offensive ones (Channon and Matthews 2016).

3. Alex Channon (2013) explores this difference in meaning between hitting on the mat and hitting in the world beyond in his analysis of mixed-sex martial arts training.
4. Susan Schorn (2014a), in writing about the use of the groin strike in self-defense, points out that MMA lists thirty-one possible fouls, including not only insults and faking injury but also attacks such as groin strikes, eye gouges, and flesh grabs. See also UFC Rules and Regulations.
5. UFC fighter Leslie Smith struck and restrained a man who sexually harassed her friend outside a nightclub and who preceded to spit in Smith's face, attempting to punch her when she challenged his violent behavior. Speaking of the altercation afterward, Smith commented: "I believe in the non-initiation of violence . . . I think violence like fire needs to be controlled and it's a part of us. It's an essential part of our lives and that's why we need to keep such a close rein on it while making sure to give it an outlet" (Raimondi 2015, Kowal 2015).
6. Although it's common to blame the sport rather than the aggressor, the fact that this violence often takes the forms of actions that are not permissible in the ring signals that these aggressors are intentionally violating boundaries rather than slipping into a habituated response. Floyd Mayweather's multiple attacks on several of his partners (and their family members) are a clear indication of this phenomenon, where he hit at least one woman on the back of the neck, a strike illegal in boxing because of its likelihood of causing serious damage.
7. John Gottschall (2015) assumes that martial art competition is best understood by treating it as analogous to real-world violence.
8. Corrections officer and author Rory Miller (2008) calls challenge fights the "monkey dance." Miller's phrase is catchy, but it's not terribly accurate. I've had several confrontations with monkeys and I've found them to be more of what Miller would call resource predators: they attack, or more commonly startle, to get what they want.
9. Bateson 1985: 132.
10. Bateson 1985: 133.
11. Channon 2013.
12. Dogs are also more limited in their movement options. Their primary means of attack consists of sharp objects (teeth), which can be used in play only if the attack is intentionally modulated. Thanks to Ann Lane for pointing this out. Greg Downey has taken up the versatility of the human body in his project The Athletic Animal.

13. This is particularly true of modern and experimental arts as well as traditional, non-Western arts concerned with thematic and abstract concerns rather than with literal representation. It is not, however, exclusive to them.
14. Wacquant 2004: 15.
15. Greg Downey (2016) makes this point when he discusses the telegenic aspect of UFC fights.
16. I have drawn my understanding of the OODA loop from Rory Miller (2008). Military strategist John Boyd initially proposed the concept.
17. As we'll see, this assumption of an unaltered script can be used against an aggressor.
18. I've reconstructed this account of the fatal fight through reference to several articles that came out after Griffith's death (Klores 2012, McRae 2015). The Griffith–Paret fight was a perfect storm of errors. Paret had been badly injured in a previous match and was cleared for participation when he was not fully healed. The referee was recovering from a heart attack and, by some accounts, had been criticized for stopping fights too soon (although some accounts suggest that he had been praised for protecting contenders). Paret's manager refused to throw in the towel as Griffith pummeled his opponent. Griffith's story has a tragic addendum. In 1992, Griffith left a New York City gay bar and was attacked and beaten by five men armed with bats and chains. The assault, more than his boxing career, cased the dementia he suffered from in later years.
19. This is not to say, of course, that Griffith was not responsible for his actions. This situation was particularly complex, as Griffith did not seem to realize that Paret was not weathering the punches and had gone unconscious while standing.
20. In challenging the idea of violence as a baseline state, I'm drawing from Joan Roughgarden (2004).
21. Husman (1955) in Binder (2007) demonstrated a decrease in aggression with training in boxing and Regets (1990) in Binder (2007) noted correlations between an instructor's level of aggression and that of his or her students. These are older studies; updated research would be helpful to further substantiate this claim.
22. Wacquant 2004.
23. I am paraphrasing T. Colin Campbell and Thomas M. Campbell (2006).
24. Bourdieu 1977.
25. Noland 2008: X.

CHAPTER 2

1. Bullshido is a neologism used to describe fraudulent martial arts training. It's a portmanteau of bushido and bullshit.
2. The phrase "transformation of meaning within the game" comes from game theorist Jaakko Stenros's (2012) summary of Salen and Zimmerman.

3. There is, of course, also a further difference between the meaning of these actions in drills, sparring, and competition. Sparring and competition fighting are as play is to sport, a contrast I explore in chapter 7.
4. Susan Schorn (2013) recounts a similar process of learning to perform a challenging kick.
5. Judoka and self-defense instructor and advocate Yehudit Zicklin-Sidikman brought this metaphor to my attention.
6. Schorn 2013.
7. Wacquant 2004: 17.
8. Anurima Banerji (2017) makes a similar argument regarding Nrityagram, a residential training center for classical dance in Karnataka, South India. Banerji argues that the dancers and choreographers who run Nrityagram maintain a "dance utopia" (94) that allows a "severing from the quotidian" (96) via their dedication to the rigors of their practice.
9. For most game theorists the circles, bubbles, membranes, and nets are metaphorical: they are devices that signal how play separates itself from daily life. I invoke Ackerman because she focuses on physical sites of play. Huizinga's often-cited description from which discussions of the magic circle developed also refers to physical spaces: the card table, the temple, the tennis court, etc. (Huizinga 1962: 10).
10. De Certeau 1984.
11. Downey 2010; Sobchack 2005.
12. Csikszentmihalyi 1990: 41.
13. Csikszentmihalyi 1990: 46.
14. This distinction emerges out of boxing's status as a business as well as a sport. My description of boxing as simultaneously a business and a sport comes from Tjonndal's paraphrase of Mark Turley (Tjonndal 2017).
15. Wacquant 2004.
16. Foster 2016: 17.
17. Schechner 1988: 12.
18. Schechner 1988: 5.
19. Schechner (1988: 14). Schechner's labeling of nonconsensual activities such as taunting, trickery, and sustained teasing as "dark play" is problematic. Naming this kind of ambivalent activity as "dark" is racialized in its association of darkness with ambiguous actions. In addition, defining an activity via the experience of prankster rather than pranked the lines up with an oppressive discourse that emphasizes the state of the aggressor rather than the victim.
20. Bateson 1985: 135.
21. Harmon 2011.
22. Ostensibly, these conflicts have rules insofar as a fight is different from a rumble in which two large groups of people come together to fight. A rumble usually

involves fighting in pairs. A rumble is utterly different from a beat-down in which a group attacks a single person, an action that clearly annihilates consent.

23. Schorn 2014.
24. Downey 2005.
25. Caillois describes the ways in which play can model ideal behavior as play "illustrates competition in which rivalry does not survive the encounter" (1962: 58).
26. Matthews 2017.
27. Csikszentmihalyi 1990: 50.

CHAPTER 3

1. Breihan 2014.
2. The fight promoter Damon Feldman has a history of sponsoring unlicensed matches, so perhaps the rules would have been flimsier than in a licensed event. But for it to be a match, there would have had to be some rules.
3. Rules are central to game theory. Huizinga puts forward order and structure as part of his definition of play. Moreover, he argues that in play, "special rules obtain" (1962: 10). Katie Salen and Eric Zimmerman structure their study of game design around rules.
4. Even in wing chun kung fu, which is less a sport than a self-defense system and which highlights attack over defense, participants invoke the metaphor of chess. When we practiced chi sao, the dynamic, semicooperative flow drill that characterizes wing chun, Sifu Gary Lam would say, "it's like playing chess."
5. Commenting on the deaths by heart failure of two players at Norway's Chess Olympiad in August 2014, *Guardian* contributor Stephen Moss argues that chess is not only a sport but also an extreme one. Although Moss is clearly being provocative in suggesting that this most sedentary activity is on par with bungee jumping or ice climbing, he has a point: chess, like sport, requires full concentration. Any distraction, physical or mental, can result in a misstep or defeat. For this reason, Moss points out, chess can be stressful, psychologically and physically.
6. I am using the term combative game as analogous with what play theorist Roger Caillois (1962) calls agonistic play.
7. Suits 1990: 133.
8. Subsequent game theorists, such as Katie Salen and Eric Zimmerman (2003: 96) take the ideas of open and closed to consider games as systems and to reflect on their relationship to an outside world, rather than to the outcome of a game.
9. Eichberg (2013: 12). Roger Caillois maintains a stronger distinction between work and play, suggesting that "boxers, cyclists, jockeys, or actors . . . they are not players but workers. When they play, it is at some other game" (1962: 6).

10. Rodriguez 2006: 2.
11. Suits 1990: 22.
12. The examples of those who've used martial arts in self-defense are too numerous to list in full. High-profile instances include a US Merchant Marine who used her Brazilian jiu jitsu skills against a bus driver who attacked her (Al Amir 2013; "Agency" 2015), a British woman who used BJJ to thwart an assault (Agency Telegraph 2015), and a seventy-two-year-old British former junior boxer who used his sport fight skills to subdue a knife-wielding neighbor who broke into his home (Daily Mail Reporter 2009).
13. Raimondi 2015; Kowal 2015.
14. Suits 1990: 20–21. Caillois (1962) comments on rule-breaking as threatening the game but not challenging its basic premises.
15. Suits 1990: 32.
16. Salen and Zimmerman (2004: 116) quote Suits on this point.
17. DeKoeven 1978: 161.
18. Csikszentmihalyi also points out that competition can add complexity to experience but that its ability to produce pleasure hinges on a balance between playing and winning: "Competition is enjoyable only when it is a means to perfect one's skills; when it becomes an end in itself, it ceases to be fun" (1990: 50).
19. Suits 1990: 76.
20. This isn't always the case, of course. Grudge matches all too often end with gloating or disdain on one side and resentment on the other. Also, when one contender perceives him or herself as insufficiently competitive, the response is obvious disappointment rather than graceful loss. Sufficient, apparent competitive tension is such an issue in sport fighting that it's become commonplace for contenders in professional combat sport to apologize to the crowd for losing too quickly and even for winning too quickly. Several pieces on the Love Fighting Hate Violence blog make the point that professional athletes are expected to put on a satisfying show while achieving their personal best and protecting their well-being.
21. Suits 1990: 77. Caillois likewise notes that agonistic games sometimes allow a less accomplished player an initial advantage as a way of reintroducing equality (1962: 14).
22. Guro Burton Richardson recently shared an image on Facebook, outlining his ground rules for sparring: "1) Playful; 2) Take Care of Partner; 3) OK to Make Mistakes; 4) No Trading" (October 5, 2016). Trading refers to taking a hit in order to land one.
23. As Mischa Merz (2011) points out, sparring can be more perilous than ring fighting, because it can act as a territory struggle as fighters establish their status within the gym; these social and emotional concerns represent higher stakes than a win or loss in the ring. Loïc Wacquant (2004: 78, n 65) describes

conditions in undersupervised boxing clubs when sparring consists of more competent fighters terrorizing less skilled ones.

Some of the dangers of sparring have to do with its status as a more open game than competition fighting. Rounds are not always timed; opponents are not necessarily well matched; there is no referee, no corner man or corner woman, the coach or instructor is tasked with watching several pairs of fighters at once, and the space may be a multipurpose one with obstacles and other dangers that are absent in the ring.

24. As sociologist D. Stanley Eitzen (2006) points out, sports are not fair in that advantages in access, training, and funding accrue along the lines of race, class, and gender.
25. For example, Sisonke Msimang (2016) critiqued the Caster Semenya controversy by pointing to the enormous advantage held by athletes from larger, wealthier countries and Semenya's disadvantage as a black South African.
26. Camporesi 2016; Moran 2016.
27. Caillois 1962: 14.
28. As noted above, a clear example is the policing of intersex athletes' participation in the Olympics. Another consists of the attempts to exclude transgender MMA fighter Falon Fox from competing.
29. Duina 2011.
30. Kru Atticus commented on this during an MMA class at the Inosanto Academy: "A fight with a white belt is sometimes the hardest because they're doing stuff and you're busy thinking, 'you can't do that; that's not a move.'" Memoirist Sam Sheridan (2006) also comments on this, using the unfortunately ableist expression of "fighting a spazzy opponent" but expressing the same sentiment.
31. Beyer 2015.
32. Manning 2007.
33. Eichberg 2013: 1.
34. Just because competitive games give us the opportunity to practice disagreement with respect doesn't mean that players always take this opportunity. As we've seen, competitive games have the potential to go awry.
35. This concept is the central focus of a talk by Susan Schorn (2015) titled "Fighting Machines."
36. I'm paraphrasing Henning Eichberg's (2013) suggestion that games remind us that we are not alone.
37. Susan Schorn (2009b) makes a similar comparison, likening sparring to marriage in the way that both require vulnerability, trust, the willingness to teach and to learn, and the acknowledgment of ground rules.
38. Game theorists comment on the pleasure of being "in on" the game versus their visibility. Huizinga (1962) highlights secrecy while Caillois (1962) emphasizes the overt nature of most games.

39. Schorn (2014) also discusses, in her terms, how "consensual violence" can create powerful bonding opportunities.

CHAPTER 4

1. Urquidez, a nearly undefeated fighter who premiered full-contact competition in the United States, offered trainees at Team Karate Centers in Woodland Hills an insightful and nuanced account of what fighters stake when they spar. The full talk can be seen at https://www.youtube.com/watch?v=-K71KlHvEBk.
2. Butler 2016: 22.
3. I am grateful to musicologist Olivia Bloechl for this phrasing. Philosopher Erinn Gilson describes this social distribution as follows: "The ideal of invulnerability is an oppressive one because it ties vulnerability to those people, social positions, and qualities that are deemed inferior, devaluating those positioned as 'lower' or less capable" (2014: 7).
4. Erinn Gilson (2014: 33) quotes Kate Brown in pointing out those who are feared are not seen as vulnerable and are therefore denied protection. Sara Ahmed (2014) sums this idea up as follows: "There can be nothing more dangerous to a body than the social agreement that that body is dangerous."
5. Butler 2016: 25.
6. Gilson 2014: 23–24.
7. Butler 2016: 25.
8. This is a parallel move to disability studies scholars who propose a social model of disability in which an impairment, a physical condition, is juxtaposed against disability, a status imposed by social circumstances such as the absence of wheelchair ramps or instructions in Braille. I'm deriving my understanding of the social model of disability from Snyder and Mitchell (2005).
9. Butler 2016: 24.
10. Mihaly Csikszentmihalyi defines vulnerability as a threat to the self (1990: 63). Extending this definition to an ethics of vulnerability suggests that a process of woundology can prompt a rethinking of what constitutes a self.
11. As Alex Channon and Catherine Phipps (2017) put it, pink gloves still give black eyes.
12. As in previous instances, I am drawing this insight from Alex Channon and Christopher Matthews's Love Fighting Hate Violence project.
13. Schorn (2013) comments on the difference between hurting and injuring. Likewise, Veronika Partikova (2016) refers to the delicate balance between pushing a training partner hard enough to enable learning but not so hard as to injure or traumatize them. Partikova refers to the tendency to push training too far as hidden violence within martial arts training.

14. Grappling can, of course, override consent. Pinning someone for longer than they are uncomfortable with is a form of violence. This kind of violence can be hard to confront precisely because of its restricted means: wrestling is easy to pass off as "just play" even when participation is half-hearted or conscripted.
15. Judo also involves chokeholds and joint-locks. Aikido and hapkido also involve the use of joint-locks.
16. I'm moving between discussing jiu jitsu generally and Brazilian jiu jitsu specifically in recognition of the commonalities between the different forms while also relying on my own experience, which is largely of Brazilian jiu jitsu.
17. In contrast to Brazilian jiu jitsu, which is a sport and has rules, Japanese jiu jitsu does not have rules.
18. Sport sociologists refer to activities such as rock-climbing, mountaineering, snowboarding, and surfing as alternative, lifestyle, or risk sports rather than as the more common but misleading extreme sports (West and Allin 2010; Langseth 2011).
19. Free diving, prior to its introduction as an extreme sport, operated as a form of work in which Japanese and Korean women dove for pearls, abalone, and seaweed.
20. This doesn't mean, however, that sports avoid risk. Most sports and many games put the body in some sort of jeopardy, one that the mastery acquired through training manages.
21. Downey 2010.
22. Conventional and alternative sports meet at the point of human vulnerability, with, for example, concussions emerging as a major health concern in both American football and in combat sport.
23. Some fighting arts use open stances as a way of drawing in the opponent. Bruce Lee called this approach attack by draw.
24. Wacquant 2004.
25. As indicated in the introduction, Brandon Rios reflected on his preparation for an upcoming match with Manny Pacquiao: "If I went in there mad, I'd get knocked out" (Pugmire 2013).
26. Debate over Pacquiao's killer instinct (or lack thereof) appeared in various sports commentaries following the bout with Margarito (Pugmire 2011; Henson 2011).

    More recently, amateur MMA fighter Mike Pantangco ceded a match to an opponent who he was steadily defeating for fear of injuring him. Although praised in some sectors he was criticized in others, largely by commentators who insisted that violence is what he signed up for and that deciding when enough was enough is the remit of a referee not a fighter (Mazique 2014; Gargiulo 2014). The insistence that sports such as MMA have, or should have, no ethical limits is deeply problematic since, as Neil Hall (2016) points out, a crucial difference between fighting and violence lies in the fact that the former has parameters that are respected, acknowledged, and enforced. In addition, consent includes the ability to withdraw consent. If we maintain that competition fighters do not have this right, we subject them to social violence (Channon and Matthews 2016).

27. Wacquant 2004; Merz 2011.
28. A fighter who aims for a victory by knockout sometimes takes punches in order to try for the big win. In other instances, fighters cover and withstand punches to wear out an opponent.
29. Martial arts that counter an attack with force are understood as "hard style" and those that move with an attack to subvert it are considered "soft style." In practice, soft-style maneuvers are present in a range of arts, including those identified as hard styles.
30. Floyd Mayweather's fight strategy is probably the clearest example of how a nearly exclusive focus on defense can preclude opportunities for an opponent to strike.
31. Encouraging athletes to ignore and train through injury is one way in which athletes are objectified by the spectacle of sports (Jackson 2013; Channon 2017).
32. Scarry 1985.
33. Snortland 2001.
34. Brownell 1995; McCaughey 1997.
35. Despite this effort to construct sport and other activities around men's capacities, women have come to excel at competitive sports. Such participation is, however, policed. The surveillance of intersex and transgender athletes discriminates not only against nonbinary individuals but also against women. For example, the claim of Olympic officials that women's hormones levels should be tested because high testosterone gives athletes an unfair advantage ignores the fact that high testosterone also advantages some men over others. For these and other reasons, scholars such as Channon (2015) have urged the reconsideration of sex segregation in sport.
36. Women's magazines typically offer to tone abs and thighs and whittle down hips, while men's magazines promise massive arms and an imposing chest. The gendering of such fads as the Paleo Diet is evident in its caveman imagery and its historically questionable valorization of hunting as the basis of human evolution. McCaughey (2007) and Zuk (2013) comment on the cultural implications of caveman imagery and narratives.
37. This irony almost can't be overstated. It's reinforced in everyday language where "having balls" conjures strength and bravery and "pussy" conveys weakness with no attention to the reverse contrast in vulnerability that this reference to anatomy evokes. In light of this, feminist self-defense writers such as Susan Schorn (2011, 2014), Martha McCaughey (2014), and Ellen Snortland (2001) have produced insightful (and witty) writing around vulnerability, masculinity, and groin strikes.

38. Author and self-defense advocate Martha McCaughey, together with her colleague Neal King, has created a series of videos that show women fighting when attacked. She points out that most men who attack women do so because they believe they will get away with it (1997: 183). She argues that "if research has shown that an increased sense of vulnerability to danger leads to self-imposed behavioral restrictions, then why aren't we increasing men's perceptions of vulnerability to danger so that they'll restrict their abusive behavior?" (1997: 183).
39. Feedback from IMPACT Personal Safety trainings suggests that watching self-defense trainings can be a significant deterrent to violence. Contrary to the received wisdom that aggressors will apprehend self-defense moves and learn to circumvent them, IMPACT instructors describe how participants in boys classes speak of the trainings as a deterrent to bullying: young men comment on thinking twice about initiating violence after seeing how effectively smaller boys can fight.

    One of my instructors, Guro Atticus, reflected on such a relationship between vulnerability and compassion. In speaking of a teenage boy who trained regularly at the academy, he said: "He'll be a good man." Unsure of what he meant, I spoke about his easygoing nature and the ability of martial arts to externalize aggression. Atticus clarified: "He spent his formative years getting beat up by adult women. He's not going to mess with anyone."
40. I'm drawing this interpretation from sociologists Karen Sternheimer's (2009) and Sally Raskoff's (2008) overviews of crime statistics as well as the Bureau of Justice Statistics from which they draw their analysis.
41. McCaughey 1997.
42. Schorn 2009c.

CHAPTER 5

1. This is not an uncommon experience. Schorn (2009a) and Phillips (2017) comment on the likelihood that a woman's fight injuries will be seen as signs of abuse.
2. Douglas 1966.
3. See Gong (2015) for a summary of sociological debates regarding Norbert Elias's claim that modern sports provided evidence of his civilizing process theory.
4. West and Allin 2010.
5. I do not mean to suggest that no traditional martial arts include contact sparring. Perspectives on contact sparring vary among practices and schools. Some traditional martial arts include contact sparring; some practice touch sparring instead. Traditional martial arts typically have more rules as to what shots are to be avoided; many eschew shots to the face, for instance.

6. This is particularly true early on in training; with experience, a fighter gets calmer, inhabiting "the eye of the storm" regardless of how intense the encounter.
7. Ackerman 1999: 21.
8. Ackerman 1999: 21.
9. Csikszentmihalyi 1990: 59.
10. Csikszentmihalyi 1990: 60.
11. Csikszentmihalyi 1990: 63.
12. Arguably the most famous instance of opposing sport fighting to civilized life was in John McCain's statement that MMA was "human cockfighting." Csikszentmihalyi, despite his nuanced understanding of the autotelic state cultivated by such high risk activities as rockclimbing and mountaineering nonetheless dismisses boxing in a similar way to McCain, presenting it as a spectacle of pain, comparable to bull fighting and dog baiting (1990: 69). This comparison is particularly unfortunate for its disregard for the consent of participants.

    The larger debate among sociologists as to the status of modern combat sport as "civilized" or "violent" is beyond the scope of this discussion. As noted previously, Neil Gong (2015) summarizes the debate effectively.
13. This contrast between high-risk play and recklessness is central to most analyses of the flow state and of alternative sport (Csikszentmihalyi 1990: 60; Stranger 1999: 265; and West and Allin 2010: 1235).
14. This, too, is a common insight in analyses of alternative sport (Csikszentmihalyi 1990: 60; West and Allin 2010: 1240).
15. Csikszentmihalyi suggests that "the whole point of climbing is to avoid objective dangers as much as possible, and to eliminate subjective dangers entirely by rigorous discipline and sound preparation" (1990: 60).
16. West and Allin 2010: 1240. This is not to say, however, that an ability to manage risk in sport necessarily carries over into the nonsport context. As an amateur rock-climber of many years, I have heard more stories of climbers seriously injured or killed on the hike out from the climb than on the rock. While this is anecdotal, it does suggest that climbers are right to position the risks of climbing in proportion with other threats. It also suggests, however, that climbing does little to mitigate the dangers of life beyond the rock face and perhaps suggests that the attunement to risk in one situation can produce complacency in another.
17. Csikszentmihalyi (1990) comments on the illusion of control and Stranger (1999) reflects on the tendency, within risk play, to continually up the ante in search of thrills.
18. Csikszentmihalyi 1990: 57.
19. Csikszentmihalyi 1990: 57.
20. Kahnemann 2011: 241, 243.
21. Kahnemann 2011: 241.

22. Eitzen 2006.
23. Stranger 1999.
24. Phadke et al. 2011.
25. Phadke et al. 2011: 62.
26. Phadke et al. 2011: 60–61.
27. For example, Donald Trump's rant over football players' peaceful protests of police violence led into an invective against modifications to the game that improved its safety. This indicated a view of professional football players as expendable.
28. Peter Gray (2014) and Ellen Sandsetter (2010) are the most prominent voices among psychologists who argue for increased possibilities for risk play for children.
29. Wacquant 2004: 68.
30. Anthropologist Craig Palmer (2005), in writing about the disparate practices of mumming, disguised house-visiting, and moshing, dancing that involves the inherently risky practice of colliding with other people, argues that such activities reinforce social relationships by reminding participants that what *could* happen (violence) is not happening.
31. Gottschall (2015), for instance, characterizes joint-locking as symbolic murder. This association is particularly problematic as it assumes that violence would play out identically to a sport fight, which, as we've seen, is a flawed contention.
32. Palmer 2005.
33. Receiving generosity is pleasurable as long as that magnanimity is genuine and is not motivated by a desire for power. All too often, however, what appears to be driven by altruism is, in fact, a play for power or dominance. See Snyder and Mitchell 2005 on charity and the marginalization of the disabled in European and North American societies of the nineteenth century.
34. I use this term recognizing its root in feminist philosophy, notably in the work of Carol Gilligan (1982) and Carol Adams and Josephine Donovan (2007). I accept that feminist philosophers do not usually apply this term in reference to agonistic practices. I also use this term aware of its critiques as in Butler et al. (2016).
35. Palmer (2005) signals how moshing performs community support as well as conflict. Moshing enacts an ethic of care in the face of danger: the code of the mosh pit consists of rules as to what is allowed, shoving but not hitting, for instance, and requires that participants aid fallen dancers and catch those who stage dive.
36. Jackson 2013.
37. A number of articles on the Love Fighting Hate Violence blog address the objectification of athletes in commercial sports. Alex Channon and Christopher Matthews's entry on quitting (2016) in particular sheds light on the issue of spectacle, risk, and objectification.

38. This point is made in several Love Fighting Hate Violence entries, notably Channon and Matthews (2016).
39. Matthew Polly (2011) comments on the role of fight matchmakers in establishing and maintaining an MMA competition fighter's career. Anne Tjonndal (2017) likewise signals the role of the matchmaker in professional boxing, specifically as it relates to the risks faced by journeymen.
40. Tjonndal 2017. See also Wacquant (2004) on journeymen.
41. Hootman, Dick, and Agel 2007.
42. This account appears numerous popular descriptions of UFC history, such as Cruz 2013.
43. Glassner 1999.
44. Glassner 1999.
45. Gardner (2009) provides insights regarding which fears grab our attention and which seem inconsequential. In evoking his analysis, I am not suggesting agreement with his argument as to the origin of fear. Gardner argues for a "caveman brain" that guides our perception of fear. Commentators such as Martha McCaughey (2008) and Marlene Zuk (2013) have critiqued the idea that modern humans are cavemen improbably and haplessly catapulted into the modern age.
46. Glassner 1999: 183; Gardner 2009: 3.
47. Stranger 1999: 271.
48. Stranger 1999: 270. Stranger's example differs from my own in that he analyzes experiences of the sublime in surfing, where the object of appreciation and the media of engagement are one and the same (1999: 270). This appreciation, he argues, is part of what distorts risk assessment. While martial artists acquire a devotion to their gyms, academies, or dojos, these cluttered, dark spaces that stink of sweat rarely induce awe. However, other elements of surf culture and martial arts align, such as the overlap between the practice of the sport, the appreciation for its depiction in film, and the proliferation of "how-to" discussions in magazines and video clips (1999: 272).
49. Susan Schorn (2011b) comments on the mutual implication of risk and consequences and the ethical implications of that relationship.

CHAPTER 6

1. Downey 2010.
2. Young 1980.
3. Halberstam 2011: 100.
4. This does not just pertain to physical tasks. Hillary Clinton's surprise loss of the presidency has prompted discussion as to whether analyzing the loss will encourage women out of politics, suggesting that her failure has more to do

with her status as a woman than with, for example, her opponent accepting the assistance of a foreign government.

5. Channon 2016.
6. Social psychology studies, especially those that focus on the business workplace, indicate that men feel threatened by women's accomplishments and capacities in the workplace and that men who hold traditional gender roles are more likely to feel threatened and therefore to behave in a demanding and even hostile manner (Beinart 2016; Rahman 2017).
7. A discomfort with women's competence may explain why men who write about sport fighting frequently ignore (in writing) the presence of women on the mat and in the ring.
8. Kaba and Meiners 2014.
9. Kaba and Meiners (2014) point out that the majority of students suspended under zero-tolerance rules are accused of disobedience and fighting with their fellow students, and not with more serious acts such as premeditated assaults or bringing a weapon to school.
10. White middle-class youth escape the criminalization suffered by their black and Latinx peers. And yet they do not fully avoid carceral logic: while adolescent behavior is criminalized among youth of color, it is medicalized among white youth with, for example, the proliferation of the diagnosis of childhood bipolar disorder, a diagnosis some psychiatrists believe there is little evidence to support (Frances 2010; Kaplan 2011).

    Carceral treatment of teenage behavior has produced a proliferation of dubious mental health practices, known as the troubled teen industry (Szalavitz 2006).
11. Alexander 2010.
12. Guo 2016.
13. Journalist Lisa Davis (2017) narrates a tragicomic tale of mistaken identity in which she incurred a series of unpaid parking tickets, fix-it tickets, jaywalking, and minor traffic violation summons that led to the suspension of her driver's license and caused her to fail a criminal background search. Davis had never been ticketed for such infractions. When she located the other Lisa Davis, the woman who incurred the tickets, she realized that the two determinative differences in how they were treated by the criminal justice system were race and the neighborhoods in which they lived.
14. The mass closure of schools in black neighborhoods is a central part of this phenomenon where once middle-class neighborhoods fall into decline (Layton 2014; Rizga 2016).
15. Bennett 2017.
16. Rosin 2014; Bennett 2017.
17. Initiatives include those at Smith College, Stanford University, and Harvard University.

18. This is not to suggest, of course, that these categories of inner city and successful youth do not overlap. Sometime the students facing the sternest demand for excellence are those from underserved areas who achieve upward mobility through their successes: they see the consequences of failure and have been conditioned that their worth lies in their success (Bennett 2017).
19. The various incarnations of the celebration of failure are too many to list here. See Martin (2014) for a summary of "failing up" in the dot com sector and Losse (2016) for a critique of the inability of failing up celebrators to account for the race, gender, and class privilege that enables them to turn failure rapidly into success.
20. Sarah Jane Bailes points out that failure inheres in action of every kind; that "we cannot *do* without failure" (2010: 12).
21. Rosenau 2006: 6.
22. Kahneman (2011: 281). Social psychologist Daniel Kahneman has determined that loss aversion can be quantified as a ratio of between 1.5 and 2.5 to 1 (2011: 284), meaning that most participants in his study avoided losses unless the potential gains were 1.5 to 2.5 times higher than potential losses, suggest an in-built negative association with loss, even in hypothetical situations.
23. Kahneman 2011: 281–284.
24. Ibid.
25. As author and choreographer Emilyn Claid points out, when failure gets incorporated into a success narrative, it is easy for it to operate as another benchmark so that it is possible to "fail to fail" (personal correspondence 2017).
26. Halberstam 2011: 23.
27. Halberstam 2011: 2.
28. Although the scientific method acknowledges failure as a very real possibility, the sciences, like other professions, demand a record of success.
29. "What works" and "try to find it in sparring" are phrases used habitually within martial arts training.
30. Interestingly, the dictionary definition of live, as in live ammunition, pertains to the presence of an electrical charge. So, for instance, live ammunition is described as "using undetonated explosives" and is listed under definition 3—"connected to a live current." *Oxford English Dictionary*, s.v. "Live," https://en.oxforddictionaries.com/definition/live#live_Adjective_200.
31. See https://en.oxforddictionaries.com/definition/live#live_Adjective_200.
32. Emilyn Claid (2006), points out that in ballet, pain is often a signal of doing something right, in contrast to many sports, where pain is an indication of doing something wrong.
33. Sara Jane Bailes, in writing specifically about representational failure, cites embarrassment as one of its consequences (2011: xvi). Greg Downey (2005) discusses the need, in capoeira training, for shedding shame. Sagar and Stoeber

(2009) comment on the role of shame and embarrassment as related to a fear of failure in sport.

34. Bailes 2011: xvi.
35. Bailes 2011: xvi.
36. Rosin 2014.
37. The celebration of failure, like the disavowal of failure, has reached hyperbolic proportions in contemporary society. Peculiarly, we celebrate high-profile instances of failing up without attending to their consequences. One of the most disturbing instances of the denial of consequence is the popularity of Allan Savory's TED talk in which he admits to engineering a devastating policy that led to the slaughter of 40,000 elephants in an East African national park. He based his policy on the assumption that the elephants were causing desertification. The desertification got worse after the ecosystem had been so profoundly disrupted. Although Savory admits to this mistake, he does not acknowledge that its consequences were far worse for others, human and nonhuman, than for him, nor did he face its fundamentally colonialist assumptions, that his intervention would improve the indigenous environment.

    Indeed, he used this failure to assert a scientifically questionable and even more colonialist assumption that non-native domesticated animals should be brought in to (primarily Third World) desert ecosystems, where they would graze until they are killed for meat and sold for profit. This, he suggests, would replicate the influence the elephants had on their desert environment before he initiated their slaughter. Rather than work toward protecting and rebuilding the elephant herds he destroyed, Savory argues for further disruption of their environment in the interest of profit making. Savory's inability to confront the consequences of this failure led to a willingness to accept a scientifically faulty, environmentally dangerous, and colonialist proposal. I am not linking to the TED talk here, because it has already received much more attention that it deserves given the dubious science behind its claims and its callous disregard for human and animal suffering.
38. Kahnemann 2011: 214.
39. Kahnemann 2011.
40. Lewis 2014: 13.
41. "There is a pedagogy in failure" in that "we learn by mistake, by accident, by getting things wrong" (Bailes 2011: xix–xx).
42. Tales of folk artists deliberately erring in their work abound, with reports of Amish quilters and Islamic artists inserting deliberate errors to signal their humility. Such reports, however, seem to be apocryphal.

    Reflections on early photographer Margaret Cameron attend to the errors that ostensibly marred her work but, in retrospect, lend it character (Ruggeri 2016). Art critic Mostafa Heddaya (2013), in discussing an exhibition of installation art, suggests that "by liberating the act of creation from the strains of perfection, an artistic intelligence of a different order is achieved."

43. Although the terms I use here, contract and release and fall and recover, refer to specific techniques within modern dance (Graham and Humphrey respectively), I also use them to invoke larger patterns of tension and relaxation that extend to characterize postmodern as well as modern dance. Author and choreographer Emilyn Claid is currently researching the politics and poetics of failure in dance.
44. Journalist Malcolm Gladwell (2000) and sociologist Francesco Duina (2011: 27) comment on failure as central to the "drama" of sport.
45. Duina 2011.
46. Emilyn Claid, personal correspondence 2017.
47. Ehrenreich 2009; Ahmed 2010.
48. The Oxford English Dictionary defines optimism as "hopefulness and confidence about the future or the successful outcome of something." Oxford English Dictionary, s.v. "Optimism," http://www.oed.com/?authRejection=true&url=%2Fview%2FEntry%2F132073%3FredirectedFrom%3Doptimism#eid.
49. Alloy et al. 1990.
50. Fine 2008.
51. Ehrenreich 2009.
52. Ahmed 2010.
53. Kahnemann 2011: 259.
54. Ehrenreich (2009) argues that positive thinking allows us to accept the corporate downsizing that has resulted in the casualization of labor for much of the population, as well as its related precarity.
55. Berlant 2011.
56. Kahneman concludes that "optimism is widespread, stubborn, and costly" (2011: 257).
57. Halberstam argues that a new kind of optimism (2011: 5) can come about through an attention to losing as it destabilizes self-importance (68). Halberstam also links failure to struggle (92).
58. Duina 2011.
59. Duina 2011.
60. Eitzen 2006: 55.
61. See Halberstam (2011: 93) on losing as a defining characteristic.
62. Mackay 2002.
63. The phrase "courage, determination, fairness, and respect" comes from Eitzen (2006: 54). Eitzen is quick to point out that sport participation also induces negative socialization, encouraging "rule breaking, selfishness, greed, contempt for opponents, and violence on the field as well as deviant behavior off the field" (2006: 54).

64. Excessive competition in children's sports is a point of concern for educators, sports administrators, parents, and public health researchers. Children's sport has become increasingly oriented toward competition while participation is in decline (Atkinson 2014; Rosenwald 2015). Commentator Ashley Merryman (2013) argues that the ability to "overcome setbacks" and lose graciously are important life skills that current approaches to children's participation overlook.
65. Duina 2011: 169.
66. As indicated above, these ideas come from Csikszentmihalyi (1990).
67. Not all successes or failures depend on the presence of another person or group. Some successes and failures are personal rather than interpersonal. However, personal failures can invoke the accomplishments of another person even if that person is imaginary: someone who has achieved more, won more, completed more.

CHAPTER 7

1. Young and Pain 1999.
2. Gladwell 2000.
3. Duina 2011: 27.
4. Jackson 2013.
5. Claid 2006.
6. While Duina argues that sports viewing is a form of sadism, he nonetheless admits that if the suffering is particularly serious "we do not feel pleasure" (2011: 27). He also acknowledges that we long to see suffering and its opposite: "pain and joy," "failures, victories, and hopes" (2011: 28).
7. See http://media.npr.org/documents/2015/june/sportsandhealthpoll.pdf.
8. Laborde 2011.
9. Adult Participation in Aerobic and Muscle-Strengthening Physical Activities 2013.
10. Sports for children have shifted from training and competing for enjoyment and personal improvement to competing to achieve a series of wins. Children's sports focus increasingly on outcome with kids under pressure to perform well and to achieve results. Adults react in peculiarly strong ways to losses in kids' sports (Duina 2011: 43) and children, pushed too hard, too soon, develop repetitive strain injuries. Children have also seen a reduction of their free time and a channeling of their energies into structured sports (Anderson and Doherty in Duina 2011: 171). Perhaps adults now place such a strong emphasis on outcome precisely because they are not participating in sports and other games themselves, and therefore have neglected experiential aspects of play.
11. Professional sports can encourage emulation and, therefore, participation, where amateurs imitate their heroes on the playing field. In India, boys of

all ages play cricket in alleys and fields, matched only in their enthusiasm by viewers watching national teams vying for titles. In Los Angeles, young men from South America set up soccer games in public parks. Adults, as well as kids, play pick-up games of basketball at the local park. Spectacle in sport can feed into participation even as it more frequently overrides it.

12. Eichberg 2013.
13. Eichberg 2013: 12.
14. Eitzen 2006: 228.
15. Eitzen 2006: 99.
16. Stuart Brown, in his TED talk on play, gives an example of a crowd at a sports event celebrating as an instance of play.
17. Laborde 2011.
18. White Hutchinson 2012; Saccaro 2015.
19. Laborde 2011.
20. This insight also applies to food injustice. Legal scholar Andrea Freeman (2013) refers to this phenomenon as biological individualism.
21. Sixty-four percent of Danish adults participate in athletic activities regularly, while the Swedish and the Finnish play even more at a rate of 72 percent.
22. Foucault 1995.
23. Ackerman 1999: 85.
24. Brownell 1995: 146.
25. This is not exclusive to sports. Dance can also serve such a purpose.
26. Astute observers will note that I referred to Alain as "coach" above and "sifu" here. Because I have trained with Alain in multiple forms, I would refer to him as coach, guro, or sifu, depending on what we're practicing at a particular time. This convention comes from the Inosanto Academy, where multiple martial arts are taught: the same person may be referred to as sifu, guro, kru, coach, or professor depending on the art that they are instructing.
27. This is my translation and it's a paraphrase of the original, rendering it gender-neutral. The original reads: "Through action without attention to results a man achieves enlightenment." The gender-specific language makes sense within the narrative, as Krishna draws parallels between Arjuna's specific situation and larger phenomena and need not be understood as a conflation of the masculine singular with the universal.
28. Scarry 1985: 169.
29. Scarry 1985: 162.
30. Scarry 1985: 169.
31. Ackerman 1999: 85; Lewis 2014: 152.
32. Lewis 2014: 141.
33. Lewis 2014: 147.
34. Lewis 2014: 151.

35. Lewis 2014: 151.
36. Lewis 2014: 163.
37. As I've indicated in the introduction, I base my understanding of Bruce Lee's approach to fight training from my experience of Bruce Lee's martial art jeet kune do with Sifus Yori Nakamura, Atticus Todd, and Alain Rono, instructors in JKD at the Inosanto Academy of Martial Arts. I also draw from Guro Dan Inosanto's references to Bruce Lee in his teaching of martial arts such as muay Thai and Filipino martial arts. Inosanto's approach aligns with Lee's jeet kune do teaching philosophy, which emphasizes a critical, analytical, and personalized approach to training in the combat arts; for Inosanto and his students, Lee's dictum "take what is useful, leave what is useful, and make it your own" is the backbone of the JKD system. Some of Lee's other students teach only jun fan kung fu, a training system that preserves the material developed by Bruce Lee.
38. Duina 2011: 168.
39. For Duina, this act of imagination through pursuit seems to hinge primarily on the anticipation of success (2011: 169). But I think his ideas can be extended to consider how the act of pursuing a goal can be enjoyable and satisfying on its own, regardless of its outcome.
40. Manning 2007.
41. Duina (2011) points out that American sports demand a winner and that ties tend to be avoided.
42. This assertion is based on Sara Jane Bailes's claim that failure "undermines the perceived stability of mainstream capitalist ideology's preferred aspiration to achieve, succeed, or win, and the accumulation of material wealth as proof and effect arranged by those aims" (2011: 2).
43. Barbara Ehrenreich (2009) comments on the ways in which public austerity has shifted the responsibility for success from society to the individual, noting an additional Calvinist tone to the insistence on personal responsibility for misfortune.
44. This suggestion is inspired by Erin Manning's (2007) assertion that intersubjectivity allows space for dissent and disagreement and not only for consensus.

CHAPTER 8

1. McCaughey 1997.
2. De Becker 2000. Women who initiate violence typically work from a more straightforward motive, that of harm, rather than manipulation in the interest of provocation or domination (Miller 2008).
3. McCaughey 1997.
4. The use of the term fight is not specific to IMPACT. Susan Schorn's *MacSweeney's* column on feminism, self-defense, and cultural critique is titled "Bitchslap: A Column About Women and Fighting."

5. It's worth noting that of the terms used for gendered violence, only one conjures humanity. "Prey" is typically reserved for animals while a target is an object. A victim is human, but one whose status is defined wholly by the violence she encounters, not by her response. So invested are we in the terminology of victimhood that law enforcement typically refers to defenders as "victims" even when they successful injure and escape from assailants. As a counterbalance, I refer to individuals in self-defense situations as defenders.
6. As Martha McCaughey (1997) points out, it is important to reiterate that defenders do not chose or cause the violence they encounter even when they win the fight.
7. I use the term "predatory" reluctantly, because such terminology glamorizes manipulation-based assaults by associating it with charismatic mega-fauna, their striking physical abilities, and effective strategies. Although animal predators, like human sexual aggressors, do target the young, the old, the sick, and the injured, they do not manipulate behavior as to make physical retaliation unlikely. Instead, they expose themselves to physical risk.
8. Live stick competitions are usually referred to as no-rules fighting, but as Neil Gong (2015) points out, they are replete with rules. Nonetheless, fighting with live sticks is bound to toughen a person in the ways I've discussed in chapter 5.
9. The padded instructors assume an alter ego, complete with a different name that they adopt to play the role of the assailant in fight scenarios. This allows instructors to fully commit to acting as the aggressor without feeling that identity seep into themselves; it also allows the students to hit, kick, eye gouge, and shout at the assailant without feeling remorse for striking their instructor. Padded instructors identify the head of the padded suit by their "mugger name." In Michael's case, he has two alter egos, Wade and Chad, each with their own suit head. Wade is an inappropriate guy with a poor sense of boundaries. Chad is angry and aggressive.
10. As we've seen, practices such as shooto and MMA are often referred to as no-rules fighting. But they do, in fact, have rules that are standardized, respected by participants, and enforced by referees.
11. Rory Miller (2008) is among the authors who make this point. Self-defense instructors sometimes draw this comparison between combat sport and self-defense in their classes.
12. The assumption of niceness is not only gendered but also classed and raced. Middle-class white women tend to have the most difficulty overcoming the need for politeness (McCaughey 1997). As a woman who grew up working-class, I typically experience less discomfort with physical and verbal confrontation than my middle-class counterparts.
13. This is not true of all self-defense courses. When a group signs up for self-defense together, often they are excited and enthusiastic about a chance to learn to fight. I have taught two self-defense classes for dancers, which also had a very

different atmosphere than a typical introductory self-defense class. I suspect that's because dancers are more accustomed to using their bodies in a multiplicity of ways and to managing physical risk.

14. McCaughey (1997) explores in detail the many ways in which self-defense training can produce pleasure and, in the process, create a new habitus.
15. Following the controversy, *The Hairpin* article was taken down.
16. Senn et al. 2013, 2015.
17. The response that "women shouldn't have to defend themselves" appeared frequently on Twitter in response to Sanchez's suggestion that women learn self-defense, as in, for instance, in @annabethwest's tweet of June 8, 2014, maintaining that "Women shouldn't need to learn to protect themselves against rape #missnevada educate and respect yourself as a woman." Likewise, it is the central claim of Rebecca "Burt" Rose's (2014) short Jezebel article insisting that women "shouldn't have to learn to protect themselves." There is, of course, a level of unquestioned privilege in this claim.
18. Here, too, a proliferation of Tweets revealed ire over the idea that women defend themselves against men's violence rather than "teaching men not to rape." They did not address the possibility that a broken nose or smashed testicles might teach a rapist to think twice about future attempts at aggression.
19. McCaughey 1997; Snortland 2001.
20. Empowerment self-defense training is the only intervention that has consistently been shown to dramatically reduce violence against women. Jocelyn Hollander (2009) summarizes the small but robust literature that signals the effectiveness of women's self-defense training. Hollander's review preceded Senn's study, which is the largest of its kind.
21. Snortland 2001.
22. Snortland 2001; Fine 2010.
23. McCaughey 1997: 181.
24. McCaughey 1997.
25. Yehudit Zicklin-Sidikman's El HaLev system is particularly good at introducing self-defense skills through games.
26. IMPACT trainings differ from other ESD trainings in that they typically emphasize working through the pain and trauma induced by a particular drill or fight scenario.
27. Sport fights do not typically include age classes.
28. "No protected" is short for "no protected areas."
29. Greg Downey (2005) comments on the importance of coaching in physical training.
30. IMPACT trainings used to have participants chant "911," but this has been changed recently to reflect the fact that it is not safe for all defenders to call the police.

31. Young 1980.
32. As in the previous chapters, the phrase "games remind us that we are not alone in the world" is a paraphrase of Henning Eichberg (2013).
33. McCaughey 1997: 114.
34. Snortland and Gaeta 2014: 153.
35. This idea of creating a new sense of self through the mastery and accomplishment induced by self-defense training is central to Martha McCaughey's (1997) analysis of women's self-defense training.
36. De Becker 2000.
37. Hollander (2009: 583) identifies several studies that indicate that women who fight when attacked blame themselves less and experience a faster psychological recovery than women who don't fight.

CONCLUSION

1. Putnam 1995.
2. Lemann 1996.
3. Duina 2011.
4. Ripley 2013; Friedman 2013.
5. Atkinson 2014; Rosenwald 2015.
6. Gregory 2017.
7. Eitzen 2006.
8. Coleman 1961.
9. Friedman 2013.
10. Ripley 2013.
11. Ripley 2013.
12. Ripley 2013.
13. US colleges pour large sums of money into student recreation at the expense of scholastic concerns. "Recreation" in university parlance refers to structural provisions for leisure, such as movie theaters and "lazy rivers" rather than for unstructured, noncompetitive athletics. The emphasis on campus life as an economic growth area occurs in conjunction with a crisis in academic employment, where casualized employees increasingly teach most courses.
14. I don't mean to suggest that all informal play is inherently cooperative. Fully unstructured play can devolve into violence. As I hope to have suggested here, rules make the game and so are crucial to the experience of unity in play. The line between competition in play and violence is a fine one and it needs management. Ideally, rules should protect the experience and not just guarantee a "fair" outcome.
15. Ripley 2013.
16. Tierney 2013.

17. Tierney 2013.
18. Atkinson 2014 maintains that 75% of children play sports. Wallace 2016 cites researchers who claim that, by high school, 70% of kids have quit sports.
19. Hua Yongmin (2006), in a sustained study of sport in Germany, links sport clubs to Germany's welfare state through sport's ability to facilitate equal opportunity, build social networks, promote integration, and produce personal empowerment.
20. As in the case of failure, however, the ability to extract an understanding of respectful disagreement and cooperation from sports requires reflection on the practice. Duina (2011) argues that reflection is central, pointing out that the Danes love competitive sport despite their status as the most communal people in the world because they emphasize the unifying aspects of participating.
21. The problem with holding up Scandinavian societies as a model for democracy, however, is that they are not pluralistic.
22. Brown 2010.
23. Levitksy and Ziblatt 2016.
24. This was the case with the 2016 North Carolina gubernatorial election.
25. Legitimate competition is, of course, also the underlying framework of capitalism. As I hope is now obvious, my recourse to competition is neither wholehearted nor unqualified. Competition—like risk, failure, and vulnerability—is value-neutral in that it can take many forms that have divergent ethical and political implications. Capitalism is, by its nature, paradoxical, insofar as an unchecked operation of the market favors the concentration of wealth, unbalancing the system and obliterating competition. Such unchecked operation of the market eventually overrides the possibility of a free market. In order to have true economic competition we need restraint: self-imposed, imposed from without, or both. The economic system we have now is not, in a true sense, capitalist. It is corporatist. Just as we have a winner-takes-all political system, we have a winner-takes-all economy.

References

Ackerman, Diane. 1999. *Deep Play*. New York: Random House.

Agency Telegraph. 2015. "Female Kickboxer Knocks Out Sex Attacker who Pounces as She Walks Home." *Telegraph*, May 20. http://www.telegraph.co.uk/news/uknews/crime/11617129/Female-kickboxer-knocks-out-sex-attacker-who-pounces-as-she-walks-home.html.

Ahmed, Sara. 2010. *The Promise of Happiness*. Durham, NC: Duke University Press.

Ahmed, Sara. 2014. "Making Strangers." *Feministkilljoys*, August 4. https://feministkilljoys.com/2014/08/04/making-strangers/.

Al Amir, Salam. 2013. "Woman Sailor Thwarts Dubai Rape Attempt with Leg Stranglehold." *The National*, April 24. https://www.thenational.ae/uae/courts/woman-sailor-thwarts-dubai-rape-attempt-with-leg-stranglehold-1.290047.

Alexander, Michelle. 2010. *The New Jim Crow: Mass Incarceration in the Age of Colorblindness*. New York: The New Press.

Alloy, Lauren B., Jeanne S. Albright, Lyn Y. Abramson, and Benjamin M. Dykman. 1990. "Depressive Realism and Nondepressive Optimistic Illusions: The Role of the Self." In *Contemporary Psychological Approaches to Depression*, edited by Rick E. Ingram, 71–86. Boston: Springer.

Alvarez, Linda. 2017. "Neoliberalism: The Terror of Profit Over People." *People's Harvest Forum*. December 9. (Presentation).

Atkinson, Jay. 2014. "How Parents Are Ruining Youth Sports." *The Boston Globe*. https://www.bostonglobe.com/magazine/2014/05/03/how-parents-are-ruining-youth-sports/vbRln8qYXkrrNFJcsuvNyM/story.html.

Bailes, Sara Jane. 2011. *Performance Theatre and the Poetics of Failure*. New York: Routledge.

Bakhtin, Mikhail. 1984. *Rabelais and His World*. Bloomington: Indiana University Press.

Banerji, Anurima. 2017. "Nrityagram: Tradition and the Aesthetics of Transgression." In *How To Do Politics With Art*, edited by Anurima Banerji and Violane Roussel, 88–113. New York: Routledge.

Bateson, Gregory. 1985. "A Theory of Play and Fantasy." In *Semiotics: An Introductory Anthology*, edited by Robert Innis, 129–144. Bloomington: Indiana University Press.

Beinart, Peter. 2016. "Fear of a Female President." *The Atlantic*, October. https://www.theatlantic.com/magazine/archive/2016/10/fear-of-a-female-president/497564.

Bennett, Jessica. 2017. "On Campus, Failure Is on the Syllabus." *New York Times*, June 24. https://www.nytimes.com/2017/06/24/fashion/fear-of-failure.html.

Berlant, Laura. 2011. *Cruel Optimism*. Durham, North Carolina: Duke University Press.

Beyer, Christian. 2015. "Edmund Husserl." In *The Stanford Encyclopedia of Philosophy*, edited by Edward N. Zalta. Summer edition. http://plato.stanford.edu/archives/sum2015/entries/husserl.

Bhumika, K. 2016. "In Step with Bruce Lee: Jeet Kune Do." *The Hindu*, July 30. http://www.thehindu.com/features/metroplus/In-step-with-Bruce-Lee-Jeet-Kune-Do/article14517021.ece.

Binder, Brad. 2007. "Psycholosocial Benefits of Martial Arts: Myth or Reality? A Literature Review." https://www.virginiatkd.com/wp-content/uploads/benefits.pdf.

Bourdieu, Pierre. 1977. *Outline of a Theory of Practice*. Cambridge: Cambridge University Press.

Breihan, Tom. 2014. "DMX to Fight George Zimmerman in Celebrity Boxing Match." *Stereogum*, February 5. https://www.stereogum.com/1657452/dmx-to-fight-george-zimmerman-in-celebrity-boxing-match/news.

Brown, Stuart. 2008. "Play Is More Than Just Fun." TED Talk. https://www.ted.com/talks/stuart_brown_says_play_is_more_than_fun_it_s_vital.

Brown, Stuart, with Christopher Vaughan. 2010. *Play: How it Shapes the Brain, Opens the Imagination, and Invigorates the Soul*. New York: Avery.

Brownell, Susan. 1995. *Training the Body for China: Sports in the Moral Order of the People's Republic of China*. Chicago: University of Chicago Press.

Bureau of Justice Statistics. 2015. Data Collection National Crime Victimization Survey. https://www.bjs.gov/index.cfm?ty=dcdetail&iid=245.

Butler, Judith. 2016. "Rethinking Vulnerability and Resistance." In *Vulnerability in Resistance*, edited by Judith Butler, Zeynep Gambetti, and Leticia Sabsay, 12–27. Durham, NC: Duke University Press.

Caillois, Roger. 1962. *Man, Play, and Games*. London: Thames and Hudson.

Campbell, T. Colin, and Thomas M. Campbell II. 2006. *The China Study*. Dallas, Texas: BenBella Books.

Camporesi, Silvia. 2016. "Why Caster Semenya and Dutee Chand Deserve to Compete (and Win) at Rio 2016." *The Conversation*. http://theconversation.com/why-caster-semenya-and-dutee-chand-deserve-to-compete-and-win-at-rio-2016-63727.

Centers for Disease Control and Prevention. 2013. "Adult Participation in Aerobic and Muscle-Strengthening Physical Activities—United States 2011." *Morbidity and Mortality Weekly Report,* May 3, 62 (17): 326–330. https://www.cdc.gov/mmwr/preview/mmwrhtml/mm6217a2.htm?s_cid=mm6217a2_w.

Channon, Alex. 2013. "'Do You Hit Girls?' Some Striking Moments in the Career of a Male Martial Artist." In *Fighting Scholars: Habitus and Ethnographies of Martial Arts and Combats Sports,* edited by Raul Sanchez and Dale C. Spencer, 95–110. London: Anthem Press.

Channon, Alex. 2015. "Why Sex Segregation Is Bad for Society." *On The Issues Magazine: A Magazine of Progressive, Feminist Thinking.*
http://ontheissuesmagazine.com/2012spring/2012spring_Channon.php.

Channon, Alex 2016. "Sexualisation, Female Fighters, and the UFC: #feminism?" Conference paper delivered at the Martial Arts Studies Conference, Cardiff, Wales.

Channon, Alex. 2017. "On the Objectification of Athletes and the Throwing of Metal Buckets at Boxers' Heads." *Love Fighting, Hate Violence,* February 24. http://lfhv.org/2017/02/24/on-the-objectification-of-athletes-and-the-throwing-of-metal-buckets-at-boxers-heads.

Channon, Alex, and Christopher Matthews. 2016. "Nicholas Walters, Boxing, and 'Quitting': A Case of the Violence of Interpretation." *Love Fighting Hate Violence,* November 30. http://lfhv.org/2016/11/30/nicholas-walters-boxing-and-quitting-a-case-of-the-violence-of-interpretation.

Channon, Alex, and Christopher Matthews. n.d. "Love Fighting Hate Violence Manifesto." *Love Fighting Hate Violence.* http://lfhv.org/wp-content/uploads/lfhv-manifesto.pdf.

Channon, Alex, and Catherine Phipps. 2017. "'Pink Gloves Still Give Black Eyes': Exploring 'Alternative' Femininity in Women's Combat Sports." *Martial Arts Studies* (3): 24–37.

Claid, Emilyn. 2006. *Yes? No! Maybe . . . : Seductive Ambiguity in Dance.* New York: Routledge.

Coleman, James S. 1961. "Athletics in High School." *The ANNALS of the American Academy of Political and Social Science* 338 (1): 33–43.

Connolly, William E. 1993. *The Augustinian Imperative: A Reflection on the Politics of Morality.* Vol. 1. Thousand Oaks, CA: Sage Publications.

Cruz, Guilherme. 2013. "Rorion Gracie and the Day He Created the UFC." MMA Fighting, November 12. https://www.mmafighting.com/2013/11/12/5043630/rorion-gracie-and-the-day-he-created-the-ufc.

Csikszentmihalyi, Mihaly. 1990. *Flow: The Psychology of Optimal Experience.* New York: Harper Perennial.

Daily Mail Reporter. 2009. "Pictured: The Battered and Bruised Face of a Burglar Who Got on the Wrong Side of a 72-Year-Old Former Boxer." June 30. http://

www.dailymail.co.uk/news/article-1196479/Pictured-The-battered-bruised-face-burglar-got-wrong-72-year-old-boxer.html.

Davis, Lisa. 2017. "For 18 Years, I Thought She Was Stealing My Identity. Until I Found Her." *The Guardian*, April 3. https://www.theguardian.com/us-news/2017/apr/03/identity-theft-racial-justice.

DeBecker, Gavin. 2000. *Gift of Fear: Survival Signals That Protect Us from Violence*. London: Bloomsbury.

DeCerteau, Michel. 1984. *The Practice of Everyday Life*. Berkeley: University of California Press.

DeKoeven, Bernard. 1978. *A Well-Played Game: A Player's Philosophy*. Garden City, NY: Anchor Books.

Donovan, Josephine, and Carol Adams (eds.) 2007. *The Feminist Care Tradition in Animal Ethics*. New York: Columbia University Press.

Douglas, Mary. 1966. *Purity and Danger: An Analysis of Concept of Pollution and Taboo*. New York: Routledge.

Downey, Greg. 2005. *Learning Capoeira: Lessons in Cunning from an Afro-Brazilian Art*. New York: Oxford University Press.

Downey, Greg. 2006. "The Information Economy in No-Holds-Barred Fighting." In *Frontiers of Capital: Ethnographic Reflections on the New Economy*, edited by Melissa Fisher and Greg Downey, 108–132. Durham, NC: Duke University Press.

Downey, Greg. 2010. "Throwing Like a Brazilian: On Ineptness and a Skill-Shaped Body." In *Anthropology of Sport and Human Movement*, edited by Robert Sands, 297–326. Lanham, MD: Lexington Books.

Downey, Greg. 2016. "'As Real As It Gets!' Producing Hyperviolence in Mixed Martial Arts." *JOMEC Journal* (5).

Duggan, Lisa. 2003. *The Twilight of Equality?: Neoliberalism, Cultural Politics, and the Attack on Democracy*. Boston: Beacon Press.

Duina, Francesco. 2011. *Winning: Reflections on an American Obsession*. Princeton, NJ: Princeton University Press.

Ehrenreich, Barbara. 2009. *Bright-Sided: How the Relentless Promotion of Positive Thinking Has Undermined America*. New York: Metropolitan Books.

Eichberg, Henning. 2013. "Another Globality of Sport: Towards a Differential Phenomenology of Play and Laughter." *East Asian Sport Thoughts* 3: 115–137.

Eitzen, Stanley. 2006. *Fair and Foul: Beyond the Myths and Paradoxes of Sport*. Lanham, MD: Rowman & Littlefield Publishers.

Elias, Norbert. 1994. *The Civilizing Process*. Oxford: Blackwell.

Fairey, Shephard. 2016. "A Dark Turn." https://obeygiant.com/a-dark-turn.

Fine, Cordelia. 2008. *A Mind of Its Own: How Your Brain Distorts and Deceives*. New York: Norton.

Fine, Cordelia. 2010. *Delusions of Gender: How Our Minds, Society, and Neurosexism Create Difference*. New York: Norton.

Flock, Elizabeth. 2017. "Why Shepard Fairey's Inauguration Protest Posters Won't Have Trump on Them." PBS News Hour, January 13. https://www.pbs.org/newshour/arts/shepard-fairey-launches-people-poster-campaign-trumps-inauguration.

Foster, Susan. 2016. "Why Is There Always Energy for Dancing?" *Dance Research Journal* 48 (3): 12–26.

Freeman, Andrea. 2013. "The Unbearable Whiteness of Milk: Food Oppression and the USDA." *UC Irvine Law Review* 3: 1251–1279.

Friedman, Hilary Levey. 2013. "When Did Competitive Sports Take Over American Childhood?" *The Atlantic*, September 20. https://www.theatlantic.com/education/archive/2013/09/when-did-competitive-sports-take-over-american-childhood/279868.

Foucault, Michel. 1995. *Discipline and Punish: The Birth of the Prison*. New York: Vintage Books.

Frances, Allen. 2010. "Psychiatric Diagnosis Gone Wild: The 'Epidemic' of Childhood Bipolar Disorder." *Psychiatric Times*, April 8. http://www.psychiatrictimes.com/articles/psychiatric-diagnosis-gone-wild-epidemic-childhood-bipolar-disorder.

Gardner, Daniel. 2009. *The Science of Fear: How the Culture of Fear Manipulates your Brain*. New York: Plume.

Gargiulo, Juan Pablo. 2014. "Is Mike Patangco a Hero, Douche, or Marketing Genius?" *Medium*, May 21. https://medium.com/@juanpgargiulo/is-mike-pantangco-a-hero-douche-or-marketing-genius-f25c31dc994f.

Gilligan, Carol. 1982. *In a Different Voice*. Cambridge, MA: Harvard University Press.

Gilson, Erinn C. 2014. *The Ethics of Vulnerability: A Feminist Analysis of Social Life and Practice*. New York: Routledge.

Gladwell, Malcolm. 2000. "The Art of Failure." *The New Yorker*, August 14. https://www.newyorker.com/magazine/2000/08/21/the-art-of-failure.

Glassner, Barry. 1999. *The Culture of Fear: Why Americans Are Afraid of the Wrong Things*. New York: Basic Books.

Gong, Neil. 2015. "How to Fight Without Rules: On Civilized Violence in 'De-Civilized' Spaces." *Social Problems* 62 (4): 605–622.

Gottschall, John. 2015. *The Professor in the Cage: Why Men Fight and Why We Like to Watch*. New York: Penguin.

Gray, Peter. 2014. "Risky Play: Why Children Love It and Need It." *Psychology Today*, April 7. https://www.psychologytoday.com/blog/freedom-learn/201404/risky-play-why-children-love-it-and-need-it.

Gregory, Sean. 2017. "How Kids' Sports Became a $15 Billion Industry." *Time*. http://time.com/4913687/how-kids-sports-became-15-billion-industry.

Guo, Jeff. 2016. "America Has Locked Up So Many Black People It Has Warped Our Sense of Reality." *Washington Post*, February 26. https://www.washingtonpost.com/news/wonk/wp/2016/02/26/america-has-locked-up-so-many-black-people-it-has-warped-our-sense-of-reality.

Halberstam, Judith. 2011. *The Queer Art of Failure*. Durham, NC: Duke University Press.

Hall, Neil R. 2016. Being Honest about Martial Arts Violence. *Love Fighting Hate Violence*, December 21. http://lfhv.org/2016/12/21/being-honest-about-martial-arts-and-violence.

Harmon, Choon-Ok Jade. 2011. *Iron Butterfly*. Gretna, LA: Penguin Publishing.

Harvey, David. 2007. *A Brief History of Neoliberalism*. New York: Oxford University Press.

Harwood, Anna, Michal Lavidor, and Yuri Rassovsky. 2017. "Reducing Aggression with Martial Arts: A Meta-Analysis of Child and Youth Studies." *Aggression and Violent Behavior* 34 (Supplement C): 96–101.

Henson, Joaquin. 2011. "Has Manny Lost Killer's Instinct?" *Philstar*, June 24. http://www.philstar.com/sports/699045/has-manny-lost-killers-instinct.

Heddaya, Mostafa. 2013. "Considering Errors, Omissions, and Mistakes in Art." *Hyperallergic*, September 19. https://hyperallergic.com/83933/considering-errors-omissions-and-mistakes-in-art.

Hollander, Jocelyn A. 2009. "The Roots of Resistance to Women's Self-Defense." *Violence Against Women* 15 (5): 574–594.

Hootman, Jennifer M., Randall Dick, and Julie Agel. 2007. "Epidemiology of Collegiate Injuries for 15 Sports: Summary and Recommendations for Injury Prevention Initiatives." *Journal of Athletic Training* 42 (2): 311–319.

Huizinga, Johan. 1962. *Homo Ludens; a Study of the Play-Element in Culture*. [Tr. from the German ed.] Boston: Beacon Press.

Hua Yongmin. 2006. "Ouzhou tiyu wenhua yanjiu: zhengfu, shichang he shimin shehui zhijian de tiyu" [Study on Sport Culture in Europe: Sport between State, Market and Civil Society]. PhD dissertation, Beijing Sport University.

Jackson, Nate. 2013. "My Injury File: How I Shot, Smoked, and Screwed My Way through the NFL." *Deadspin*, October 31. https://deadspin.com/my-injury-file-how-i-shot-smoked-and-screwed-my-way-1482106392.

Kaba, Mariame, and Meiers, Erica R. 2014. "Arresting the Carceral State." February 24. http://jacobinmag.com/2014/02/arresting-the-carceral-state.

Kahnemann, Daniel. 2011. *Thinking Fast and Slow*. New York: FSG.

Kaplan, Stuart L. 2011. "Mommy, Am I Really Bipolar?" *Newsweek*, June 19. http://www.newsweek.com/us-children-misdiagnosed-bipolar-disorder-67871.

Kowal, Eric. 2015. "Two Female UFC Fighters Beat Up Pervert Outside Club." *My MMA News*, June 1. https://mymmanews.com/two-female-ufc-fighters-beat-up-pervert-outside-club.

Klein, Naomi. 2014. *This Changes Everything: Capitalism versus the Climate*. New York: Simon and Schuster.

Klores, Dan. 2012. "Junior, the Kid, the Fight." *New York Times*, March 31. http://www.nytimes.com/2012/04/01/sports/emile-griffith-benny-paret-and-the-fatal-fight.html.

Laborde, José E. 2011. "The Role of Income in Determining Leisure Time Exercise." http://economia.uprrp.edu/ensayo150.pdf.

Langseth, Tommy. 2011. "Risk Sports: Social Constraints and Cultural Imperatives." *Sport in Society* 14 (5): 629–644.

Layton, Lyndsey. 2014. "Are School Closings the 'New Jim Crow'? Activists File Civil Rights Complaints." *Washington Post*, May 13. https://www.washingtonpost.com/local/education/2014/05/13/1a0d3ae8-dab9-11e3-b745-87d39690c5c0_story.html.

Lemann, Nicholas. 1996. "Kicking in Groups." *The Atlantic*. https://www.theatlantic.com/magazine/archive/1996/04/kicking-in-groups/376562.

Lewis, Sarah. 2014. *The Rise: Creativity, the Gift of Failure, and the Search for Mastery*. New York: Simon and Schuster.

Levitsky, Steven, and Daniel Ziblatt. 2016. "Opinion: Is Donald Trump a Threat to Democracy?" *New York Times*, December 16. https://www.nytimes.com/2016/12/16/opinion/sunday/is-donald-trump-a-threat-to-democracy.html.

Losse, Kate. 2016. "The Art of Failing Upward." *New York Times*, March 5. https://www.nytimes.com/2016/03/06/opinion/sunday/the-art-of-failing-upward.html.

Mackay, Duncan. 2002. "Marathon Effort Pays Off." *Irish Times*. https://www.irishtimes.com/sport/marathon-effort-pays-off-1.1099392.

Manning, Erin. 2007. *Politics of Touch: Sense, Movement, Sovereignty*. Minneapolis: University of Minnesota Press.

Matthews, Christopher R. 2014. "Biology Ideology and Pastiche Hegemony." *Men and Masculinities* 17 (2): 99–119.

Matthews, Christopher R. 2017. "We Need to Talk about the Worst Bits of the 'Best Fights.'" *Love Fighting, Hate Violence*, February 11. http://lfhv.org/2017/02/11/we-need-to-talk-about-the-worst-bits-of-the-best-fights.

Matthews, Christopher R., and Alex Channon. 2016. "'It's Only Sport': The Symbolic Neutralization of 'Violence.'" *Symbolic Interaction* 39 (4): 557–576.

Martin, Claire. 2014. "Wearing Your Failures on Your Sleeve." *New York Times*, November 8. https://www.nytimes.com/2014/11/09/business/wearing-your-failures-on-your-sleeve.html.

Mazique, Brian. 2014. "Mike Patangco's Kind Act Toward Jeremy Rasner Shows Compassion and Confusion." *Bleacher Report*, May 22. http://bleacherreport.com/articles/2072308-mike-pantangcos-kind-act-toward-jeremy-rasner-shows-compassion-and-confusion.

McCaughey, Martha. 1997. *Real Knockouts: The Physical Feminism of Women's Self-Defense*. New York: NYU Press.

McCaughey, Martha. 2008. *The Caveman Mystique: Pop-Darwinism and the Debates Over Sex, Violence, and Science*. New York: Routledge.

McCaughey, Martha. 2014. "Miss Eliza Leslie's Hookup Handbook for Ladies." *See Jane Fight Back*, July 28. https://seejanefightback.com/2014/07/28/miss-eliza-leslies-hookup-handbook-for-ladies.

McRae, Donald. 2015. "The Night Boxer Emile Griffith Answered Gay Taunts with a Deadly Cortege of Punches." *The Guardian*, September 10. https://www.theguardian.com/sport/2015/sep/10/boxer-emile-griffith-gay-taunts-book-extract.

Merz, Misha. 2011. *Bruising: A Boxer's Story*. Australia, Victoria: The Vulgar Press.

Miller, Rory. 2008. *Meditations on Violence: A Comparison of Martial Arts Training & Real World Violence*. Boston: YMAA Publication Center.

Mouffe, Chantal. 2014. "Agonistic Democracy and Radical Politics." *Pavilion Magazine*. http://pavilionmagazine.org/chantal-mouffe-agonistic-democracy-and-radical-politics/

Merryman, Ashley. 2013. "Losing Is Good for You." *New York Times*, September 24. http://www.nytimes.com/2013/09/25/opinion/losing-is-good-for-you.html.

Moran, Colin N., and Yannis P. Pitsiladis. 2016. "Tour de France Champions Born or Made: Where Do We Take the Genetics of Performance?" *Journal of Sports Sciences* 35 (14): 1411–1419.

Msimang, Sisonke. 2016. "Caster Semenya Is the One at a Disadvantage." *The Guardian*, August 24. http://www.theguardian.com/world/2016/aug/24/caster-semenya-is-the-one-at-a-disadvantage.

Noland, Carrie. 2008. "Introduction." In *Migrations of Gesture*, edited by Sally Ann Ness and Carrie Noland, IX–XXVI. Minneapolis: University of Minnesota Press.

O'Shea, Janet. 2007. *At Home in the World: Bharata Natyam on the Global Stage*. Middletown, CT: Wesleyan University Press.

Palmer, Craig. 2005. "Mummers and Moshers: Two Rituals of Trust in Changing Social Environments." *Ethnology* 44 (2): 147–166.

Palumbo-Liu, David. 2014. "Civility Is for Suckers: Campus Hypocrisy and the 'Polite Behavior' Lie." *Salon*, September 10. https://www.salon.com/2014/09/10/civility_is_for_suckers_campus_hypocrisy_and_the_polite_behavior_lie.

Partikova, Veronika. 2016. "'Your Partner is Not Your Enemy': Confronting Hidden Violence in Martial Arts Schools." *Love Fighting, Hate Violence*, December 16. http://lfhv.org/2016/12/16/your-partner-is-not-your-enemy-confronting-hidden-violence-in-martial-arts-schools.

Phadke, Shilpa, Sameera Khan, and Shilpa Ranade. 2011. *Why Loiter?: Women And Risk On Mumbai Streets*. New Delhi: Penguin Books.

Phillips, Stephanie. 2017. "Fighting to Heal: How Survivors Are Finding Strength in Martial Arts." *Love Fighting Hate Violence*, April 18. http://lfhv.org/2017/04/18/fighting-to-heal-how-survivors-are-finding-strength-in-martial-arts.

Play. n.d. *OED Online*. Oxford University Press. http://www.oed.com/view/Entry/145475.

Polly, Matthew. 2007. *American Shaolin: Flying Kicks, Buddhist Monks, and the Legend of the Iron Crotch: An Odyssey in The New China*. New York: Gotham.

Polly, Matthew. 2011. *Tapped Out: Rear Naked Chokes, the Octagon, and the Last Emperor: An Odyssey in Mixed Martial Arts*. New York: Gotham.

Pugmire, Lance. 2011. "Boxer Blends Mercy, Menace." *Los Angeles Times*, May 6. http://articles.latimes.com/2011/may/06/sports/la-sp-0506-manny-pacquaio-20110506.

Pugmire, Lance. 2013. "After Margarito Failed, Can Bradon Rios Beat Manny Pacquiao?" *Los Angeles Times*, October 30. http://articles.latimes.com/2013/oct/30/sports/la-sp-sn-boxing-brandon-rios-manny-pacquiao-20131030.

Putnam, Robert. 1995. "Bowling Alone." *Journal of Democracy* 6 (1). http://xroads.virginia.edu/~hyper/DETOC/assoc/bowling.html.

Rahman, Sophia. 2017. "Why Men Treat Female Bosses Differently Than Their Male Counterparts." *Vice*, April 11. https://www.vice.com/en_us/article/53vmp8/how-to-stop-male-workers-feeling-threatened-by-female-managers.

Raimondi, Marc. 2015. "UFC's Leslie Smith Defends Female Friend by Beating the Crap out of Male Groper." *MMA Fighting*, June 1. https://www.mmafighting.com/2015/6/1/8696347/ufcs-leslie-smith-defends-female-friend-by-beating-the-crap-out-of.

Raskoff, Sally. 2008. "Girls, Boys, and Violence: Who's Really at Risk?" *Everyday Sociology*. http://nortonbooks.typepad.com/everydaysociology/2008/06/girls-boys-and.html.

Ripley, Amanda. 2013. "The Case Against High-School Sports." *The Atlantic*, October. https://www.theatlantic.com/magazine/archive/2013/10/the-case-against-high-school-sports/309447.

Rizga, Kristina. 2016. "We're Losing Tens of Thousands of Black Teachers: Here's Why That's Bad for Everyone." *Mother Jones*. http://www.motherjones.com/politics/2016/09/black-teachers-public-schools-education-system-philadelphia/2.

Rodriguez, Hector. 2006. "The Playful and the Serious." *The International Journal of Computer Game Research* 6 (1). http://gamestudies.org/0601/articles/rodriges.

Rosin, Hanna. 2014. "The Overprotected Kid." *The Atlantic*, April. https://www.theatlantic.com/magazine/archive/2014/04/hey-parents-leave-those-kids-alone/358631.

Rose, Rebecca "Burt." 2014. "New Miss USA Says Women Need to 'Learn to Protect Themselves.'" *Jezebel*, June 9. https://jezebel.com/new-miss-usa-says-women-need-to-learn-to-protect-themse-1587972074.

Roughgarden, Joan. 2004. *Evolution's Rainbow: Diversity, Gender, and Sexuality in Nature and People*. Berkeley: University of California Press.

Rosenau, Pauline Vaillancourt. 2006. *The Competition Paradigm: America's Conflict, Contest, and Commerce*. Lanham, MD: Rowman & Littlefield.

Rosenwald, Michael S. 2015. "Are Parents Ruining Youth Sports? Fewer Kids Play Amid Pressure." *Washington Post*, October 4. https://www.washingtonpost.com/local/are-parents-ruining-youth-sports-fewer-kids-play-amid-pressure/

2015/10/04/eb1460dc-686e-11e5-9ef3-fde182507eac_story.html?utm_term=.1306ead8a748.

Ruggeri, Amanda. 2016. "When Mistakes Make the Art." *BBC Culture*, January 12. http://www.bbc.com/culture/story/20160112-when-mistakes-make-the-art.

Russo, Charles. 2017. "Bruce Lee and the Art of Scientific Street Fighting." *Vice Sports*. https://sports.vice.com/en_us/article/pae7v9/bruce-lee-and-the-art-of-scientific-street-fighting.

Salen, Katie, and Eric Zimmerman. 2003. *Rules of Play: Game Design Fundamentals*. Cambridge, MA: The MIT Press.

Sandsetter, Ellen. 2010. "Scaryfunny: A Qualitative Study of Risky Play Among Preschool Children." PhD dissertation, Norwegian University of Science and Technology, Trondheim, Norway.

Saccaro, Matt. 2015. "America's 'Free Time' Problem: Why Nearly Half of US Workers Don't Get Enough of It." *Salon*, February 4. https://www.salon.com/2015/02/04/americas_free_time_problem_why_nearly_half_of_u_s_workers_dont_get_enough_of_it.

Sagar, Sam S., and Joachim Stoeber. 2009. "Perfectionism, Fear of Failure, and Affective Responses to Success and Failure: The Central Role of Fear of Experiencing Shame and Embarrassment." *Journal of Sport & Exercise Psychology* 31 (5): 602–627.

Scary, Elaine. 1985. *The Body in Pain: The Making and Unmaking of the World*. New York: Oxford University Press.

Schechner, Richard. 1988. "Playing." *Play and Culture* 1: 3–19.

Schorn, Susan. 2009a. "Column 1: The Rules. Bitchslap: A Column About Women and Fighting." *McSweeney's Internet Tendency*. https://www.mcsweeneys.net/articles/column-1-the-rules.

Schorn, Susan. 2009b. "Column 5: Women Beware Women. Bitchslap: A Column About Women and Fighting." *McSweeney's Internet Tendency*. https://www.mcsweeneys.net/articles/column-5-women-beware-women.

Schorn, Susan. 2009c. "Column 6: Tidings of Comfort and Uh . . . Bitchslap: A Column About Women and Fighting." *McSweeney's Internet Tendency*. https://www.mcsweeneys.net/articles/column-6-tidings-of-comfort-and-uh%E2%80%A6.

Schorn, Susan. 2011a. "Column 26: Below the Belt. Bitchslap: A Column About Women and Fighting." *McSweeney's Internet Tendency*. https://www.mcsweeneys.net/articles/column-26-below-the-belt.

Schorn, Susan. 2011b. "Column 31: Moral Hazard and the Chubby Blue Line. Bitchslap: A Column About Women and Fighting." *McSweeney's Internet Tendency*. https://www.mcsweeneys.net/articles/column-31-moral-hazard-and-the-chubby-blue-line

Schorn, Susan. 2013. *Smile at Strangers: And Other Lessons in the Art of Living Fearlessly*. Boston: Houghton Mifflin Harcourt.

Schorn, Susan. 2014a. "How to Kick a Guy in the Balls: An Illustrated Guide." *Jezebel*, November 12. http://jezebel.com/how-to-kick-a-guy-in-the-balls-an-illustrated-guide-1657810297.

Schorn, Susan. 2014b. "Violence Incognito. Bitchslap: A Column About Women and Fighting." *McSweeney's Internet Tendency*. https://www.mcsweeneys.net/articles/column-50-violence-incognito.

Schorn, Susan. 2015. "Fighting Machines: Re-imagining Physical Conflict and Gender Disparities through the Martial Arts." *Women's and Gender Studies, Department of Sociology*, Virginia Tech. October 5 (Presentation).

Senn, Charlene Y., Misha Eliasziw, Paula C. Barata, Wilfreda E. Thurston, Ian R. Newby-Clark, H. Lorraine Radtke, and Karen L. Hobden. 2013. "Sexual Assault Resistance Education for University Women: Study Protocol for a Randomized Controlled Trial (SARE Trial)." *BMC Women's Health* 13 (May): 25. https://doi.org/10.1186/1472-6874-13-25.

Senn, Charlene Y., Misha Eliasziw, Paula C. Barata, Wilfreda E. Thurston, Ian R. Newby-Clark, H. Lorraine Radtke, and Karen L. Hobden. 2015. "Efficacy of a Sexual Assault Resistance Program for University Women." *New England Journal of Medicine* 372 (24): 2326–2335. https://doi.org/10.1056/NEJMsa1411131.

Sheridan, Sam. 2006. *A Fighter's Heart: One Man's Journey through the World of Fighting*. New York: Atlantic Books.

Snortland, Ellen B. 2001. *Beauty Bites Beast: Awakening the Warrior Within Women and Girls*. 2nd ed. Sunland, CA: B3 Books.

Snortland, Ellen, Lisa Gaeta, and Gavin de Becker. 2014. *The Safety Godmothers: The ABCs of Awareness, Boundaries and Confidence for Teens*. Edited by Ken Gruberman. Sunland, CA: B3 Books.

Snyder, Sharon L., and David T. Mitchell. *Cultural Locations of Disability*. Chicago: University of Chicago Press.

Sobchack, Vivian. 2005. "'Choreography for One, Two, and Three Legs' (A Phenomenological Meditation in Movements)." *Topoi* 24 (1): 55–66.

Stenros, Jaakko. 2012. "In Defence of a Magic Circle: The Social and Mental Boundaries of Play." *Proceedings of DiGRA Nordic 2012 Conference: Local and Global—Games in Society*. http://www.digra.org/digital-library/publications/in-defence-of-a-magic-circle-the-social-and-mental-boundaries-of-play/

Sternheimer, Karen. 2009. "Who Is Most Likely to Be a Crime Victim?" *Everyday Sociology*, May 1. http://nortonbooks.typepad.com/everydaysociology/2009/05/who-is-most-likely-to-be-a-crime-victim.html.

Stranger, Mark. 1999. "The Aesthetics of Risk: A Study of Surfing." *International Review for the Sociology of Sport* 34 (3): 265–276.

Suits, Bernard. 1990. *The Grasshopper: Games, Life, and Utopia*. Boston: D. R. Godine.

Szalavitz, Maia. 2006. *Help at Any Cost: How the Troubled-Teen Industry Cons Parents and Hurts Kids*. New York: Riverhead Books.

Tierney, Mike. 2013. "At a College, Dropping Sports in Favor of Fitness." *New York Times*, April 13. http://www.nytimes.com/2013/04/14/sports/at-spelman-dropping-sports-in-favor-of-fitness.html.

Tjonndal, Anne. 2017. "Journeymen, Health Risks, and Commercialization in Professional Boxing." *Love Fighting, Hate Violence*, May 15. http://lfhv.org/2017/05/15/journeymen-health-risks-and-commercialization-in-professional-boxing.

Turner, Victor. 1983. "Body, Brain, and Culture." *Zygon* 18 (3): 221–245.

Twigger, Robert. 1997. *Angry White Pajamas: An Oxford Poet Trains with the Tokyo Riot Police*. London: Indigo.

UFC Rules and Regulations. http://www.ufc.com/discover/sport/rules-and-regulations#15.

Urquidez, Benny. 2012. "Sensei Benny the Jet Talks about Sparring." February 1. https://www.youtube.com/watch?v=-K71KlHvEBk.

Vertonghen, Jikkemien, and Marc Theeboom. 2010. "The Social-Psychological Outcomes of Martial Arts Practise Among Youth: A Review." *Journal of Sports Science and Medicine* 9 (4): 528–537.

Wacquant, Loïc. 2004. *Body and Soul: Notebooks of an Apprentice Boxer*. New York: Oxford University Press.

Wallace, Kelly. 2016. "Why Are So Many Kids Dropping Out of Sports?" CNN, January 21. http://www.cnn.com/2016/01/21/health/kids-youth-sports-parents/index.html.

West, Amanda, and Linda Allin. 2010. "Chancing Your Arm: The Meaning of Risk in Rock Climbing." *Sport in Society* 13 (7–8): 1234–1248.

White Hutchinson Leisure and Learning Group. 2012. "The Rise of Leisure Time Inequality." https://www.whitehutchinson.com/leisure/articles/rise.shtml.

Young, Iris Marion. 1980. "Throwing Like a Girl: A Phenomenology of Feminine Body Comportment, Motility, and Spatiality." *Human Studies* 3 (2): 137–156.

Young, Janet A., and Michelle D. Pain. 1999. "The Zone: Evidence of a Universal Phenomenon for Athletes Across Sports." *Athletic Insight* 1 (3): 21–30. http://www.athleticinsight.com/Vol1Iss3/Empirical_Zone.htm.

Zuk, Marlene. 2013. *Paleofantasy: What Evolution Really Tells Us about Sex, Diet, and How We Live*. New York: Norton.

Index

CPSIA information can be obtained
at www.ICGtesting.com
Printed in the USA
BVHW072247210319
543388BV00002B/5/P

9 780190 871543